# CERTANE TRACTATIS

## FOR REFORMATIOUN

## OF DOCTRYNE AND MANERIS

### IN SCOTLAND.

#### BY NINIANE WINZET.

M.D.LXII.—M.D.LXIII.

REPRINTED AT EDINBURGH.
M.DCCC.XXXV.

PRESENTED TO

THE MAITLAND CLUB

BY

JOHN BLACK GRACIE.

# THE MAITLAND CLUB.

M.DCCC.XXXV.

THE RIGHT HONOURABLE
## THE EARL OF GLASGOW,
PRESIDENT.

    HIS ROYAL HIGHNESS THE DUKE OF SUSSEX.
    ROBERT ADAM, ESQ.
    JOHN BAIN, ESQ.
5 ROBERT BELL, ESQ.
    SIR DAVID HUNTER BLAIR, BART.
    BERIAH BOTFIELD, ESQ.
    WALTER BUCHANAN, ESQ.
    THE MOST NOBLE THE MARQUIS OF BUTE.
10 ALEXANDER CAMPBELL, ESQ.
    ARCHIBALD CAMPBELL, ESQ.
    THE HONOURABLE LORD JOHN CAMPBELL.
    JOHN DONALD CARRICK, ESQ.
    THE HONOURABLE LORD COCKBURN.
15 JAMES DENNISTOUN, ESQ.
    JAMES DOBIE, ESQ.
    RICHARD DUNCAN, ESQ., TREASURER.

WILLIAM JAMES DUNCAN, ESQ.
JAMES DUNLOP, ESQ.
20 JOHN DUNLOP, ESQ.
JAMES EWING. ESQ.
KIRKMAN FINLAY, ESQ.
THE REV. WILLIAM FLEMING, D.D.
WILLIAM MALCOLM FLEMING, ESQ
25 JOHN FULLARTON, ESQ.
JOHN BLACK GRACIE, ESQ.
THE RIGHT HONOURABLE THOMAS GRENVILLE.
JAMES HILL, ESQ.
LAURENCE HILL, ESQ.
30 GEORGE HOUSTOUN, ESQ.
JOHN KERR, ESQ.
ROBERT ALEXANDER KIDSTON, ESQ.
GEORGE RITCHIE KINLOCH, ESQ.
JOHN GIBSON LOCKHART, ESQ.
35 ALEXANDER MACDONALD, ESQ.
WILLIAM MACDOWALL, ESQ., VICE PRESIDENT.
THE VERY REV. DUNCAN MACFARLAN, D.D.
ANDREW MACGEORGE, ESQ.
ALEXANDER MACGRIGOR, ESQ.
40 GEORGE MACINTOSH, ESQ.
DONALD MACINTYRE, ESQ.
JOHN WHITEFOORD MACKENZIE, ESQ.
ALEXANDER MACNEILL, ESQ.
JAMES MAIDMENT, ESQ.
45 THOMAS MAITLAND, ESQ.
WILLIAM MEIKLEHAM, ESQ.
WILLIAM HENRY MILLER, ESQ.

WILLIAM MURE, ESQ.
ALEXANDER OSWALD, ESQ.,
50 JOHN MACMICHAN PAGAN, ESQ.
WILLIAM PATRICK, ESQ.
EDWARD PIPER, ESQ.
ROBERT PITCAIRN, ESQ.
JAMES CORBET PORTERFIELD, ESQ.
55 HAMILTON PYPER, ESQ.
PHILIP A. RAMSAY, ESQ.
JOHN RICHARDSON, ESQ.
WILLIAM ROBERTSON, ESQ.
ANDREW RUTHERFURD, ESQ.
60 JAMES SMITH, ESQ.
JOHN SMITH, ESQ.
JOHN SMITH, ESQ., YOUNGEST, SECRETARY.
WILLIAM SMITH, ESQ.
MOSES STEVEN, ESQ.
65 SIR MICHAEL SHAW STEWART, BART.
DUNCAN STEWART, ESQ.
SYLVESTER DOUGLAS STIRLING, ESQ.
JOHN STRANG, ESQ.,
THOMAS THOMSON, ESQ.
70 W. B. D. D. TURNBULL, ESQ.
PATRICK FRASER TYTLER, ESQ.
ADAM URQUHART, ESQ.
SIR PATRICK WALKER, KNIGHT.
WILSON DOBIE WILSON, ESQ.

# LIFE OF NINIAN WINZET.

DURING the ascendancy of Cardinal Beaton, attempts were made with a high hand to arrest the progress of reformed opinions in Scotland; and after the downfall of that ambitious prelate, in 1546, if sanguinary measures were less frequently resorted to, it was not owing to any change in the character or spirit of the Romish priesthood. Still it is singular that no efforts on their part should have been made to direct the spirit of inquiry which was then making daily progress, by instructing the people in religious knowledge; and that the force of argument should have been altogether neglected as a means of preventing the spread of "heresy."[1]

At the subsequent period of the Reformation, there were also but few of the Catholic clergy[2] who made themselves conspicuous either by their

---

[1] The reading of the Scriptures in the vernacular tongue had been allowed in 1543, but that permission was soon withdrawn, and it is not known that any work appeared in Scotland calculated to instruct the people in religious knowledge, prior to 1552. In August that year was published the work usually called "Hamilton's Catechism," from having been "set furth,"—that is, printed "be the command and at the expensis of the most Reverend Father in God, Johne Archbishop of Sanct Andrews." It is entitled "THE CATECHISME, That is to say, ane commone and catholik instructioun of the Christin pepill in materis of our catholik faith and religioun, *quhilk na gud Christin man or woman suld misknaw*;" and it evinced a commendable design on the part of the Romish clergy to instruct "the Christian pepill in the faith and law of God, agreabill in all points to the catholyk veritie of Halie kirk."

[2] The only controversial writer among the Roman catholics prior to the Reformation, whose writings have descended to our time, was Quintin Kennedy, Abbot of Crossraguel, and uncle

x  LIFE OF NINIAN WINZET.

public disputations or writings in support of the Romish church. Among these the Author of the following works held a prominent place, although possessed of no title to distinction, either on account of birth, genius, or ecclesiastical preferment. His various "Tractatis" are now collected for the first time, and besides the interest attached to them on account of their vernacular dialect, and the circumstances under which they were originally published, they have still higher claims, as in some measure connected with the progress of events in the establishment of the Protestant faith in this kingdom. Bishop Keith was so much impressed with this idea, as to insert such of them as he had met with, in the Appendix to his " History of the Church and State in Scotland."[3] The original of the " Tractatis," printed in May 1562, he says, "is indeed so exceedingly rare to be found, that I am told there is not another copy of it now extant besides that one from which this is taken;"[4] and he tells us he reckoned it to be " one of the most valuable monuments of ecclesiastical affairs in Scotland in the sixteenth century, so far as it contains and discovers the causes and manner of the eversion of the ancient form of religion in this kingdom, and treats the bishops and nobles of that time with a freedom which their unconcernedness for the religion they professed, and their vicious manner of living, did justly deserve." The honest zeal and boldness with which Winzet " soundit the trumpet of Godis word" in these Tractatis is indeed remarkable; and, as a late eminent and lamented biographer observes, "they contain a strong testimony in support of the extreme corruption which prevailed among the superior Popish clergy, against which Wingate in-

---

of the Earl of Cassilis. In 1558, he published a volume on the subject of implicit faith in the decisions of the church and clergy, under the title of " Ane Compendious Tractive conforme to the Scriptures, of Almychtie God, Ressoun, and Authoritie, declaring the nerrest and only way to establyche the conscience of ane Christiane man in all matters (quhilks ar in debate) concerning Faith and Religion." It has no printer's name or place, but was evidently printed at Edinburgh by John Scott, in 1558, 4to. His " Oratione," in 1561, and his dispute with Knox concerning the mass, in 1562, are known by the tracts published by the late Sir Alexander Boswell of Auchinleck, Bart.

[3] Page 203, &c. Edinburgh, 1734, folio.

[4] This copy, which then belonged to the Scotish College at Paris, is now in the library belonging to the Roman Catholic Bishops in Scotland.

veighs as keenly as any reformer."[5] Some particulars of the Author's life, so far as these can be recovered, may form a suitable introduction to the present volume.

NINIAN WINZET, or Wingate, was a native of the shire and town of Renfrew, and was born in the year 1518.[6] Of his parentage, education, or his employment in the earlier period of his life, no other information has been discovered, excepting that Dr. Mackenzie informs us, he was " of an honest parentage, and had his education at the University of Glasgow; where, after he had finished the course of his studies, he was made Schoolmaster of the town of Linlithgow."[7] Part of this statement requires to be confirmed, as Winzet's name is not found in any of the contemporary registers of the Glasgow University. It cannot, however, be doubted, from the subsequent tenor of his life, and his having entered into holy orders, that he must have received a liberal education. From his own words we learn that his appointment as Schoolmaster of the royal borough of Linlithgow was about the year 1551, when he had reached the mature age of thirty-two. In this situation he might have continued for the rest of his life in the quiet and unobtrusive discharge of its duties, as he had done for the space of ten years, instructing, (as one of its biographers expresses it,) " the children of that town, to the great satisfaction of the inhabitants," had not the religious discussions at that eventful period brought him, evidently with reluctance, more prominently forward on the public stage.

According to Winzet's statement in his third Tractate, the state of education in Scotland had been very much neglected; and he expresses his surprise, that among all the charitable endowments for religious purposes, so little should have been done for so important an object. But no sooner was Popery abolished, than the Reformers displayed great and

---

[5] M'Crie's Life of Knox, vol. ii. p. 74.

[6] Dempster styles him " Ninianus Winzetus aut Winchetus Glascuensis," (Hist. Eccl. Gentis Scotorum, p. 659. Bonon. 1627, 4to,) but his own words on the title page of " The Last Blast," &c. are of course preferable authority.

[7] Lives and Characters of Scottish Writers, vol. iii. p. 148.

commendable anxiety to secure in a permanent manner the benefits of parochial education to every part of the country. As they could not be insensible of the danger of leaving youth under teachers who had not conformed to their principles, it was thought expedient that all persons who then held such offices should be examined, and required to sign the Confession of Faith, under pain of dismissal. In this way Winzet was cited, probably in May or June 1561, before John Spotswood Superintendent of Lothian,[8] and Patrick Kinloquhy Minister of Linlithgow. "Divers conferences," we are told, were "kept with him, to make him acknowledge his errors, but he continued obstinate, and was therefore sentenced by the Church."[9] That is, he was deprived of his situation, and was even "expellit and schott out of that his kindly town, and from his tender freindis thair," after having spent about ten years "of his most flourishing age," and "nocht without manifest utilitie of thair commonwelth."

Previous to this event, Winzet had received priest's orders, and he laments that his own studies had been too much neglected in consequence of his time being entirely occupied in teaching youth. But he now set himself, by diligent application, to inquire into the grounds of dispute between the Protestants and his own party; and while still at Linlithgow, he addressed various papers "familiarlie in a pleasand manner," to Spotswood and Kinloquhy, in regard to what he termed "novations" in religion. From the first he received no answer; and the other, he says, replied "in sindrie writtings void of all humanitie and compatience, and taistand nocht only of contention bot of contempt;" at the same time making various promises of an answer, with great boastings of victory. For this confutation, Winzet says he waited in vain seven or eight months. At length having collected together his various questions in matters of controversy, and these being approved by several of his brethren to whose judgment they had been submitted, he was emboldened to address himself to Knox, "as to him quha was haldin in the partis principall patriark of

---

[8] He was admitted Superintendent of Lothian on the ninth of March 1561. (Diurnal of Remarkable Occurents, &c. p. 64. Edin. 1833. 4to.)

[9] Spotswood's History of the Church of Scotland, p. 183, edit: Lond. 1655, folio.

the Calvineane court." It has been alleged that Winzet held a public disputation with Knox in Linlithgow; but for this statement there is no good authority.[10] It was not until Winzet had taken up his residence in Edinburgh, where the presence of the young queen gave some countenance and protection to the Roman catholics, that his correspondence with our Reformer commenced; and it is curious to observe the respectful or even courteous and flattering style in which he addresses Knox, compared with some of his subsequent allusions.[11]

Soon after Queen Mary's arrival in Scotland in August 1561, as a proclamation had been issued, prohibiting controversial disputes for a time; Winzet, on the 15th of February 1561-2, presented an exhortation to her Majesty, on the subject of reformation of doctrine and manners, and soliciting permission to propose in writing, certain articles to the reformed clergy. This liberty seems to have been granted; and the request had evidently a special reference to his Buke of Four-scoir three Questions, upon the principal topics of dispute between the catholics and protestants, which was drawn up in the name of the inferior catholic clergy and laity in Scotland. These Questions were then handed about in manuscript, and were highly extolled by those of his own persuasion.[12] But in order more pointedly to draw the Reformer's notice, Winzet, on the 22d of Feb-

---

[10] See Geo. Conaeus de Duplici Statu Religionis apud Scotos, p. 135. Romae 1628, 4to. His authority probably was Bishop Lesley, who is not always minutely accurate.

[11] In his "Certane Tractatis," 1562, his letters to Knox are thus addressed; "Rarae eruditionis facundiaeque viro Johanni Knox." But in 1563, among other abusive epithets applied to Knox and his brethren, he speaks of "the phrenesie of thir proud pestilent Protestantis, *every day descending a step farther to thare master in hell.*" And in 1582, when considering whether the Dialogue on the Right of Kings, was really the production of Buchanan, he tells us he began to imagine, *inter alia*, "*An cruentus ille caedium rebelliorumque minister,* Ion. Nox, *sit ab inferis revocatus?*"

[12] One of these manuscript copies is preserved in the University Library at Edinburgh. It corresponds very closely with the printed text, excepting that it has not the address "To the Christian Reider," and the letter to John Knox, both of which were added by the author after leaving Scotland. It also wants that addition to the 21st Question, which according to the marginal note in the printed edition, the Author says, "We ar nocht assuirit gif this wes in John Knoxis copie."

ruary, transmitted to Knox the 33d, 34th, and 35th Questions regarding his vocation to the ministry, seeing that he had renounced his ordination to the priesthood, under the popish dispensation by which "he had sumtyme been called Schir Johne Knox;" and on three successive occasions, by missive letters dated the 3d, 10th, and 12th of March 1562, he requested that the answer which Knox promised, should be in writing. Knox, however, at the time, paid no other attention to such solicitations than by giving from the pulpit a verbal reply, to the evident disappointment of Winzet and his brethren, at "getting na answer in wryt, but waist wynd agane." These Tractatis, in which he had "soundit the trompit of God's word, in three wrytingis according to his [Knox's] preching on sindry dayis,—and that very schortlie, as it had bene be three sindry soundis blawin almaist at ane tyme," were committed to the press on the 21st of May, and on the 24th, he added the third Tractate, occasioned by the tumults in Edinburgh on that day.

The publication of these "Certane Tractatis," in May 1562, we may suppose, excited more than ordinary attention. The zeal and freedom with which he inveighs against the scandalous ignorance and corruption of the popish clergy, with their neglect of professional duty, comparing them to dumb dogs, lazy mariners, and sleeping helmsmen in the time of danger,—and likewise against the rapacity of the nobles, the unwarrantable claims of the protestant ministers, and the hypocrisy of numbers who had embraced the new opinions from the most selfish motives,—could not have been acceptable to either party. Bishop Keith and other writers, not aware of the existence of Winzet's "Last Blast of the Trumpet," supposed that the "Certane Tractatis" was the work to which Bishop Lesley alludes as having been seized in the printing office. But the publication of that work in May, and the report that he had another in the press, may have led to the suppression of both, in the beginning of August that year, by the civil magistrate, while it also had the effect of forcing the author to leave his native country. The particulars of this occurrence have been detailed with some minuteness by Lesley, in his History of Scotland. After mentioning Winzet's Buke of Questions in terms of high commendation, he alludes in particular to Knox having undertaken to answer them, but that, sensible of his utter inability to do so, he, from the pulpit, on successive days, endeavoured to persuade the people that he had an extraordinary call to the ministry. Lesley then proceeds to state that the protestants were so enraged against Winzet, when they heard he intended to publish an expostulation addressed to the nobility, on Knox having broken faith with him, that they resolved in a summary manner to interrupt its progress, to seize the author, and subject the printer to a heavy penalty. For this purpose, he says, the magistrates of Edinburgh, with their officers, broke into the printing office, seized the copies of the work, and dragged the printer, John Scott, to prison; while Winzet, whom they chiefly desired to lay hold of, meeting them at the door of the office, escaped in disguise, to the great joy of his friends and the disappointment of his enemies.[14]

"The Last Blast of the Trumpet," was undoubtedly Winzet's latest publication before leaving Scotland, and it seems very evident that it was the identical work of which the printing was thus interrupted. It is dated July 31, 1562, two months subsequent to the "Certane Tractatis;" and the only copy known to be extant, is a fragment of five

---

[13] Another Popish writer, Nicol Burne, in his "Disputation concerning the controversit headdis of religion, &c." printed at Parise, in 1581, 8vo. has a chapter entitled, "Of the calling of Knnox and the fals Ministeris of Scotland." He refers in particular to Knox's defence of the validity of the Protestant Ministry, in the pulpit, and says "sua that being demandit of [him be] the reuerend father Maister NINIANE VINGZET nou Abbot of Ratinsburgh of his authoritie, he ansuerit that he vas extraordinarilie callit euin as vas S. Johne the Baptist, And this he ansuerit in publik befoir the peple: Bot privatlie he scheu himself to be so called in ane vther maner, that is be gunnes and pistolis, &c." (fol. 128.)

[14] "Haec res NINIANO WINZETO maximam apud Haereticos invidiam conflavit. Unde cum andirent illum jam apud Typographum calere in libro excudendo, quo cogitarat cum KNOXIO de fide violata ad nobilitatem expostulare (hac sola ratione putabat haereticos ad responsionem posse elici) consilium ineunt de opere disturbando, Winzeto capiendo, Typographo mulctando. Magistratus cum satellibus irruit in Typographiam, libros, quos reperit, aufert, JOANNEM SCOTUM Typographum bonis mulctatum in carcerem abripit; sed WINZETUM, quem tantopere cupiebant, prae foribus Magistratui occurrentem, quod incognitus elapsus fuerat, dolent haeretici, rident Catholici." (Leslaeus de Origine, Moribus, et Rebus Gestis Scotorum, p. 584. Romae, 1578, 4to.) It is highly probable that Scott's licence was taken from him, as no books printed by him for a considerable time subsequent to 1562 are to be met with.

# LIFE OF NINIAN WINZET.

leaves, which breaks off abruptly, thus rendering it extremely probable that it was never completed.[15] Although neither of these works has any printer's name, it is certain from the typography and wood-cut ornaments, that they issued from the press of John Scott. As typographical curiosities, therefore, the appearance of the original has been closely imitated in this re-publication.

Winzet, in his flight from Scotland, took "the occasion of a ship that was bound for Flanders, where he safely arrived, and stayed for some time at the university of Louvain."[16] During this residence, while he occupied himself in translating the works of some of the Fathers, which he considered to bear upon the matters then in dispute, he also, straitened as he was in circumstances, set about the publication of his Buke of Fourscoir-three Questions. It contains an address " to the Christiane Reider," from Louvain, 7th October 1563; and a postscript, addressed to John Knox, reminding him of his promise to answer the work, dated on the 27th of that month, when the printing of the volume was completed"[17]— summing up the whole with this exclamation, " *Och for mair paper or pennyis!*"

It is quite evident that Knox intended to publish an answer to Winzet's Questions, and to defend the validity of the protestant ministry, but that more important matters prevented him carrying such an intention into effect. In the narrative of his Reasoning with the Abbot of Crossraguell, printed at Edinburgh in 1563, he adverts to the circumstance of the papists denying the lawfulness of the reformed ministers' vocation, and says, " But, my Lorde, perchance, requireth miracles to prove our laughfull vocation. *For so doeth Winzet, procuter of the Papistes*. To bothe I answer, that a treuth by itself, without myracles, hath sufficient strength to prove the

---

[15] The original is in the Library of the University of Edinburgh, in fair preservation, bound with Winzet's " Certane Tractatis," and a MS. copy of the Questions, (See Note 12,) written undoubtedly at the time, and not transcribed from the printed edition. The volume was presented to the Library by William Hog of Hercus, in the year 1700.

[16] Mackenzie's Lives, vol. iii. p. 149.

[17] The original is in small 8vo. printed in Italic type, A to H 4 in eights, or 60 leaves not paged. The date 1563, on the 13th line of the title page, is an evident blunder for 1561-2.

laughful vocation of the teachers thereof; but miracles destitute of treuth have efficacie to deceave, but never to bring to God. *But this, by the grace of God, shalbe more fully entreated in the answer to Winzetes Questiones thereupon.*"[18] In a later work, entitled "Ane Breif Gathering of the Halie Signes, Sacrifices, &c. translatit out of Frenche into Scottis be ane faithful Brother," printed at Edinburgh in 1565; the translator also alludes to the recent publication of the 83 Questions, and assigns as one reason for this translation, that as "the tractat is sa proper and perfite an answer to syndrie of the said Winzet's Questiounis," he had therefore "causit this litle buike be set furthe in our Scottis toung to make the treuth knawin to all our countrie men that hes not the knawlege of the uther leid [language], *and that it may be partely ane answer to Winzets Questiouns quhil the compleit answer be prepared for the rest.* Sua that in my judgement, Papis men sal not haif greit occasioun, God willing, to brag thaim self in this behalfe."

The publication of the Buke of Fourscoir Three Questionis, was speedily followed by his translation of the well-known work of Vincentius Lirinensis, on the Antiquity and Truth of the Catholic Faith, which he dedicated to Mary, Queen of Scots.[19] Both these works were printed at Antwerp in 1563, and form part of the present volume. They furnish curious specimens of our vernacular language at the time, being written in a plain and homely style, for which Winzet showed a marked fondness. Addressing Knox, who wrote English with great purity and terseness, he says, "Gif ze throw curiositie of novationis hes forgot our auld plane Scottis, quhilk zour mother larit zou, in tymes cuming I sall wryte to zou my mind in Latin, for I am nocht acquaintit with zour Southeroun."

Winzet translated for the benefit of his countrymen, other "Tractatis, written by ancient Fathers many years ago." Some of these were pro-

---

[18] Fol. 8 of "The Reasoning," &c. Edinburgh, 1563, reprint 1812, 4to.

[19] In small 8vo. printed in Italic letter. A to I 4 in eights, or twelve leaves of title and dedication, and sixty leaves of text. Winzet probably was not aware that the work had been more than once translated into English. See Ames's Typogr. Antiq. by Herbert, vol. iii. pp. 1575, 1600, and 1796.

## LIFE OF NINIAN WINZET.

bably also printed at Antwerp, although no copies are known to have been preserved. In the marginal notes to the first of his 83 Questions, he refers the Christian reader to Vincentius, "newlie put in Scottis," being the work just alluded to. In like manner, on the second Question, he says, " Reid for this quaestioun the sext buik of Optatus, putt in Scottis, with utheris tractatis for this purpose." And on the third Question, he says, " Quha pleiss to reid Tertulliane de Praescriptionibus adversus Haereticos, newlie putt in Scottis (quha wrait about 1400 zeris passit,) sall knaw quha is now a Catholik, and quha is an haeretik."

Another work translated by Winzet, was a discourse by "Renatus Benedictus, concerning composing Discords in Religion," which was printed at Paris, 1565, 8vo,[20] but no copy of the book itself has been met with. The author, René Benoist, was in the train of Mary Queen of Scots, when she arrived from France in August 1561; and he remained in Scotland, for two years in the capacity of preacher and father confessor to the Queen. An Epistle to Knox and the rest of his brethren, written by him while at Holyrood, in December 1561, was translated from the Latin, " by ane certane Frier," but whose name is not mentioned by David Fergusson, the first Protestant minister of Dunfermline, in his Answer to it April 1562, which was printed at Edinburgh in May 1563.

In the year 1565, Winzet, we are informed, proceeded from Flanders to France, and took the degree of Master of Arts in the University of Paris; and he taught philosophy there with great applause, in the year 1569.[21] It is also stated that he was chosen three times Procurator in that University; but the period of his residence in Paris, has not been ascertained. In the course of his varied life, he appears to have gone to Italy, and it was perhaps upon the recommendation of Bishop Lesley, that he obtained the favour and patronage of Pope Gregory XIII. In the year 1576, the abbacy of the Scotish monastery of St. James, Ratis-

---

[20] Ames's Typogr. Antiq. by Herbert, vol. iii. p. 1614. It is also mentioned by Dr. Mackenzie under the same title, among Winzet's works, vol. iii. p. 156.

[21] Dempsteri Hist. Eccl. p. 569.

[22] Mackenzie's Lives, vol. iii. p. 149.

# LIFE OF NINIAN WINZET.

bon, having become vacant by the decease of Thomas Anderson, this office was conferred on Winzet by the Pope. Upon his appointment, he set himself sedulously to discharge its duties, and besides introducing a stricter observance of monastic discipline, he renovated the buildings which were much dilapidated, and secured for the monastery various privileges,[23] at the time when Bishop Lesley obtained from the Emperor Rodolpus the Second, an edict, dated October 8, 1578, for the restitution of the Scotish monasteries in Germany.

In this situation, Winzet, who had received the degree of Doctor of Divinity, continued his literary labours, and published two elaborate works, which were highly commended at the time.[24] They were printed together at Ingolstadt in 1582, the one, called The Scourge of Sectarians, was on the subject of Obedience to the Civil Magistrate; the other, written " rudi penicello," was in answer to Buchanan's Dialogue, " De Jure Regni apud Scotos."[25] Neither of these works is likely to excite much

---

[23] "At Ratisbon, there is a monastery of St. James, a Scots Benedictine. The pretence of Benedictines coming from Scotland to Germany in the 12th century, and erecting that monastery, was to entertain Scots pilgrims, who travelled through Germany to the Holy Land. But after pilgrimages and crusades ceased, Scots, English and Irish monasteries remained for another purpose. Great Britain is the country, the loss of which the Pope seems most to regret, and which he uses every possible means to recover to Catholicism. For this purpose, secret Romish missionaries are employed, and monasteries are made seminaries for qualifying the children of British or Irish Catholics for such missions, and for secretly sowing the seeds of popery. Immediately after the Reformation, the Benedictines got the direction of these missions. See Reineri Apostolatus Benedictorum in Anglia. Dusci 1626." (Extract from Reise van Nicolai. 2 Band. Berlin, 1783, in Dr. Erskine's Sketches and Hints of Church History, vol. ii. p. 6. Edinburgh, 1790-7, 2 vols. 12mo.)

[24] See in particular Gul. Barclaius I. C. de Regno et Regali Potestate, p. 2, 183, &c. Paris. 1600, 4to. Another countryman, David Chalmers, in his work " De Scotorum Fortitudine, &c. Paris. 1631, 4to. styles Winzet " doctissimus Theologus."

[25] The title runs thus; " FLAGELLUM SECTARIORUM, qui Religionis praetextu seditiones iam in Caesarem, aut in alios orthodoxos Principes excitare student; quaerentes ineptissimè quidem Deóne magis, an Principibus sit obediendum? Accessit Velitatio in Georgium Buchananum circa Dialogum, quem scripsit de Iure regni apud Scotos. NINIANO VVINZETO, Renfroo, S. Theologiae Doctore, et ad Sancti Iacobi apud Scotos Ratisponae Abbate, Autore.

" Summam suarum vtriusque libelli rerum secundae paginae continent. Quibus omnibus

xx                    LIFE OF NINIAN WINZET.

interest at the present day, although a learned prelate, when he remarks that " the kingdom of Scotland has never wanted able advocates to plead in defence of monarchy," has added, " The first man that drew his pen against Buchanan was Ninian Winzet, a Popish schoolmaster at Linlithgow, who was afterwards banished for writing against the Reformation, and was at last made Abbot of a Scotch Monastery in Germany. He called his book *Velitatio* in Geo. Buchananum circa Dialogum, &c., and showed himself as great a master of the imperial law as of critical learning."[26]

In the list of the Abbot's works, Dempster, along with " In D. Paulum Commentaria, lib. i." has enumerated, " Epigrammata, lib. i. Poemata, lib. i." It might perhaps be difficult to enlarge these " books" by the addition of any other verses than the lines subjoined to Vincentius Lirinensis (at page 182 of this volume,) and the commendatory poem addressed to Bishop Lesley in 1578.[27]

At length, Winzet, having enjoyed for a period of sixteen years, the peaceful retirement of a monastic life,[28] died at the advanced age of

---

additus est in fine utriusque, rerum praecipuarum index copiosissimus. Rogate, quae ad pacem sunt Jerusalem. Psal. cxxi. Cum gratia et priuilegio Caesareae Maiestatis.

" INGOLSTADII : Ex Officina Typographica Davidis Sartorii. Anno M. D. LXXXII."

In 4to. pp. 284, inscribed by the author, " Illustr. et Seren. Principi ac Domino, Domino Gvilielmo, Comiti Palatino Rheni, superioris et inferioris Bauariae Duci," &c.

" VELITATIO IN GEORGIVM BVCHANANVM circa Dialogum, quem scripsit de iure regni apud Scotos. Eodem Niniano VVinzeto, Renfroo, S. Theologiae Doctore, &c. Autore. Domine saluum fac regem, et exaudi nos in die, in qua inuocauerimus te. Psal. xix. Ingolstadii, ex Typographia Davidis Sartorii. Anno M. D. LXXXII."

The dedication, " Illustr. Seren. Principi ac Domino, D. Gulielmo, Comiti Palatino Rheni, ac vtriusque Bauariae Duci, &c." is dated, Ratisponae, Idibus Maij 1581.

[26] Nicolson's Scottish Historical Library, p. 39, Lond. 1705, 8vo.

[27] " De Jo. Leslaeo Episcopo Rossensi adversis rebus in dies magis inclarescente, Niniani Vuinzeti, Monasterii Scotorum Ratisbonensis, Abbatis, Decastiction." (De Origine, Moribus, et Rebus Gestis Scotorum. b. 4. Romae, 1578, 4to.)

[28] F. Bonifacii Strachani Monasterii Scotorum Sancti Jacobi ordinis Sancti Benedicti Ratisbonae Descriptio, 1684. p. 97. 4to. MS. in Advocates Library. Dempster and other writers were ignorant of the period of the Abbot's death. His words are ; " Quando obierit, aut quando Abbas sederit, et an in Germania excesserit, an in patria, pro comperto non habeo."

seventy-four, on the 21st of September 1592. A monument was erected to his memory, with the following epitaph, expressing the regard that was entertained for his piety and learning.

### D. O. M.

NINIANUS WINZETUS, SACRO-SANCTAE THEOLOGIAE DOCTOR, VIR ·PIUS ET ZELOSUS MONASTICAM HIC DISCIPLINAM RESTAURAVIT, MULTAQUE VERBO, SCRIPTO, ET VITAE EXEMPLO AD AEDIFICATIONEM PROXIMORUM PRAESTITIT, QUI POSTQUAM HUIC MONASTERIO SEXDECIM ANNOS SUMMA CUM LAUDE PRAEFUISSET, AC SUCCESSOREM CANONICE ET LEGITIME SIBI PROSPEXISSET, TANDEM XXI. SEPTEMBRIS ANNO CHRISTI MILLESIMO QUINGENTESIMO NONAGESIMO SECUNDO, AETATIS VERO SUAE SEPTUAGESIMO QUARTO, PIE ET PLACIDE OBDORMIVIT IN DOMINO.

# Certane tractatis for

Reformatioun of Doctryne and maneris, set furth at the desyre, ãd in ye name of ẏ afflictit Catholikis, of inferiour ordour of Clergie, and layit men in Scotland, be *Niniane Winzet, ane Catholike Preist borne in Renfrevv.*

☞(✽)☜

❡ Quhilkis be name this leif turnit sall schaw.

*Murus aheneus, sana conscientia.*

*Edinburgi. 21. Maij.*
1562.

## THE FIRST

ANE Exhortatioun to the maist excellent and gracius Souerane, Marie Quene of Scottis. &c. To the Bischoipes, and vtheris Pastores, and to al thaim of the nobilitie within this hir graces Realme: For vnfenʒeit reformation of doctrine and maneris, and for obtening of licence, to propone in wryt to the Precheours of the Protestantis, certane Artyculis tweching doctrine, ordour, and maneris approuin be thame.

## THE SECVND.

THRE Questionis, tweching the lauchful vocation of Johne Knox, & his brether Precheours to the Protestantis, in Scotlande: quhilks ar in noumbre the xxxiii. xxxiiii. ād xxxv. of the four score thre questionis proponit to thaim be the saidis Catholickis, togidder with thre wryttingis deliuerit to ye said Johne: quhairin is replyit aganis his ansueris maid to ane part of ye said thre questiōis.

## THE THIRD.

ANe declamatioun to the honourable Prouest Baillies, and Counsell of Edinburgh, for the obseruatioun of the glaid solemniteis off the blyssit Natiuitie, Circūcissoun, Epiphanie, Resurrectioun, and Ascenssoun of our Saluioour, with the feist of Witsonday: haistelie maid one Pasche twisday. *Anno*. 1562. Quhē thair apperit ane daingerous seditioun in Edinburgh, throw calking of the durris on euery syde: as efter sall follow.

*Dominus mihi adiutor, non timebo, quid faciat mihi homo.*

¶ The first Tractat to the Quenes Ma=
iestie, Pastouris, and Nobililitie.

EFTER that we thy graces humill Sub= *To the que-*
ditis, Marie maist excellent and gracius *nes maies.*
Quene, be our small Iugement hes con=
siderit the stait of this thy Realme, at this
present, tweching religion (quhair vpō the weilfair thairof is onely groundit) can esteme it, to
na thing mair lyke, thā to ane schip in ane dede=
ly storme, enforsed be contrarius wyndis, betuix
maist daingerus sanddy beddis on ye rycht hād,
and terrible rolkis presenting deth alrady on the
left. Quhilk gydit thir mony zeris be sleuthfull
Marinaris, and sleipand sterismen (we mein of
þ Pastores of the kirk, ᴁ in that part of thair p-
moueris) is eupl crast on the schaldis. Quhair-
at su effrayit, and almaist desperat of thair awin
and vtheris lyues in the samyn schip, hes pullit
the rudder and gouernmēt fra the formare rewlaris, maist vnworthy yir mony zeris of that name: and be our Iugement sleing fra the sanddy
beddis, speidis baith with airis and erect salis,
to brek in splēderis the schip on the feirful rokis.
For the quhilk perrel, we now mair effrayit, than
we and thay wes for the vther, may not contene
vs for na feir of man, sen þ mater standis in dainger of our bodeis ād saulis, bot exhort the latter Marinaris, albeit impatient other of repreif,
or aduertisment, to lat down ane gret dele, thair

[4]

<small>Reassonis collectit aganis thee last reularis intent.</small>

hie sailis, and hald to wyndwart, returning thair course set by the first sett compasse, and direct it to sũ mair sure harbery place, than thay first intendit to. To that end we haue collectit, as we mycht for schortnes of tyme, our apperand resonis, that the passage and dew course is partlie tyll vs knawin: Exhorting thaim to assent to our counsell, or to schaw mair plane demonstratioun of strenthiar reasonis for thair interpryse: or to be iugeit wylfull and led be sum phrenesse, & thairfor not to be hard. Zit sen the godlye wysedome of thi Maiesᵗ. hes be ane edict inhibit ony question or controuersie to be mouit in this action for a tyme, to the end that seditioun be eschewit: we differ to present our said aduertisment and ressoning to the craibit rewlaris foresadis, quhill thy gracious licence be had thairto: quhilk we hope to obtene, our ressonable despris being knawin, alrady presēt in wryt, as we for schortnes mycht collect to that effect: hoipand þ thay sall ansueir w̃ mair expeditioun & circũspect aduismēt to ye samyn (quhilk thing we maist ernestlie despre) fra thay psaue our ressonis to be knawin to thy maiesᵗ. And also war not ye vrgēt schortnes of tyme ãd imminēt dainger of deth afore our eis, thunderis in our earis to hald ãd defend vs but delay fra the rolkis of errour, heresse, and manifest seditioun in this thy Realme, manassing alrady destructioun, of zour reuling misreulit ãd misgydit gouernmẽt, Fatheris Bischoipis ãd vtheris Pastores, we wald lamēt afore god, & cry for remeid afore the warld: Suppose vtherwayis for honour of zour offices we dar not cõtemne zour selfis. And albeit þ time be schort, suthing of zour prais

<small>To the bischopis and vtheris pastores.</small>

mā we speik. Bot quhidder sal we begin zour cō-
mēdation & louing at zour haly lyfes, oz at zoure
helthful doctrine, we ar doutfū: Sē zour godly  Of thare
leving garnisit w̄ chastitie, fasting, prayer, & so- commenda-
brietie, be þ worthi frutis parof (quhat nedȝ mair) tioun.
is patēt to al mā. Zour mchādrice, zour symonie, Of thare
zour glorious estait, zour solicitude be mariage, lyfes.
efter to haif brocht þ baronis to be impis of zour
posteritie, & witnessing in all aiges to cum of zour
godlines, quhay speikis not of it? Zour liberalitie to ye pure, zour magnific Collegeis of godly
learnit ī zour cūpanie, zour nurissing of pure stu-
dentis, of ryche igynis able efter to reull ye kirk
of God, in helthfull teachemēt, all cuntreis and
Collegis dois deplore. Zour godly & circūspect
distributiō of beneficeȝ, to zour babeis ignorātis
& filthy anis, al Ethnik, Turk, & Jow may lauch
at it, þ being þ special grōnd of al impietie & divi-
siō þis day w̄in ye O Scotland. Zour wyse, saige
& grave familiar servādȝ, void of al vanitie, bo-
dely lustis, & heresie, ar spokin of to zour praysé,
god wate. Zour dum doctrine in exaltig ceremo- Of thare
neis only, w̄out ony declaratiō of ye samin. And doctryne.
ȝit mair keipig in silence ye trew word of god necessar to al mānis saluatiō, & not refusing manifest errours, to ye warld is knawin. Quhat yt of
ye trew religiō, be zour sleuthful dominiō & princelie estait is not corruptit oz obscurit? Hes not
mony throw slak of techemēt ī mad ignorāce mys-
knawi pair deuty quhilk we al aucht to our Lord
god, & sua ī pair psite beleif hes sairlye stūmerit?
Wes not ye sacramētis of christ Jesᵃ pphanit be
ignorātis, & wikit psones, nother able to psuade
to godlines be lernig noz be leuig? Of þ quhilk
nūmer,

we confesse the maist part of vs of the Eclesiasticall stait to haue bene, in our ignorant and inerpert zouthe vnworthelie be zow admittit to the
ministratioun thairof. Geue thir thingis maiste
speciall throw ignorance and Auarice be brocht
fra thair puritie: quhate maruell is it, that materis of les pryce, as of Ymages, the inuocationis of sanctis to praye for vs, the prayar for the
saulis departit, and mony siclyke thingis in sobrietie and learnit simplicitie Iesum, to be at this
tyme corruptit, and prophanit fra the mynde of
our auncient Elderis, be the sampn vices? War

*Ezechie. 33.*
ze cōmandit in vaine of God be the mouthis off
his Prophetis and Apostolis to walke attentlie
and continualie vpon zour flok, and knaw dili

*Actu. 20.*
*Proue. 27.*
gētlie the sampn be face? Or gaif the Princes of
the erth zow zeirly rentis (as the Disciplis in the

*Of the disponyng off thare rentes.*
beginnyng, sauld thair landis, ād gaif the pryces thairof to the Apostolis) to the end, that euery ane of zow, mot spend the sampn vpon his da

*Actu. 4.*
me Dalida and bastard browis? And albeit it
chance oft to the infirmitie of man, that he fal on
sleip, quhē he suld erast walk, ād he gevin to pastyme, quhē he sulde maist diligētlie labour: Bot
zit O mrcyful god, quhat deidly sleip is this, that
hes opprestit zow, that in sa gret vproir, tumult,
& terrible clamour, ze walkin nocht furth of zour
dreme? And in sa gret dainger of deth, ze haif na
regard of zour awin lyues nor vtheris? Awalke,
awalk we say, and put to zour hande stoutlie to

*Psal. 120.*
*Hebre. 4.*
saif Petiris schip: For he nother slepis nor slummeris, quha behaldis al zour doingis, and seis

zoure thochtis: bot fall require the blude oute
of zour handis, of the smallaste ane that fall pe=  Eze. 3. and
rise throw zour negligēce. Bot the tyme not per=  33.
mitting vs to speik ferder in this mater, occasiō  To þe nobi-
prouokis vs to schaw sū thing to zour honouris,  litie.
O worthy Nobilis, of ilke degre withī this realme: and that in hope of reformatioun in all thee
partis of Godis kirk. The speciall rutis of all
mischeif we suspect nocht zour prudent nobilitie  Ecclia. 10.
to myſknaw, to be þ twa infernal monstris Pryde  1. Timo. 6.
and Auarice: of the quhilkis vnhappelie hes
vpſprung the electioun of vnqualifeit biſchopis
and vtheris pastores in Scotland: And that laitlie, as we cā collect, within thir hundreth zeris,
in the gret destructioun of the trew religioun off
chriſtianis, and in prouocatioun of Godis wraith
contrare vs. For afore thay dayis, na man gentle nor vther for feir of conscience, ād dout of his
inhabilitie, wald resaue ye office of ane pastour,
quhil he wes almaist compellit thairto. Ane wit=
nessing of the sampn may be the ceremonie obser
uit be mony now in hypocrisie, *Nolens volo.* And zit
we may nocht dout of the lauchfull ordinatiō ād
auctoritie of al: as we may not of our lauchful so
uerane be name. For i doutig thairof, quhat ellis
is it, bot to plant but rutis of ordour, ane mani=
fest confusion & vter exterminion of this realme:
setting vp ane peple heidles left of God, as thee  Ose. 3.
Prophetis speikis, A*b/q; rege, ab/q; lege, & ab/q; sacer*  2. Para. 15.
*dote*: that is without ane king, without ane law,
and without ane preist? Bot geue ony spote, or
blek be in the lauchfull ordination of our pasto=

toris: we maye nawayis of reasone, bot impute that cryme to the hie reproche of zour nobilitie. Call heirfor to remembrance, we beseik zour humanitie, that zour selfis on lyue togidder ȝ zour Eldaris in the lait aige foresaid, fra the lawaste to the hieast degree, to haif bene the inuentaris, nurissaris, and Simoniacall merchandis of the sampyn miſcheif, playand to zour inferiouris the part of lippit Giezi in this mater, sayād: Quhat wyll þ geue me. And to the kingis of this realme (bot god impute not that to zow and zour posteritie playande the part of Symon his companzone, sayand, schir, quhat sall we geue the? And sua ze nobilis specialie, ɋ zouris lait pgenitouris blyndit be carnal effectioun of zouris babis, brether, or vtheris freindis, or be Auarice, hes destropit the trew religioun and triumphand kingdome of Chriſte, sa fer as ze mycht : putand in the place of godly Miniſteris, and trew succeſſouris of the Apostolis, dū doggis. Quha for the maiſt part in extreme dainger of thair maiſteris houſſe the kirk of Chriſte, quhair ennimeis ar without and within, dar not only nocht barke, bot maiſt schamefullie popit with ſtaff ɋ ſting, dar nother quhryne nor quhynge. Bot of the rigour to thee pure dune on zour awin landis, and of the appropryping ye kirk lādis ȝ vtheris dewiteis thairof, to zour awin kechingis: of the depaupering thee tennentis be zour fewis, augmētationis ɋ utheris exactionis: or of the schuiting of honeſte men fra thair native roumes, be tytle off zoure newe quhirlie fewis, tyme ſeruis not to schaw. Heirfor

*The Symonie off thee Nobilis.*

*4. Reg. 5.*

*Actu. 3.*

*Of the rigour done to the pure.*

sen be his iustice god punissis oftymes, in ye sa= *Sapi.* II.
myn thing, quhairin man offendis: That sū off **Of ye pla-**
ʒour houssis hes bene laitlie, aluterlie destroyit, **gis on thee**
and put out of memorie: And the vtheris deiec- **nobilitie.**
tit to pouertie, is not that ye iustice of God? And
that vtheris degenerat fra ye auncient nobilitie
of thair Eldaris, be fallin in extreme ignorance
of god, and in obstinat stubbirnes to leir vnceirlie his law, or walk thairin ʒforme to yair knawlege: bot hauād regarde to ye wrek of this warld
or lustis of thair bodyis, leuis as Epicurianis,
but faith or lufe to god or man. And vtheris cōtrarie reioyses to be callit Gospellaris, and cunning in Scripture: quha rest vp in hie curiositie
of questionis, and (as apperis tyll vs) in manifest errours and presumption, makis of the gos-
pell ane takin craft but ferder practise off godis
law in deid. Quha albeit thay cry out fast vpon
ydolatrie: ʒit thay ar na les thā the vtheris degenerat ignorantis abone specifeit, as wikit E-
thnikis, and bund subditis to ye monstrous ydolatrie of Auarice, neuir intendand to clenge yair
handis of ye kirk rentis, nor of ye blude ād sueit
of the pure anis, spurrande fast vtheris to reformatioun, bot in deid neuir reformand thaim selfis fra the ydolatrie of Auarice: neuir change-
and in this daingerus battel of religioun, thair
babis with men, thair ignorantis with learnit:
except in ane clokit maner to sustene ane Minister, quhare three hundreth ryche & pure wes sus-
tenit afore. O Immortall God, quhy perfaue
ʒe nocht thir three plaigis to be the scurge of thee

B

diuine iustice for ȝour former impietie, ād deuilische simonie? Sen ȝe and ȝour last forefatheris in the wyldsū way of this daingerous lyfe chesit ȝour selfis sa blynd gydis: quhate meruell is it, that ȝe sa lang indurat but repentance, be fallin in the pot of ignorāce errour or vice? Quhy clenge ȝe not ȝour hart & handis fra ydolatrie, quha (with idolatrie, with ane simple.) be toung cōdamnis ydolatrie sa mekle? Sen god geuis vs libertie efter our vnderstande frelie to think: sall this ȝour ydolatricall auarice psuaid our cōscience (albeit we be ruid of letteris ād iugemēt) that ȝe intend only to trampe doun ydolatrie, and set vp Chrystis kingdome? Or thate ȝour forbearis quha distributit thair awin iuste geris and landis to exercise the louing of god, ād to sustene the pure, to haue bene ignorantis off god ād ydolatouris: And ȝow (saifing ȝour dew honoris we speik) quha rugis, as ȝe may, fra god & al godly vse, to ȝour awi keching): to be þ trew Discipulis of Chryste? Na na, trewlie: sen ȝe veritie pronunces this: *Non potestis deo seruire & mammone.* And againe, *Nisi quis renunciauerit omnibus quæ possidet, non potest meus esse discipulus.* Nochtheles we psaue mony amāgis ȝow (to god be glore) quha with humil spirit, wald flee fra al Idolatrie, superstition and abuse: and siclyke fra errour, heresie, and curious presumptioun to vaine babling: and practissis the law of god, leuing sobirlie, godlie, and iustlie. To quhome we commit this regiment: *Qui se existimat stare, uideat ne cadat:* As we do to the warldly ignorantis abone specifiit, this vther of the Prophet: *Nolite fieri sicut*

Luc. 16.
Luc. 14.

I. Cor. 10.

Psal. 31.

[ 11 ]

*equus & mulus, in quibus non est intellectus.* And as we haue schawin sum thing, as we may for tyme to our Pastoris, exhortyng thame to refoꝛmatiõn: swa we suspect nocht zoure gentle humanitie, zee Noble potēt Loꝛdis, Baronis, & vtheris quhat sumeuir of the Nobilitie of Scotlande, to be offendit with vs zour pure anis, bot our Souerane Ladyis fre liegis, to zet in vnfenzetlie the beray selfis affectionis of oure myndis, as in thee bosūis of paim mony wayis deirbelufit: sē we of the law sorte ar to gidder with zour excellence, in the samyn schipe of thee commoun welth of this realme, participant confoꝛme to oure small part of all pꝛosperitie and aduerstie thairof.   And thairfoꝛ of nature and of conscience ar mouit to wys gude to al in the samyn.   And zit we attempt this mair bauldlye, that we ar compellit be ane part of zour nobilitie and zoure Pꝛechouris, as we efter sall schaw.

Bot to thy Maiestie maist excellent Soue- *To ye que-*
rane we returne, besetkand maist humlie thy G. *nes maies.*
and thy nobilis foꝛesaidis, to impute nocht that
tyl vs as a falt, that we speik in ye cause of God
sa frely: desyrande licence that we may but iuste *The peti-*
offence of ony persoun, ypone in wꝛyt to the pꝛe- *tioun to ye*
chouris of thaim callit the congregatioun, thay *wryttaris.*
thingis quhairin specialie we ar offedit, tweching doctryne, oꝛdour and maneris appꝛouin bee
thaim: to the intent that all errour ād abuse being cuttit away, we al ō baith sydis mot knaw þ
veritie and glaidlye ād vnfēzeitlie embꝛace the
samyn, as the peir belouit dochter of God.

*Twa causis of ye petitioun.*

The quhilkis we set furth for twa causis. The ane is, that we intending to be faithfull chriſtianis, and reddy to ſuffer thy graces lawis for ony cryme committit be vs, ar compellit other to affirme in religioun afore man contrare our conſcience: or to be incarcerat or exilit, and haldin be the warld as Infidelis, heretykis, apoſtatis, or wikit perſones vnworthy the companie of chriſtianis: And i ye mein tyme at ſic extreme pouertie all we of the clergye, that we ar almaiſte loſit to out ony mercy of mã. The vther cauſe is: that we being of ſmal learning, and ȝit laith to be hypocritis to our cõdemnation, hes lang abydit for reſſoning of the Biſchopes, Theologis ãd vtheris weill learnit tyl ane godly reformation rycht neceſſare. Quhilk thing not cũande to paſſe, bot mair cure had of the keching nor of the queir, we may nawayis langer contene vs, bot expreſſe on al ſydis, as we think: referring our iugemẽt to ẏ haly catholik kirk and that without eloquence or manly perſuaſion, of ye quhilk we haue lytle regarde in reſpect of the diuine veritie: knawand yat lyke as ane beutiful perſoun is luſtie aneuch in ane ſobir rayment, that ſa is the veritie in ane ruid ſtyle. Bot ſen this controuerſie and tumult, O gracius Soueranc, cũis but dout of the formare iniquitie, and contempt of God in vs, and

☞ \*

our forbearis: quha of his gudnes beſydis * his mony maiſt excellẽt giftis geuin to the amangis al Princis, hes geuin to thy hienes ane maiſt excellẽt of all: in ẏ preſeruing to this day thy bewtifull body & ſaule, fra al ſpot of notorius cryme in ony of baith: We may not, bot exhort the our maist excellent Souerane to haue ye gudnes of thy God in memorie intendyng be his grace to perseuere sa to the ende, walkande and panceand in his lawis day and nycht. Quhilk thing consistis nocht in the reidyng of mony cheptours (albeit that be proffetable to ane humill mynde) bot in haly feir, trew faith wyrkād be charitie: quhair on dependis sure hope of temperal prosperitie, & blys eternall. For the kingdome of god is nocht * in word bot in worke. Bot because gret cōtrouersie is new for the dountraping of Ydolatrie: to ye outruiting of ye quhilk we beseik thy princelie Maies. maist effectuslie. for ye lufe of Christ (quhome in word we all professe) to bent vp thy mynd maist ernestlie: sen that is the falt, quhair with the maiestie of God is maist greuouslie offendit. For albeit mony in thir dayis hes laborit to abolise, and pull the sampn mercyles vp be ye rutis, and erd the leist memoriall thairof oute of the mynd of man: and in the name of it in thare greif, hes destroyit mony thingis nawayis ydolatricall: Zit thay left to thy victorious hand amang vtheris mair smal, thre of the gretast ydolis but controuersie vntwechit, verray ydolis in deid, ʒe, ye rute, top, & body of all vtheris ydolis. Of the quhilkis ane we haue schawin the monstruus ydoll of Auarice: to the quhilk the Princes of the erd maist cōmonlie cōmittis Fornication. To the end that thy Maies. be neuir thairwith pollutit, nother in Ciuill nor Ecclesiasticall essaris, euery day we pray war in thy mynde the

The soum of our christiane religioun.
I. Pet. I.
Galat. 5.
I. Timo. 4.
I. Cor. 4.
\* 🙰
Of ydolatrie.

Thre ydolis lefte ʒit vntwechit.

The ydoll of auarice.

<small>3. Reg. 21.
Art. 5.</small>

histoꝛie of Naboth, of Ananias, and Saphira, pꝛaying that wikit persoun quhatsūeuir, quhay wald defyle thy conscience ād faime thairwith, haistelie to returne to oppin repentance: oꝛ to haue the reward of wickit Jezabell in exemple and terrour of vtheris. The secunde idoll is, the wickit dum pastour: of the quhilk we mak thꝛe kyndis.

<small>The Idoll of the dum Pastores.</small>

Sum foꝛ saying only to our ruid refoꝛmearis: My maisteris zour doctryne plesis vs: hes libertie to bꝛuke the kirk rentis, and leue als dum in godis cause, as ony fische in the watter, and in mair licentius lyfe, than euir thay did afore. Ane vthir soꝛte startis vpe faithles, euery ʒeit embꝛaissyng to gret bꝛak the faith of the starkast pty. And vtheris foꝛ not saying this ane woꝛd: My maisteris vs lufe zou and zour doctryne: ar deposit of thair offices, denudit of thair rentis: ⁊ h apperandlye be the pmissioun oꝛ exar reuenge of god, sen thay being afflictit, hes na compūcitioun noꝛ dolour of pair foꝛmer necligence, noꝛ intent to refoꝛmatioun, bot only luckis bakwart to the Israelitis to thee potis of flesche in Egypt: that is to thare foꝛmer licentius leuing. Quhilk soꝛt ar les prossitabyll to godis kirk, than wes Lothis wyfe to him, efter pat scho wes turnit in ane stane of salt.

<small>Zacha. II. the kindis of pis fool at pis present.</small>

The thꝛid Idoll and werst of all is the fals Pꝛecheour sittand in the temple of god schawād him self (as S. Paule speikis of his maister the Antichꝛist) as he war god: that is exaltit in the cōsait ⁊ cōssence of mā, and estemit to haue that pfectioun that he can nocht noꝛ may nocht lie.

<small>The Idoll of the fals Pꝛechours. 2. Theff. 2.</small>

Thir thꝛee Idolis be the mycht of thy Maiestie and bauld assistence of thy nobilis ād trew Pastores, being with the speciall grace of god, anis in ȝis ȝi realme suppℓit: we dout not bot al Idolatrie, quhilk is now in controuersie in religion, be men of mein learning, amang al peaceble mē, salbe pacifiit be small labouris, to ane godly cōcorde. We speikād frelie in the cause of our god to his glore, ād in feruent zele, efter our small iugement, to the weilfair of thy maiestie, nixt efter god to vs thy trew Subditis maist deirbelouit in erth, suspectis na godly persoun to be offendit with vs. For geue we had kepit langer silence, we ferit baith the offence of our god, and our cōscience to be smotit to the cryme of lese maiestie, for not assisting to the veritie, in this daingerus tumult. Farder sen all man hes this word reformatioun in mothe, willing to reforme vtheris: that al man haue iuste occassoun also to reforme ane, that is him self: We maist humelie and erneistlie beseikis thy Maiestie, maist gratious souerane for the supporte of vtheris, ād euery ane within this realme quha vnfenzetlie lufis God, and ane godly reformatioun, to luke in the mirrour vnderwryttin set vp be the finger of God, & ȝe mouth of his haly Prophet Ezechiel: quhair in euery stait may see his smot, and haue iust occassoun to reforme hym self first, and thairefter be mair able to help his nychtbour or inferiour. The spirit of Iesus Christe our only Saluiour & mediatour mot conuoye the hert of thy Maies. & al christiane Princes to ȝour Subditis in euery degre, to behald attentlie euery day ȝ sampn mirrour, & to purge & wesche all smotis exprest be it. Amen.

*Ane cleir Mirrour for the Reformatioun of all
Eſtatis.   Ezech. 22.*

To all Eſ-
tatis.

THE worde of the Lorde come vnto mee, ſaying thow Sone of man, the houſe of Iſraell is turnit into droſſe, or rouſt. Al thay that ſuld be tin, Irne, ād led, ar in the fyre becum droſſe. &c. *And a lytle efter,* thow art ane vnclene land, quhilk is not raynit vpō in the day of the creuell wraith.   The Prophetis

The gredy
prechouris.

that ar in it ar lyke ane lyone rorying and takand ў pray: thay haue deuorit ў ſaulis, thay haif re-ſauit ryches and glore, & multipliit the wedowis in ye middis of it.   The preiſtis of it hes contem-

The wikit
Preiſtis.

nit my lawe, hes defylit my Sanctuarie, betuix the haly, and the vnhaly, thay haue had na dif-ference: and fra my haly dayis thay haue turnit away thair Ein: And I wes vnhallowit in thee middis of thaim.   The reularis in the middis of

The prin-
ces.

it, ar lyke woulfīs rauiſching pair pray, to ſched blud, to deſtroy ſaulis, & gredelie to ſearce lucre.

Thee fals
prechores.

Bot the Prophetis of it, ſpargeonit thaim with vntemperit morter, ſeing vaniteis, and prophe-ciing leis vnto thaim, ſayand: The Lord hes ſaid this, quhen the Lord hes not ſpokin.   The peple

The peple.

of the land bût wikit extorſſoun and rubberie. Thay verit the pure and nedy and oppreſſit the ſtrainger aganis rycht.   I ſocht of thaim ane mā that wald mak vp the haige, & ſet hym ſelf in ye ſlope before me in the landis behaif, that I ſuld

The puniſ-
ment.

not vterlie deſtroy it: bot I could fynd naine. Thairfore I haue pourit oute my creuell diſple-

foure vpon thaim, in the fyre of my wyraith haif I
slumit thaim. Thair awin wayis haif I recom=
pencit vpon thair heidis, sayis the Lord God.

*Delyuerit to the Quenes Grace, the 15.
of Fabruar.* 1561.

### THE SECVND TRACTATE.

☞ **Gene Johne Knox be lauchfull Minister.
the xxxiii. Questioun.**

SEn we reid that nane suld tak the honour
of Ministratioun of Godis word ād Sa= Rom. 10.
cramentis on him, except he be lauchfullie Heb. 5.
callit thairto: other be God imediatlie, or be mā
haisand power to promot hym to that office. And
sen we reid nane callit be god ōlie, except sick as
schew pair power geui to paim be him,* be pow= * Quhate
er of ye spirit, or in signis & wounderis. Heirfor is menit be
giue zow, Johne Knox we say, be callit immedi= pir wordis
atly be God: quhair ar zour meruellis wrocht be clarit.
the haly spirit? For the meruellis of woltring of
realmes to vngodlie seditioun and discorde, we
abnūber nocht to be of his gyftis: Bot giue ze be
callit be man: ze moist schaw thaim to haue had
lauchful power thairto: as ÿ Apostolis ordinatit Act. 13.
S. Paule and Barnabas, albeit chosin be God Act. 9.
afore: and thay siclyke vtheris in the xiiii. of the
Actis: and as S. Paule ordinatit Timothe ād I. Tim. 4.
Cite, geuand thaim power & cōmand to ordour 2. Tim. I.
vtheris: quharin apperis the lauchfull ordinatiō Titum. I.
of Ministeris. Zour lauchful ordination be ane
of thir twa wayis, we desyre zow to schaw: sen ze

C

renunce and estemis that ordinatioun null, or e=
rar wickit, be the quhilk sumtyme ʒe ware callit
Schir Iohne.

Giue Iohne Knox be not lauchfull Bischope,<br>
quhow can thay be lauchfull ordinatit be<br>
him, the xxxiii. Questioun.

**Iohne Kno=**
**ris ansuer**
**to this wes**
**I ordinat**
**nane super**
**intendentis**
**nor minis=**
**teris.**

Giue he can nocht schaw him self ane lauch=
full ordinatit bischope, nocht onlie ane pre=
ist or inferiour minister? quhow can ʒe Super=
itendentis or vther inferiour prechouris ordina=
tit and electit be him not haifand power thairto,
iuge ʒoure selfis to be lauchfull ministeris in the
kirk of god?

Quhy ar not the Lordis and vtheris, lauchfull mi=<br>
nisteris as Iohne Knox and his Complices.<br>
the xxxv. Questioun.

**His answer**
**heir wes sa**
**schort and**
**obscur yat**
**we vnder=**
**stude it not.**

Giue Iohne Knox and ʒe affirmis ʒour sel=
fis lauchful, be ressoun of ʒour science: ād
that ʒe ar ꝑmittit alwayis, giue ʒe be not admit=
tit, be thay kirkis quhome ʒe serue: Quhy haue
ʒe techit manifestlie ane gret errour and schisme
in ʒour congregatioun, contending tō tuith and
naill (as is the prouerb) sū lordis ād gentil mē,
to haue gretumlie failʒeit, ministrand ʒour com=
munioun in tymes bypaste, to thair awin hous=
hald seruandis and tenentis: sen the saidis lor=
dis and gentilmen being men of science, be thair
awin iugement, in that case wes ꝑmittit be thair
sadis seruandis to þ office: quha affirmis yame
selfis to be ane kirk of god?

*The Copie of ane vvrytting delyuerit to Iohne Knox, on tuifday the thrid of* Marche. 1561.

SChir it mote pleis 3ow, for3amekle as we delyuerit certane articulis to 3ow, tweching 3our doctryne, or̃dour &c. Quhairin specialie we war offendit: And that priuatlie be ane honorabyll perſoun of 3our awin religioun: quha of his cheritie (as he thocht) had oft exhortit ſũ of vs, tyll ane vnioun tõ 3ow. And albeit we onlp defpr̃it ane anfweir thairoff in wr̃yt priuatlpe ẁout contentioun as we pponit to 3ou: Nochttheles 3e haue oppinnit the ſamyn in the pulpet, and reherſit ſum thingis thairof in oure name, nocht ſa ſinceirlp, as we pponit thaim, nor 3it in that mynd. Heirfor we exhor̃te 3ou 3it, as afor̃e, that we maye haue 3our anſweir in wr̃yit. And giue it ſal pleis 3ou alſo to anſueir to paim in ye pulpet: We wald that firſt 3e red our wr̃yttings fullelie and ſinceirlie: And thairefter anſweir thairto. *Sicut ex deo, coram deo, & in chriſto.* Quhare 2. Cor. 2. 3e ſperit, quhat we menit to be ſend of god imediatlie, be power of the ſpirit, or &c. This is our trew mening and mynd: that almychtie god teſtifiis thair power geuin to ſick be his worde & expreſſe ſcripture, pnunceit be inſpiratioun of the halp ſpirit, that he ſend thaim as his trew miniſteris of his worde and ſacramentis: As he teſtifiit of S. Johne Baptiſt, be the Prophetis Ma- Malac. 3. 4. lachias, Eſaias, and Zacharie, his father, be ye Eſa. 40. Angell, and the mouthe alſo of our ſaluiour ſelf: Luc. I. Or as he teſtifiit that he ſend his Apoſtolis and
ſeuinty twa

Matth. II. Discipulis be the samin his word, geuand thaim also power to wyrk wounderis. Joh. 20. Luc. 9. And sa ȝe sall fynd nane in the lawe of grace, sed imediatlie of god, bot be ane of thir twa wayis: of the quhilkis nane (as we vnderstande ȝit) conuenis to ȝow. And as twechinge S. Johne Baptist, we think his lauchfull vocatioun sufficientlye schawin to the People, be Gode in signis and wounderis, wrocht afore his conceptioun, & efter his Natiuitie in Zacharie his father, and be Elizabeth and him self in hir wamb, þat thair nedit na mair signis of his lauchfull office: sen thay wounderis wes knawin and keipit in memorie

Luc. I. as it is wryttin. Luc, 1. *In tota montana Iudææ diuulgabantur omnia uerba hæc. Et poserunt oēs qui audierāt, in corde suo dicentes: Quis putas puer iste erit? Etenim man⁹ domini erat cū eo.* Bot se ȝe haif harpit sa lang on that ane string, tweching ȝour lauchfull vocatioun: we exhorte ȝow to schaw it iustlie toneit, or ȝe leif it. Quhilk geue ȝe may do, & assuir the peple and vs heirof, it is the radiast waye, to psuade al ȝour aduersaris to delyte in the rest of ȝour melodie. *In Christo vale, & operā da, ut ueritas, & non homo uincat.* 3. Mart. Be ȝours in all godlines.

Niniane vvinzet *at the desyre of
his afflictit brether.*

☞ Geue ony wryttingis be put furthe ony wayis contrare ȝow or ȝouris without subscriptioun, impute nocht that to me. For I testifie to ȝow that I wes neuir participant of sic wryttingis to þis hour.

Idem Ninianus.

Swa it is wryttin on the bak as on the btheris.

*Raræ eruditionis facundiæq; uiro Ioanni Knox.*

*The Copie of the vvrytting delyuerit to Iohne Knox, the tent day of* Marche. 1561.

Schir it mot pleis zow be rememberit, that we declarit zow i our laſt wryttivg at zour deſyre, quhat we meanit to be imediatlye callit of god, to be ane lauchfull Paſtour: quhilk is ony man to haue the ſpecial cōmand of godis word at the left, chargeand him to that vocatiō: Or ellis to haue the ſampn cōmand with power to wyrk ſignis and wounderis: & ſchew that S. Johne Baptiſt (be quhois exemple, ze apperit to intend to preue zour lauchfull vocation) had the auctoritie of godis worde: ād that ſignis alſo war ſchawin be god, that he wes ſend be him. Bot quhair ze denyit þ S. Johne, wrocht ony ſigne; Io. 10. ze affirm þ wt the Jowis: quhilk albeit be trew, of þ exteriour ſigne requirit be Infidelis, zit in þ ſampn place, ze maye collect, that he wrocht that ſigne ſufficient to ane faithfull: quhilk wes that al thing quhilk he ſpak in ye ſpirit of Prophecie of Chriſte, wes trew. Quhair ze intendit to preue zour lauchfull vocatioun be exemple of the Prophet Amos: þ proffetis zow na thing. For quhat chriſtiane man may dout but Infidelitie (as all mē may dout of zour doctryne but al perrell) bot the Prophecie of Amos is the worde of god? For the ſcripture teſtifiis yat Amos wes ſend be god, Amos. 7, & that viſible ſignis wes ſchawin to him be god. &. 8. And ane ſufficient ſigne to ye peple wes, that al thing quhilk he foreſpak, come to pas. And ſuppoſe Amos, as the reſt of ye prophetis: war ſend namelie, to ſchaw ſum ſpeciall thing off goddis

wyll cõforme to the tyme : Zit he vsurpit not the
auctoritie of the hie Bischope in Hierusalem, as
ze do at this present of the primat of Scotlande
in Edinburgh. Quharefor chearitie moueis vs
to aduertis zou of thre thingis : The first is of þ
terrible punisement of Core, Dathan, & Abiron,
being of that tribe appoyntit onely of God to be
preistis, ãd allegeand the scriptur also for yaim,

Numi. 16.

Exod. 19. sayand: *Sufficiat vobis quòd omnis multitudo sacta est, &*
*in ipsis est dominus :* As ze do this place off the scrip-
Apoca. I. ture for zow, *Fecit nos (christus) reges et sacerdotes deo*
*& patri,* with siclyke. Be ye quhilk auctoritie giue
ze be ane lauchfull preist or bischope in Edinburgh,
ze ar be the sampn auctoritie also lauchfull king
of Scottis. The secund is to remẽber zow, *quòd*
luco. 3. *sapientia quæ est desursum, a patre luminũ, pudica est pa-*
*cifica, modesta, tractabilis, &c. & nihil simulans. Et quòd*
*domini seruũ non oportet litigare, sed placidũ esse ad oẽs,*
2. Tim. 2. *propensũ ad docendũ, patientem, cũ modestia corripientẽ*
*eos, etiam, qui resistunt veritati :* And sen we allegeit
na thing in our last byll, bot vnceirlie the expres
word of god, but wrystig, wryig, gloissig, or clo-
kig as ze cuid not preue þ gtrare : par ar sidry offendit tô zour terrible exclamatioun towart vs,
quhilk wes, *Progenies viperarum &c.* The thrid is,
that we exhort zow, and adiuris zow also, in thee
name of our Lorde Jesus, giue ze haue na mair
testimonie, for zour lauchfull vocatioun imedi-
at, than ze haue schawin, to descend from the hie
skyis, but ferder contentious cauillation, amãg
men : And schaw zour power gewin zow of yaim

For vtherwayis we freindlie aduerteis zow, that zour awin scoleris thinkis, þ that ane mistoneit string confoundis all zour harmonie. The lorde of peace mot geue you his peace and cheritie, tó vs, and mynd to wyll, that veritie win the victorie. 10. Marc. 1561. Be zours in all godlines.

*Niniane VVynzet at the defyre of his brether.*

Ane vther delyuerit the xii. of Marche. &c.

Schir it mot pleis zour prudence to haue in mynd þ we send zow ane wrytting this last twisday: exhortyng zow to testifie tyll vs, mair planelie zour ordinatioun to be lauchfull. Of the quhilk ze spak na thing in zoure nixt sermon. Heirfor sen ze by our first desyre and counsell, hes spokin sa braid thairof in the pulpet, ād as zit not assurit not only not vs, bot nocht zour awin best learnit scoleris of the sampn: we pray zou and exhortis zou, and ais be al power geuin to mony of vs be ye auctoritie of preistheid, commandis ād chargeis zou in the name of our lord Jesus, & in ye power of his maist mychtie spirit, that ze other mak demonstration to the people ād vs, of zour lauchfull ministerie geuin be god immediatlie, as had the Apostolis. Or be man in þ cause haifand the power of God, as S. Paule ordinatit Timothie and Tite: Or be baith, as ye said S. Paule wes first callit be god, and syne ordinatit be men. Or vtherwayis that ze aluterlie desiste, fra the vsurpyng of

I. Tim. 4.

Io: 20.
I. Tim. 4.
2. Tim. 1.
Act. 9.
4. 13.

ane vther mannis office, quhill ʒe be lauchfullie cal=
lit thairto: and heir ʒit the Apostill sayand, Nec
quisquā vsurpat sibi honorē, nisi qui vocatur a deo. The

*Hebre.* 5.
*Numi.* 16.

seueir punisment of Core Dathan and Abiron, & 
the feirfull Plaige that come on thay people, 
quha fulesshelie assentit to thair prydefull arro=
gance (as we supart schew in our laste wrytting) 
thunderis swa throw al our senssis, and peirsis to
feir oure heartis, that we dar nocht bott in com=
patience brotherlie aduerteis ʒow, and ʒour sco=
leris to be (as we think) in the perrell of the sa=
myn punischement. We beseik ʒow also to remē=
ber of the plaige of the king Oʒias: quha in his

2. *Paral.*
26.

presumptioun ingerit him self to offer the brynt
sacrifice at þ alter of god, to quhilk office he wes
not callit. And ʒit his falt wes a smal thig in re=
spect of ʒouris, giue ʒe want godis auctoritie as
he did: Sen he intendit to offer the signe onelie,
and ʒe to treit the veritie self of the Sacrifice off
the kirk, at ʒour cōmuniōn cōforme to our Sal=
uiouris institutioun, togidder to all the vtheris
Sacramentis ād mysteriis. For we can persaue
be ʒour awin allegeāce na power þat euir ʒe had,
except it, quhilk wes geuin to ʒow in þ sacramēt
of ordinatiōn be auctoritie of Preisthed. Quhilk

1. *Tim.* 4.

auctoritie geue ʒe esteme as nochtis, be reasoun
it wes geuin to ʒow (as ʒe speik) be ane papiste
Bischope, ād thairfor renunceis it, & seikis ane
vther ordinatioun of secularis: It followis con=
sequentlie that ʒe (quhilk god forbid) sulde re=
nunce ʒour Baptism also, geuin to ʒow be ane pa=
pist preist, as ʒe allege on lyke maner. For as S.

Auguſtine maiſt cūniglie ād godlie wryttis, As ane man throw ſchiſme and hereſſe amittis nocht the ſacrament of Baptim: ſiclyke, ſayis he, for þ ſampyn ſaltis, he amittis nocht the Sacrament to geue baptime, quhilk is ye ſacramēt of ordinatioun: conferring the ppetuitie of the ane ſacramēt anis reſſauit to the vther, mairouer that ʒee may be pſuadit, that we ſpeik vnfenʒetlie, ād ſinceirlie of cōſcience, we pray the oipotent to be mercyfull tyll vs all, and to dit and cloſe ye mouthis of ʒow or ws, quha ſpeakis iniquitie in dowble mid. *Vale, & in dei ſapiētia vince, aut reſipiſce.* 12. Mart. 1561. Be ʒouris in all godlines,

*Aug. li. i. ca. l. de bapt. cōt. donat. & li. 2. ca. 13. contra epiſt. permenie.*

Niniane vvinzet *at the deſyre of his brether.*

## THE THRID TRACTAT.

Niniane Winʒet to the redar wyſſis grace & peace.

Quhen it come to my earis, gentill reidar, of the ſeditious calking of the buith durris of certane catholiks in Edinburgh at the cōmand of the reularis thairof, on Paſche monūday laſt paſſit: And quhow at that nycht at euin the durris of certane Caluinianis wes calkit alſo with ſum notes of diſhonour, I wes panceād, quhou happy ane thing it war, giue euerie man mycht leue according to his vocatiō, at ane tranquillitie in godlines. And throw that reuolueād in mynd yat maiſt fluriſſād part of my aige, ſpēt i ye teching of ye grāmar ſcule of linlpchtquow, about the ſpace of ten ʒeris, I iugeit the teching of the ʒouthed in vertew and ſcience, nixt efter ye auctoritie to þ ministerſ of iustice vnder it (& efter þ angilicall office of godlie Pastours, to obtene þ thrid principal place maist commodious and necessare to the kirk of god. Ze, sa necessar thocht I it, that the dewe charge and office off the prince and prelate woute it, is to thaim efter my iugemēt, wonderous pynefull and almaist iportable, ād zit lytle cōmodius to ye cōmoun welth, till vnfenzeit obedience and trew godlines, quhē the peple is ruid and ignorant: and cōtrarie be the help of it to the zouthed, the office of all Potestatis is lycht to thaim and plesand to the subiectis. For the mynd of man of ane gude inclination (as ane auncient wryttar rycht warly notis) obeyis not, nor submittis not ye self willinglie to ony cōmandar or techear, bot to sick quhōe it is psuadit, to cōmand iustlie for vtiliteis cause. Quhilk psuassioun throw ignorance it maye not weill haue, woutt the lycht of vnderstanding. Bot as vnderstāding to sciēce is maist specialye & happelie cōquest in zouthe sua nane doutis it at yat tyme obtenit, maist firmlie to be reseruit ī memorie, & maist fruit to cū thairof. The singular vtiltie thairof to the cōmoun welth causit me to muell gretulie, quhou in tymes passit amang sa gret liberalitie, & ryche dotatiōs maid ī scotlād of sindry fundationis to religiō & science, that sa litle respect hes euir bene had to the grāmar sculis (quhairī cōmonlie þ maist happy & first sedis of ye said cōmon welth ar sawin) þ in mony townis thair is not sa mekle puidit thairto, as a cōmō house: And in nane almaist of al ane sufficiēt life to ane techear: Albeit ma be requirit to vn-

*Cice. li. I. offic.*

dertak þ cuir deulie, as beculis of ony a scuil. And
agane quhou it mȳ be, þ at þis time, quhē mē pꝛe-
sſis to refoꝛme al cause of ignoꝛāce & abuse, þ sa
few childer war haldin at þ studie of ony scīēce &
specialie of grāmm. The cōtēpt heirfoꝛ of þis smal
enteres to scīēce, wout þ quhilk na ferder ꝓgres
may be had pairto, I cōiecturit to be ane gret poꝛ-
tēt & foꝛetalkig of ignoꝛāce & ma cōfusſt errouris
(quhilk god auert) schoꝛtlie tocū : namelie sē now
al mē wil be theologis, & curius seircearis of the
hie mysteriis of god. In remēbꝛing yir thigis, I
callit thā to memoꝛie, quhou be þ mcyful ꝓuidē-
ce of ye almȳtie (quha be in all & foꝛ euer pꝛaisſt)
þair wes sūtyme submittit to my techemēt (albeit
my eruditiō wes smal) humane childer of happy
igynis, mair able to leir than I wes to teche: to
quhō I vsſt to ꝓpone almaisſt dalie sū theme, ar-
gumēt, oꝛ sētence, of þ quhilk I wald haif þaim in-
tēding to mak oꝛisone oꝛ episſtil in latin tong : ād
thocht þ yis mater of seditiō afoꝛe nawit had bene
ane verray cōueniēt theme to þ purpose. Heirfoꝛ I
being dꝛery and doloꝛus for þ schisme & diuisiō pꝛe-
sentlie i godis kirk, & apperād tēpoꝛal calamiteis to vpꝛyse parthꝛou, & als haifād affectiō to my
kynd discipulis, & my glaid & godlye exercise sūtyme w paim, began I almaisſt foꝛ pastyme, ād sū
mitigatiō of my displesur to wꝛit yis declamatiō
followig : þ is ane foꝛm of ditemēt maid foꝛ caus
of exeꝛcise & pꝛiuat studie, as vsſs to be in sculis.
Notheles quhē ane of our bꝛeder chāceit to reid
it, he diuulgat it in þ contre in my name, bot sub-
scriuit, as efter folouis, & gaif copiis thairof as it
had bene ane ernisſt mater. Bot quhen I vnder-
sſude that sum wes offendit thairw & w me also

for it, I seik the coppy thairof & consideris it. And as I psaue rethozik thairof verray small: swa I cā espy na thing thairin abhozring fra ye treuth. Of the quhilk I (geuing the honour of learning tyll vtheris) intending to be ane faithful Christiane, & ane sone of þ haly kirk vniuersale, he only regaird. Heirfoz sen I neuer sett furth ony wrytting cōtrare the Protestātis, suppressing my name, that I maye saue me ȝit in þ innocence, void of all detraction. I confesse me to haue wrytting the samin tractate ād na thing penitēt thairof as ȝit, except that I strenthit not my purpose tō ma sufficient ressonis and auctoriteis. Quhilkis I differ quhill oure aduersaris mak answeir heirto: Praying god maist gratius to moue thame tō the spirit off humilitie, þ thay be not eschamit to recant pair errour in pis mater and all vtheris, bot thay be aluterlie cōfoundit to maling in ane iote aganis the knawin veritie. I nameit the twa psonis following by vtheris, becaufe the ane is knawin to be the principall defozmare of his allegeit refozmatioun: And to certifie the vther, that erar or I condemnit of idolatrie Hierome ād Augustine as leand wytnesses, & the haill kirk of God i pis a poynct wout cause: that I had leuir be banisst furthe of Europe as be his assistence I wes banisst fra Linlychtquow, for not assenting to his factioun generalie in all poynctis. This far gentyll redar haue I schawin, that I may be clein fra all smot of blame in þ putting furth of priuat wryttingis wout subscriptiō: Praying þ to fair weil in þ Lord. Of Edinburgh ye 24. of may 1562.

*To the honorable Prouest baillies and counsall
of Edinburgh.*

When I remember, honorabyll schirs, þ Solon þ law maker of Athenis amangis the rest commãdit þis i special, þ gif ony of þ town in ane publict seditioun or tumult, quhẽ on baith sydis thai ran to armour, hid him self, as ane cowart at hame, not takand part to the ane syde, he sould be denudit of his gudis & banissit the Citie: it strykis me not to lytle feir, that I sõlyke in this controuersie of religioun, as ane soldiour of ye kirk of Laodicea, þat is, nother haet noȝ cauld, be expellit (quhilk god forbid) out of my citie of heuinlie Hierusalẽ, for not assisting to þ assurit veritie, in gainsaying leis, the father thairof ye deuyll, and all his mẽberis. Quhairfoȝe quhẽ I se the seditioun amãgis ȝou & ȝoure Citiȝanis, for the celebratioun of the solennitie off Pasche, ãd quhou ȝe cõmand to calk the closst buith durris, at this tyme of certane nocht dissonit fra ye haly kirk vniuersale to ȝou, and haldis ye sampn mẽ Idolatouris & worthy of punismẽt, it apperis to my waik iugemẽt, that to attempt sic proude misordour, sall not only dig vp ane wal betuix vs & ȝou in religioun, bot also sall engener (quhilk ye mercy of god stay) mair temporal seditioun, cũmeris, ãd debait, I thocht that I ane priuat mã could do na better at þat tyme, bot pray for peace amangis all professing our lord Jesus. Quhilk quhen I did, and thairefter castand vp ye dukis

*Apoca.* 3.

of sũ aũciẽt fatheris, to seik þ mid of godis kirk i þis mater: I fynd maist cleir witnessing of famous fatheris & specialie of S. Hierome & Augustine, þ þe haill kirk of god to ane cõsent, hes ʒeirlie celebratit þe solennitie of ʒule & pasche, to vtheris feistis of our saluiour, & ũclyke kepit þe ʒeirlie abstinẽce of fourty dayis afore pasche, callit lentren, in al contreis in þe warld pfessing christ afore þir dayis: & affirmis þ þir, & ũclyke thingis vniuersaly obseruit, & ʒit not erpressli cõtenit in scripture, ar traditiõs of þ Apostolis, or decreis, of gñral cunselis, & thairfor na wayis be ony pticulare cũtre to be changeit. Ane notable cause of þir solennit dayis geuis the said renownit father Augustine, & worthy to be lokit in þe memorie of thaim, quha knawis thaim selfis to be men in þis flesche, & waik & frail as ʒit in þis warld. *Ne curriculo temporũ* (sayis he) *ingrata subrepat obliuio*, þat be þe proces of tyme vnthãkful forʒetfulnes steil not vpon vs. Quhen I reid þis maist cleir testimonie of sa renownit fatheris, of þe vniuersale cõsent of godis kirk i this mater, sen our saluiours dayis, I begin to mucl at þe arrogãt temeritie of ʒour haly pphete Johne Knor, quha cõmãdis to abolise þir solẽniteis as papistrie: be þe quhilk name he vnderstãdis, as I cã collect, idolatric sup̃stitiõ, or doctryne cõtrare þ scriptur. And gif he vnderstãdis þai vices be þis name: I think þ þar is na treu christiãe, bot he dar affirme baldly in þ face of al þe warld, þ i þis mater (quhair he callis þ saidis solẽniteis idolatrical, sup̃stitius or cõtrari° to godis law) he spekis blasphemie aganis þe haly gaist, & agais þ essẽtial veritie our lord

---

Hiero.3.parte *epist. epist.* 80. *& parte* l. *episto. ad Marcellam.* Aug. *ad Ianuarium. li.* 1. *& 2. reid* þir workis and be not dissauit.

Aug. de ciuitate dei. li. 10. ca. 4.

Joh. Knor in his buke of discipline.

& kig chrift Jeſ⁰: quha pmittit his ſaid ſpirit of
treuth to teche his kirk ād be tō it to the warldis
end: For Johne Knox & his ſcolers ſchrynkis not  Matth. vlti.
to rail, & lie þ it hes bene euer in idolatrie i þis caſe  Io. 14.
of yir feſtual dayis amāgis vtheris ma. Bot I
miſknaw not ſū of ʒow to obiect ye cōmād, charg-
and *Sex dayis to laubour, & the ſeuint day to ſanctifie to
ye lord,* thairfoʒe I defyʒe þ doutſū mā to cauſe his
doctour & pphete foʒeſaid, tō all ye aſſiſtence of
his beſt learnit ſcolers, to anſueir in wʒit, quhat
ſcripture hes he oʒ vther authoʒitie, by ye cōſēt of
ye haly kirk vniuerſal to ſāctiſie ye ſonday to be
þ ſeuint day. And gif he aboliſſis tō vs ye ſater-
day, as ceremoniall & not requiſit i ye law of the
euangel: quhat hes he by ye cōſent of godis kirk,
to ſāctiſie ony day of ye vii. & not to labour al ye
ſeuin days: ye ſert day, becauſe it is ſua cōmādit,
& þ ſabbaoth, becauſe it is aboliſſit be ye euāgel?
& gif he cā ſchaw na expʒes ſcriptur parfoʒ: quhi
aboliſſis he not ye ſonday, as he dois ʒule paſche
& ye reſt vniuerſalie obſeruit be al chriſtianis as
ye ſōday? Bot note honoʒable ſchirs (þ þ veritie be
not loſſt be altercatiō) ye hiſtoʒie of Judith, quhow
ye Jowis by ye ſolēniteis of yai dayis geūn þam
afoʒe i ye ſcriptur, iſtitute ane ʒeirly ſolēnitie to  Iudith. vlti.
gloʒifie god for þ deliuerig Bethulia & yaim fra
ye crudelitie of Holofernes. Reid alſo þ Mardo-
cheus, Heſter, ād ye reſt of ye Jowis captiues vn-
der ye king Aſſuerus, inſtitutit ſic ʒeirly ſolennitie of blyth- Hester. 9.
nes, in remembrance yat be ye mychtie hand of God thay wer
delyuerit fra ye tyrannie of wikit Amman. Gyf ſic ʒeirlie memorial in blythnes & thankis gefting wes haldin for ye delyuer-
ance of yair bodeis: had not ye Apoſtolis, and the haill kirk of

god gydit vndouttitlie be the haly gaist, siclyke
aucthoritie to institut sic festual dayis for the de=
lyuering of thair bodeis and saulis, not fra twa
eirdlie tyrannis, Holofernes & Ammon, bot frō
the deupll, hell, and syn, : not be twa wemē Ju=
dith and Hester, bot be the pretious blude of the
immaculat lamb the Sone of God? ȝe reid sick=
lyke the fest of the dedication callit Encenia, in=

Io. 10.

stitute be the Hebreuis without ony cōmand cō=
tenit in ony canonicall scripture : quhilk solenni=
tie wes approuin and decorit be our Saluiours
awin presence. Sall the haill peple of god heir=
for of al aiges, in the libertie of ye Euangel haif
les libertie in the lyke materis, thā had þ Jowis
vnder the ȝok of the Mosaical law? Ze may re=

2. Para. 7.

id also that Salomon at the dedicatioun of thee
tempyll celebratit in gret solennitie sewin festu=
all dayis together, and trow ȝe, that he brak the
cōmād thairthrow, *Sex dayis fall thou laubour?* quhē
we heir ȝour prophete cast in dout, sayand quha
wat quhat day Christ wes borne on? Can ȝe thik
hi in ony vther gre, bot nyrt efter to speir gif christ
be borne? O mad mā and maist fulische wald he
psuade ane faithful christiane, that ye haill vni=
uersall kirk, is mair vnthankfull, ād les mynd=
full of the byrth of hir spouse and king the sonne
of God, thā ony realme is of thair tēporal king:
quhais day of Natiuitie, na cōtre forȝettis, in=
during his lyfetyme? Bot our kyng and maiste
sweit spouse leuis for euer. Quhairfore euer sall
ye day of his blissit natiuitie, circumcūtiō, passiō,
resurrectioun, ascensioun, and his manifestatiō

[ 33 ]

to the warld callit Epiphanie in the dispyte of ye deupll and all his furius mēberis (quha * euer hes laborit to abolish his name out of pis warld) be i freche memorie of his deirbelouit spouse his haly kirk vniuersall. Bot allace quhow mony in pir dayis repetis pis haly kirk vniuersal, as ane necessare articule of yar beleif (as it is but dout) and zit othir throw ignorance dissauit, or throw malice blyndit, impugnis the trew vnderstand= ing yairof? Amāgis mony materis rycht wechty lat this sampn grosse exemple of the abolitioun of thir solennit dayis, as idolatricall, be ane cō= trare the vniforme cōsent in all tyme ād place of the sampn kirk. Bot allace for pietie, honorable schiris, quhy remēber we not, þ for þ abusing of thir dayis, amangis vtheris faultis, God is at wrayith tō vs, and not for the institutioun and godlye obseruance of the sampn: bot because we haue mispent thaim fra the seruice of our god, to the seruice of our Bellis, and of thay memberis vnder the bellie: fra ye honour of our lord christ to the vaine glorious pompe of our awi bodyis: frome cheritie, to carnalitie, bestowand that per= tenit to the pure nedy mēberis of Christis bodye on our sinfull flesche tō the ryche Glotton: And sa fra humilitie, to pryde: fra sobriete, to drūkin= nes: fra peace and lufe, to contentioun & debait, fra louing of God, to māsuering of his name: fra godly talk of pace, amitie, & frendschip, to scurri= litie, stryfe, & detractioun? Finallie fra al the ser= uice of god, requirit on the haly daye, to the ser=

E

uice of Sathan, or of the warld. And last of all, quhē we sould lamēt for our impietie, & returne to god and the rycht vse of thir solenniteis, ʒe eik this mischeif to all ʒour former wickitnes, quhē ʒe pnunce ƥis blasphemie to the spirit of god, af‑ firming that his haly kirk vniuersall hes bene euer pollutit tō idolatrie in the obseruing of thir dayis. O mcyful god wyl ʒe not remēber quhay spekis sa mekle of the scripture, that god for the wickitnes of the peple, wes not appleūt tō thay festuall dayis, quhilkis he in the scripture afore had cōmandit be ƥe Jowis to be obseruit, quhill the cūming of Chrift: & that for thair abusing of ƥe sampn to ane vther fine, thā he institute ƥam? On this maner he complenis be his prophete, I

Amos, 5. haue hait (sayis the lord) ʒour festuall dayis: I
v. 8. wyl not haue ʒour brunt Sacrificeis. And i ane vther place, I sall turne ʒoure solennit dayis in murnyng, and ʒour canticulis in sobing. The
Thren. 2. prophete Hieremie lamentis, that god for ƥe im‑ pietie and sinnis had caussit the festuall and so‑ lennit dayis in Hierusalem to be forʒet, and in ƥe wrath & idignatiō of his fury (be quhilk we vnder‑ stand his Justice aganis the wickitnes of man)

☞ had geuin the king and ƥe preiste to be despyst, his temple sanctuarie and altare to be destroyit. Be the quhilk place allane it is euident, that as the king, and all lauchfull superiour poweris, ƥ preiste bischope, and all authoritie of the kirk, wes contemnit for ane tyme, according to ƥe iu‑ stice of god, bot ʒit be the wickit ād reprobat on‑

lie: that on lyke maner the ordinance of god tuecheing the saidȝ dayis in that tyme, quhil Chriftis paffioun amang ye peple of god wes to be obferuit, according to the law geuin thaim: ȝit for
the abufing of the fampn, the Lord be þ mouth
of his Prophete repellit pair folēniteis ād Sa-
crifficeis.  The caufe thairof is declarit: becaufe *Esai.* I.
thair cōgregatiō wes iniufte & wickit, and thair
handis full of blude.  And ȝit as he wald at that
tyme nane of his belufit peple to be difobedient
and nott reuerence king and preift not only ye
gude bot alfo the euyl, noȝ ȝit his peculiar peple I *Petr.* 2.
to difppfe his fanctuarie, temple, altare, noȝ his
halp dayis: fwa he wpll but dout his belouit to
obferue ye ordinance of his halp kirk vniuerfal,
twecheing thir fampn Solēniteis, quhilkis ar
now in cōtrouerffe: albeit thay be difpput be the
wickit.  Giue dew obedience and reuerēce be had
to kingis, quenis, princes, & prelatis, at this tyme: lat vper mē iuge.  For a thig fpecialy exhort
I ȝour prudence, at this prefent to cōfider, honorable fchiris, that ȝe be not of ye noumber of that
wickit gñratiō, quhō ye prophete rebukis on this
maner, *All thair generatioun faid this in thair hart, lat* *Psalm.* 73.
*vs mak all the feftuall dayis of the Lord to ceafe out of the* Reid this
*eird.*  For except ȝe be wpllighy blind, ȝe may pfaue Pfalm for
ȝir dayis, quhairof we fpeik, to be the feftuall dayis and bthers
of the lorde.  For as ȝour Prophetis be auctoritie at this ty-
of the kirk, without exprefte Scripture thairfor, in the Eng-
appreuis with vs the Sondaye to be the Saba- lis Bibill
oth daye to all Chriftianis:  Swa be aucthoritie *is the* 74.
of the fampn kirk in all

contreis and aiges, and be the eremplis also of
the scripturis aboue wryttin, appreue & affirme
we baith the ane and the vther. And that ȝe may
be mair assurit in conscience, that thair is na er⸗
rour cōmittit be the kirk in this mater, bot ȝour
pphetis to haue fallin arrogātlie in ane blynd,
arrogant and wylfull errour, quhē thay dar op⸗
pone thaim sa proudlie or erar impudētlie to the
haill kirk of god: reid in the C. rvii. Psalme,
quhare the spirit of God cōmādis þ kirk i blith⸗
nes and thankisgeuing, for hir redemptioun bee
Mar. 12.   Chrīst (quhare he exponis him self to be þ corner
or band stane, quhilk þ bigaris refusīt) to reiose &
institute solennitie of tyme thairfor in thir wordis:
Psalm. 117.   *Hæc est dies quā fecit domin°, exultemus & lætemur in ea.*
And againe, *Constituite diem solennē in condensis vsq.
ad cornu altaris.* Twa thingis remanis, quhilk J of
my small learning bot of ardēt lufe beseikis ȝow
Schiris to consider: first that ȝe be not ye scurge
of god (as wes the wickit in the dayis of Hiere⸗
Thren. 2.   mie) to dispyse king, quene, bischope, & al lauch⸗
full auctorite, to gidder tō thir solennit festuall
dayis euir obseruit in goddis haly kirk vniuer⸗
sall: and leir to prefer the sampyn kirk to the Ju⸗
gement of ony ane mā, Citie, Prouince, realme
or ony ane aige of mē of ane vther spirit, ȝe, albe⸗
it it wer ane Angell frome heuin, and knaw ȝour
fragilitie and fall & returne hame agane to ȝour
awin moder godis kirk. Secundly giue ye ruid⸗
nes of my dytemēt haistely wryttin in feruour of
spirit but eloquence may not dissuade ȝow fra ye
obstinate puersūtie of ȝoure erroure, J exhorte ȝe

cause zour pphete Johne Knox, and zour supin-
tendent Johne Spotiswod, to impreue Sanctis
Hierome ād Augustine as leand witnessis in the
premissis. And cause thaim delyuer thair answer
in wryt, for thir haly fatheris bukis ar patēt tyl
vs and thaim. And sum of our faithfull brether
hes wryttin sindry tymes to thaim baith & gettis
na answer in wryt, bot waist wynd agane. Bot p-
aduenture albeit thir twa zoure kempis dar nott
for schame answer in this mater, ze wyll appeill
to þ rest of zour lernit theologis of a gret nūber i
Scotland ād Geneua. Bot to thaim we oppone
all the Christiane catholikis in Aphrik Assa and
Europa. Bot zit, pchance ze wyll allege zour priuate misordour to haue auctoritie, as establissit
be ane lāg space, now, almaist thre zeris in scotland: heirfore to that we oppone the vniuersale
ordour throw all the warld beleuand in Christe,
thir xv. c. xxvii. zeris as the said Sʸ. Hierome,
and Augustine witnesses afore thair tyme, ād al
historiis sen syne. Desist heirfore Schiris maist
deirbelusst, desiste I pray zow in ye sycht of god
fra zour furius rage & wylful blyndnes. Think
quhat it is to maising cōtrare christ, his haly kirk
vniuersall, our souerane Lady ād zour lauchful
pastours. Be war to moue distructiō to zour selfis, and seditioun in this nobyll town be zoure
calking, and keling, and puerst mynd to puneis
the Innocent contrare all lawis of god and mā.
The potent spirit of god mot humpll zour hertis
and giue zow grace that this tumult tak rest w-
out extreme damnage. At Edinburgh ye last of

[ 38 ]

Marche. be ȝouris M.

☞ Quhais name ȝe sal knaw, quhen ȝe sal knaw ȝoure Errour, oȝ quhen Johne Knox oȝ his Bȝether answeris heirto in wȝit.
FINIS.
☙(✳)❧

# THE

LAST BLAST OF THE TROMPET OF
Godis worde aganis the vsurpit auctoritie of
Iohne Knox and his Caluiniane brether
intrudit Precheouris &c.

☞ ( ✳ ) ☜

Put furth to the Congregatioun of the
Protestantis in Scotlāde, be Mi-
niane Winʒet, ane Catho-
lik preist borne in
Renfrew:
( ✳ ✳ )

☞ At the desyre and in the name of his afflictit Catholike brether of ye inferiour
ordoure of Clergie, and laic men.
( ‡ )

*Vir impius procaciter obfirmat vultum suum: qui autem
rectus est, corrigit uiam suam.*
Prouerb. 21.

Edinburgi vltimo Iulij. 1562.

*Ane Submonitioun to the redar.*

The caus quhy we haif intitulit þis tractate on the maner preceding, is: that we first foundit the trompet of godis word, twiching this purpose in thre questions specialie, amangis mony ma proponit to Johne Knox ād his brether, & delyuerit to him in name of þam al. Quhilkis we iugeit sufficiēt occasiō to ony man in quhome had bene the feir of god, to examinat him self, and to wdraw him fra ye rolkis of errour and arrogance in this mater. And secundlie quhen this fornamit Johne wes nott mouit thairby, bot erar puft vpe tō mair prydē, intendit to preue his vocation planelie in þ pulpet (bot quhat strenth had his armour of defence thair, lat cūning mē iuge quha hard·him) we blew the samyn trompet againe in thre wrytingis according to his preching on sindry dayis: ād þat verray schortlie as it had bene be thre sindry sōndis blawin almast at ane tyme. Be þ quhilks albeit he wes abaissit, and woundit in conscience afore god (quhais worde is mair peirceand thā ony twa aigeit sworde &c.) Zit ye wylfull blyndnes & obstinat arrogance leidand all puersit erroneus men as captiuis and bunde presoneris, haldis him and his brether sa fetterit, as it war tō certane strang chenis of Jrne, that thay wyll not zit descend in thaim selfis to humilitie & penance: bot indurit as Pharao whaldis the peple of·god in thraldū aganis his expres cōmād and approuin ordinance. Quhairfor þ the blynd

Hebre. 4.

of thaim and thair scoleris be not impute tyll vs
in ye sycht of god, for not schawing our brotherlie lufe to thaim, in admonissing of thair erroure
& perrell: we put furth this thrid and last blaste,
to call abak the scoleris frome ye plaig of godis
iustice, as we callit (as we mycht) thair techa-
ris afore: thinkand this to be sufficiēt aduertis-
mēt to al thaim quha hes earis to heir ye treuth,
yat we neid not in this mater ony ofter to sound
this trompet.

      *Reid and Iuge.*

*To the Congregatioun of the Proteſtantis
in Scotlande.*

VHILL we ar aluterlie irkit, ho-
norable and deirbelouit, we haif
kepit silence, almaist aganis our
cōscience, sen the twelft of Marche, awaityng on Johne Knox
answeir in writt, of his lauchfull
vocatioun, accordinge to his promis maid in the
pulpet to our last writtyng, delpuerit to him yat
day thairupon. Quhilk promis sen he nother
fulfyllis (nother anētis this, nor our vther questionis) nor yit he nor his brether desistis fra v-
surpinge sa hie ane office, to the quhilk thay can
nocht schaw thaim lauchfullie callit conforme to
godis ordinance, nor yit mak ony answeir thairin wout thair schame (as we ar psuadit) except
thay godlie schaw thair repentāce: We may not
bot pray and beseik your prudence for the health

and saifing of zour awin saulis, that ze reid, cō‑
sider and iuge sinceirlye withoute all affectioun
our questionis & answeris maid to Johne Knox
declaratioun thairupon. And exhortis zow al‑
swa gyf ze may collect furth of the Euangell ony
defēce be precept or exemple, to assure vs of zour
precheouris lauchfull vocatioun: that ze assiste
to thaim thairwith, and mak the samyn patent
tyll vs: Quhair by that ze and we sum tyme bre‑
ther of ane kirk, may be to gidder, zit obedient
brether but schisme and discorde, to the Prophe‑
tis and ministeris of god (of zoure precheouris
we meine) fra thay be knawin vndouttitlie to be
send be him. Bot failzeing thairof (as we hope
ze sall) we exhorte zow in the bowelis of IESVS
Christe oure onelie Saluiour & Mediator that
ze set aspde all blynd affectioun, and auert zoure
earis fra the sweit venum of deuyllish eloquen‑
ce of wordis, and begin to feir and trimbe at the
Num. 16. feirfull exemplis of deid in Core ād his cumpa‑
2. Par. 26. nie, and of ye proude king Ossas quha temerus‑
lie in his arrogance ingerit him self, to make sa‑
crifice at the altare of God, woute all lauchfull
vocatioun thairto. For of thir dais now present
Iudæ. I. aduertissis zow, nocht we, bot the Apostle Iude.
Woo be to thaim (sayis he) quha in the rebelli‑
oun ād tressoun of Core hes perissit. And giue
ze think thir exemplis nocht sufficiēt to persuade
zow, quhilkz we haif writtin to Johne Knox in v‑
theris tractatis: remēber alsua maist effectuous‑
I. King. 13. lie we zou pray, þ for vsurpyng Samuelis office,
as for ane fait in special, king Saule wes repel‑

lit fra his kingdome. The mercy of god stay, þ we and ȝe for defending of sic misordour, be nott repellit fra our natiue possessionis heir, ād efter fra our kingdome eternale. Quhat? sulde nocht the arrogance & murmuring of Maria the sister of Moyses, with Aaron, & þ foule lippre quhairwith scho wes plagit thairfor, stryk ȝow ŵ feir? Quha murmuring aganis Moyses, & ascriuing auctoritie to hir self, ŵout all lauchfull vocatioun thairto, (as ȝour precheouris dois presētlie) said this: hes god spokin be Moyses onlie? hes he not spoki siclik to vs? Eui as ȝour pphetj sais now. Haue we not science knaulege, & vnderstādig þ gyft of god? Quhy ar we not thairthrow, but farder auctoritie or ordinatiō, lauchfull pastores Bischopis ād prelatis? Reid and cōsider siclyke to quhat miserable end Hieroboam wes brocht for his wickit consaitis and doingis, causing þe Isralites nocht to passe to Pierusalem, to make sacrifice to god, quhair the Arcke, Tabernakle, and prestis (as in the town quhilk god peculiarlie had elect) wes appoyntit than to remane: and nocht chesing the preistis of the tribe of Leui according to godis especiall command, bot passing with the peple to Bethel and Dan, and thair offerit sacrifice to strainge goddis, electing be his auctoritie aganis the ordināce of god, ane confussioun of wickit prestis of quhat sumeuer Tribe thairto. Mark and obserue with al diligence we exhort ȝour prudence in the name of our lord Jes., gif ȝe haif folowit Hieroboā i lyke maner or

nocht

Num. 12.

S. Reg. 14.
Ibid. 12. & 11.

nocht: drawing ye peple and zour selfis, fra our trew Hierusalem godis haly kirk vniuersal (out of ye quhilk pair is na sacrifice of prayer, louing, or rychteousnes plesand to god) to Bethel & dan to the priuat conuenticules of Schismatikis ād heretikis: ād giue ze haue thair maid sacrifice to fals godis: ye is alsua (as ancient fatheris godlie exponis it) hes embraceit fals and erroneus doctryne, for the treuth: hes worschippit, and adornit erroures, heresies and leis for the eternall veritie of godis word: & that ze mycht haif zoure awin consaitis wicketlie fulfyllit, consider giue ze *prurientes auribus* hes not electit preistis and precheoures, & *heipit vp masteris to zour selfis:* not discending of the tribe of Leui: That is not succeding to the Apostles and thair successouris efter ye ordināce appoyntit be the word of god. And gyf al thir terrouris may nocht mollifie zour hartis to knaw oure iust motiones: and that ordinare auctoritie ād obedience thairto quhilk Christe hes left i his kirk be his Apostlis & pair successours: Aduert we praye zow and mark the office of ane bischope to be sa hie & sa excellent, that our Saluiour self tuke not that office vpon him without the lauchfull vocatioun of his heuinlie fader, as S. Paule writtis, *Euin sa Christ alsua glorifeit not him self to be maid the hie preist: Bot he that said vnto hī: Thou art my sonne this day haue I begottin the: glorifeit hī. As he sais in ane vther place. Thou art ane preist for euer efter the ordour of Melchisedech.* And sen ze reding the haill new Testamēt sen Christ, & ye historiis of al cuntreis, sensyne, findis na bischope, preist, nor dea-

*Cant.* 6.

*Vincent. Lirinen.*

2. *Timo.* 4.

*Io.* 20.
*Act.* 2. 6.
13, 14.
1. *Timo.* 5.
*Tit.* 1.

*Hebre.* 5.
*Psalm.* 2. &
109.

cone institute, & ordanit be þ laic peple in ye haly catholike kirk bot be the Apostlis and thair suc cessouris bischopis alanerlie: Insamekle that þ sewin Diacones electit be the peple to be steuar tis specialie to þ pure in godis kirk, wes presen tit afore the Apostlis ād tuke thair ordinatioun and power of thaim: Ar ʒe not affrait to auante samekle that ʒe haue godis worde for ʒow, & not we: and contrare the worde of god sa expresse ād sa largelie put afore ʒour eine to manteine ād de fend sic misordoure? Wyll ʒe not schaw ane au ctoritie of godis word for ʒour misters vocatiō? Quhair find ʒe euer ony of the Apostlis writ ting to the Romanis, Corinthianis, or ony vther multitude cōmanding thaim to constitute & or dinat bischope or vther minister, as ʒe may reide ʒat he geuis expresse cōmād to ye bischopis, Ti mothe and Tite, to vse that power euery ane off thaim seuerallie. Quhair reid ʒe euer in the apo stolis dais amang sa mony thousande Christi anis turnit to the faith, or ʒit sensyne ony multi tude of laic people allane to haue ordinatit ane bischope, preist, or diacone? Bot that we appeir nocht to depriue ony part of the kirk, mēbris off Christ of ony dignitie appoyntit to thaim in the scripture. We confesse (and to that gladlye we assent) that the laic peple sumtyme hes electit sic persones, as the sewin Diaconis afore namit: & in the presence of the peple the bischopis to haue bene ordinatit: quha afore had bene cōmonlie in the law of grace, electit ād presentit to the Com prouinciall Bischops be thaim, geuing to thaim

*Act. 6.*

*I. Timo. 3. & 4. Tit. I.*

*Act. 6.*

testimonie of thair godlie conuersatiō, & cōsent of thair fauour to thaim: as to sic psonis quhō efter thay suld reuerēce, baith for thair office ād haly leuing. Sa *instituit* Moyses *the Bischope* Eleazarus *on the hyech montane* Hor *before the haill multitude: as before thaim quhay sulde testifie alwayis of his haly lyfe.* Sa wes Mathias ordinatit *in the place of* Iudas *in the middis of the discipulis:* quhome afore to Joseph thai hed electit. On the quhilk place the haly martyr Cypriane writis this: Quód vtique id circo tam diligenter & cautè, conuocata plebe tota gerebatur, ne quis ad altaris ministerium, vel ad sacerdotalem locum indignus obreperet. That is, quhilk thing verilie pairfore wes done sa diligētlie and warlie the haill peple being callit to gidder, pat na vnworthy psoun mycht quietlie creip to the ministerie off the altare: or to the preistis roum. And in the sampn place contendis he: pat be ye auctoritie of godis word it suld be obseruit, that the preist or bischope be admittit, in p psence of all the peple, that he be haldin be the iugemēt and witnessing of all to be worthie ād apt to pat office: Sē p peple (sais he) hes special power to elect the worthie preistis, & to refuse the vnworthie. peirfore sen the princes in our dayis takis on thaim the haill power of electioun vote & suffrage of the peple, presenting quhat psoun thay pleis, wald god pat thair presentation war void of all symonie, ambition, & inordinat affection: And to it wer adiunit alsua, ye testimonie & cōset of p peple in euery Diocesse & parochin, according to the auctoriteis abone rehersīt. Sa we think, that thair suld nocht be sa mony Blynd *cru-*

Num. 20.

Act. I.

Cyp. li. I. epist. 4.

Job. Vnoy quhat altar is this? and quhat preist?

Electioun, and ordination ar not ane as it is patent abone

Act. 6.

kit, & seik, smottit, mutilat, mankit, deformit, scabbit, Moabites, Amonites, and sclanderous, Mamzeres, contrare the law of god presentit, offerit, and maid preistis ād prelatis in the kirk, Giue ony of ʒow wpl obiect that the preistis bischopis ād ye clergie in oure dais hes bene blekkit w̄ the saidis deformiteis and sa ignorāt or vitious, or baith, ād alsua sclāderous, p̄ thay ar vnworthie ye name of Pastores. Allace we ar rycht sorie that this is treu for the maist part, ād mair. Bot wald ʒe consider the cause thairof to be our iniquitie, vngodlines & abominable lyfis for the quhilk god is at wraith with vs, and for the quhilkis in reuenge of our sinnis, according to his iustice, he sufferis, *Hypocrites to haif cure ouir vs, as he caussis*, Sum tyme vitious, or tyrane princes, sūtyme effeminat personis, or babis, impotent to defende vs throu iustice in quietnes and rest, sumtyme *Infidelis to haue dominioun abone vs*. We wald seik ane vther remeid thā to heip vp sin vpon sin in ye defending of sa vngodlie misordour agains p̄ ordinance ād reuelit wpl of god i his scripture sa expresse & sa largely set furth. Quhat remede speir ʒe? But dout to turne vnfenʒeitlie of al our hart fra our idolitricall and insaciable auarice, proude feirles presūptiō, fra maist auaricio' * prodigalitie (we meine specially of ye glorious bordouring of ʒoure garmentis with the blude of pure) fra the deuoring of the patrimonie of the kirk, ye tressour of indigent, fra Geschelie libertie ād brutale irreligiositie, fra vaine babling of godis worde but feir and reuerence thairoff in contentioun and

*Levit.* 21.
& 22.
*Malach.* I.
*Deut.* 23.

*Iob.* 34.
*Esa.* 3.
*Eccle.* 10.
*Hierem.* 38.
As the babilonianis had vpon ye Sowis and the Turk now vpon mony christianis. *
*Antitheton.*
*Hiere.* 2.

*Act.* 2.

curiositie, fra proude ignorāce, fra þ abominatiō of wychecraft & schameles mantening thairof in contempt of god and his law, fra fals fenzeit hypocrisie of halines, fra ingratitude and vtheris deuyllische monstres of vice regnād at this tyme: to our maist mercyfull god and trew seruing of him in haly feir and brotherlie lufe and in reiosing in him be humill dredour and reuerence.

*Psalme. 2.*

Bot of the twa proude princes Dame Herese and hir sister we wyll not talk, knawing that our maistres faithfull simplicitie, ād lufeand lawtie, tō thair seruandis, be thaim wyl nocht be hard, bot repellit & schot to the dure as sillie thingis wantand craft to circumuene, flatter, & lie. For now quha seis it nocht cum to passe, quhilk god complenis be his Prophete? quhilk is, *That mony heris and knauis his worde (in ane parte) and dois not thairefter, bot turnis it in ane sang of thair mouth, thair hartis being geuin tyl auarice, & the word of god is to thaim, as ane ballat of menstralie, quhilk hes ane sueit tone, & plesand to sing.* Lat ws turne I say and pray, *that the Lorde of the winezarde send vs lauchfull treu workmen thairto baith to schute oute the vnclene baris,* quha be filthie leuing ād sueingeing in thair stinkande styis, infectis the tender burgeounis of the zong wynis and to schut out or cut of alsua, the wyld sangleris, þ is þe proude Schismatikis and obstinat heretikis na wayis sociale to þ cōpanie of christiāe catholiks. Quha in hie arrogance of thair maister Lucifer trampis down the heuinlie incres and all decent policie of the lampn winzarde, drest and deckit, be ye former workmē vnfenzeit policiaris of ye samin,

*Ezechi. 33.*

*Luc. 10.*
*Psalme. 79.*

*Of doctrine & ordor we meaine maist specialle.*

# THE BUKE

OF

## FOUR SCOIR THRE QUESTIONS,

TUECHING

### DOCTRINE, ORDOUR, AND MANERIS,

PROPONIT TO YE PRECHEOURIS OF YE PROTESTANTS IN SCOTLAND, BE YE CATHOLIKS OF YE INFERIOUR ORDOUR OF CLERGIE AND LAYT MEN YAIR, CRUELIE AFFLICTIT AND DISPERSIT, BE PERSUASIOUN OF YE SAIDIS INTRUSIT PRECHEOURS.

---

Set furth be NINIAN WINZET a Catholik Preist,

AT YE DESYRE OF HIS FAYTHFULL AFFLICTIT BRETHIR, AND DELIUERIT TO IOHNE KNOX YE XX. OF FEBRUAR OR YAIRBY, IN YE ZERE OF THE BLISSIT BIRTH OF OUR SALUIOUR 1563.

---

Ne sis sapiens apud temetipsum. *Prouerb. iij.*
Sed interroga patres tuos, et annunciabunt tibi: maiores tuos, et dicent tibi. *Deu. xxxij.*

---

ANTVERPIÆ

EX OFFICINA ÆGIDIJ DIEST. M. D. LXIIJ. XIIJ. OCTOB.

CUM GRATIA ET PRIUILEGIO.

*REGIÆ Maieſtatis Priuilegio permiſſum eſt Niniano Winzeto, vti per aliquem Typographorum admiſſorum impune ei liceat imprimi curare, et per omnes ſuæ ditionis Regiones diſtrahere librum inſcriptum,* The buke of fourſcoirthre queſtionis, tweching doctrine, ordour, and maneris, proponit to ye precheours of ye proteſtants in Scotland : *Et omnibus aliis inhibitum, ne eius libri editionem abſque eiuſdem Niniani conſenſu imprimant, vel alibi impreſſum diſtrahant, ſub multa xx. florenorum vltra exemplaria impreſſa. Actum Bruxellis xxviij. Auguſti* 1563. *Subſcripſit.*

*Facuwez.*

NINIANE WINZET A CATHOLIK PREIST TO YE CHRISTIANE

REIDAR WISSHIS GRACE AND PEACE.

---

At ye command of Dene Patrik Kinloquhy precheour in Linlythqow and of his fuperintendent, gentil Reidar, quhen I, for denying only to fubfcriue yair phantafie and factioun of faith, wes expellit and fchott out of yat my kyndly toun, and fra my tender Freindis yair, quhais perpetuall kyndnes I hoipit yat I had conqueft, be ye fpending about ten zeris of my maift fluriffing aige, nocht without manifeft vtilitie of yair commoun welth, and be all apperance had obtenir fik fauour of yame, as ony fik man micht haif of ony communitie: I thocht I had na caufe to be efchameit, bot to reiofe and glorifie my God (according to S. Petiris reull) for yat I fufferit nocht, 1 Pet. 4. as a wickit perfoun, or an ewill doar, bot as an wnfenzeit and faithfull Chriftiane: for ye tyme is now (as ye famin Apoftill writtis) yat ye terribill iugement to cum, in a manere in yis lyfe beginnis at ye houfs of God: yat is, at ye faithfull catholikis, yat firft for yair awin finnis, and fyne for ye trewthis faik yai fuffer in yis lyfe with Chrifte yair heid, yat be diuers tribulis yai mot enter with him in ye lyfe eternall. Nochtyeles I began Act. 14. nocht litill to merwel at fa haifty, and fa fubdane a wolter of yis warlde, in fa mony grete materis, and fpecialie of ye fubdane change of fum cunning clerkis, of ye filence and fleitnes of wtheris, and of ye maift arrogant prefumptioun approwin fpecialie in ye ignorant: and amangis wtheris ftrange mutationis, quhow micht it be, yat ane kinloquhy culd be king in Linlythqow: and fpecialie fik a king, as appropriat to him felf mair large

<sub>A meruolis haifty change to be amangis Chriftianis. Of new kingis.</sub>

empyre and power in yis caice, yan euir did faithfull king or emprior in Chriftianitie. For of yame all, certane is it, yat neuir wes ane, quha attemptit to charge yair fubiectis, with ye burding of an uther religioun nor faith, yan ye vniuerfal kirk of God had euir afore profeffit: quhilk in his prefence (albeit I wes to him na fubiect) for ye gloir of Chriftis name (quha in all mot euir be praifit) before honorable perfones, maift planelie confeffit I. And fua fra I perfauit yis new proud prince, and his Caluiniane brethir on lyke manere in utheris partis, to hef fubdewit fa to yame, wnder fik thirldum yair miferable fcoleris, nocht only yat yai micht leid yame concerning yair bodyis, as yai war flawes, prefoneris, and captiues in a raip: yat is, to caufe yame to wair and hafert yair geris and bodyis, for yair plefuir: bot to hef blindit alfo yair iugement and naturall reffoun, yat yai regaird na lawis diuine nor humane, bot haldis it only law quhateuir yai raill, rattill, or trattill: be it neuir fa euident aganis Godis expres word, his manifeft ordinance, his haly Kirk, his princeis and his prelatis: and amangis ye reft to hef vsurpit to thame in maift præfumptuows bauldnes, yat plane tyrannie, for fatisfying of yair rage, to compell yair fcoleris to banies catholik and innocent men, ze, yair awin tendir freindis and kinifmen, in contempt of oure Souerane Lady and hir hienes lawis, fra yair iuft poffeffionis, natiue roumes and cieteis: I wes almaift aftoneift at yair proud præfumption in fa hiech an interprife, and in fa prydeful and arrogant procedingis: yat fa obfcuir men durft prefume to medle yame aganis all auctoritie, bayth with ye auctoritie of ye fpiritual and temporal fuorde. Bot fra I mair deiply confyderit and weyit ye hiech arrogance of men of fa law degre, and aluterlie woid of all lauchful power, be ony titill yai allege yairfor, to be aganis al lauchful pouer placeit be God, a manifeft fcurge of his wraith, for ye inundation of our fynnis, lang raigeing in euery eftate: I ceiffit ferther to merwell. For yat few catholik Kingis or Quenes, Princeis, or Prelatis almaift throw Chriftindome, hes yis day voluntare and dew obedience, according to ye expres word of God, of yair fubiects, it is ouer patent, allace for pietie: infamekle yat quhilk ye Prophete fpak afore of Ierufalem (quhilk wes a figure of ye Kirk in yis tyme of grace) apperis in yir our tribulus dayis almaift fullelie complete. *Obliuioni*, fays he, *tradidit Dominus in Sion feftiuitatem* *et sabbathum: et in opprobrium et in indignationem furoris sui Regem et Sacerdotem. Repulit Dominus altare suum, destruxit sanctuarium suum.* That is ye Lord hes forzet in Zion (that is in his haly kirk) ye solennit* tyme and ye sabboth day: and in indignatioun of his wraith, hes forzett ye king and ye preist. He hes schott away his altar, and hes destroyit his sanctuarie. Thairfor fra I wes persuadit, yat it wes ye almychty doutleslie, quha throw his iustice aganis sin, sufferis ye Prince and ye Preist (whome to in erd be ye expres word of God, we aucht maist honour) sumtyme to be dishonorit, albeit be ye wickit only, according to it yat is writtin, *Baltheum Regum dissoluit, et precingit fune renes eorum: ducit Sacerdotes inglorios, et optimates supplantat.* And in an vther place speikand of ye hie preist, *Qui honorificauerit me,* says ye almychty, *glorificabo eum: qui vero me contemnunt, erunt ignobiles:* I seirceit out ye titill, yat our new Caluiniane kingis and princelie preistis culd haif for yair auctoritie: quhiddir yis yair dominioun abone ws, wes prouideit to yame, as to a weilbeluifit peple of God, as wes ye land of Chanaan to ye Israelitis: or permittit as to an wngodly and wickit peple sterit vp to be Godis scurge, for a tyme aboue his welbeluifit peple, in his discipline and fatherlie correctioun for yair trespassis: as wes ye wngodly and confusit Babilonianis aganis ye haly citie of Ierusalem. And breuelie considering ye first part of yair titill to yis yair supreme auctoritie: I fand it nocht only sclinder and licht, bot planelie inglorius, and a thing to depriue yame of all auctoritie without delay, gif yai had hald ony afore. This first and speciall part, and almaist ye hail wair is, yat yai confessit yame selfis to hef bene afore, in ye preching of ye hevinlie and eternal word of almychty God, contrare baith yair conscience and science, schameles learis, and be fals doctrine wilfull dissauearis and poysonnaris of ye peple of God: forgeing yair sermonis for ye plesuir of euery auditour, efter ye fassoun of schipmenis breiks, mete for euery leg: any thing to hef vnderstandit and roundit priuatlie in ye mirk, and ane vther thing to hef precheit oppinlie in ye pulpet: ane thing to hef had cloisit in yair breistis, and ane vther reddy, as yai thocht tyme, in yair mowthe. Be ye quhilk schameles testimonie of yair awin toungis, of na ressoun culd I be induceit, efter to credit and reuerence yame mair yairfor, as mony yan

* Zuil pasche witsund. etc.
O Mahometical impietie.
O preparairis of ye way to ye Antichriste.
Ro. 12.
1 Pet. 2.
Heb. 13.
Iob 12.
*ab impiis procedit impietas.*
1. Re. 24.
1. Reg. 2.
Note, of superioritie.
Gen. 12. 13. 15. &
Ios. passim.
Heb. 12.
Prouer. 3.
4. Reg. 24. 25.

The titil of ye new Caluiniane kingis.

Their recantatioun.

## TO YE CHRISTIANE REIDAR.

*The botum of yair hert is declarit to be, a botumles conscience.*

*Of yair excuis. Act 9. 22.*

(bot fy on ye clekane wittit in ye caufe of God) of a maruelus facilitie did : bot to efteme yame rather at yat prefent to be ye famin felf men, quhome yai without all fchame, or appering repentance of fa horrible a cryme (gif yai had recantit yair leis vnfenzetlie, fra ye botum of yair hert, as yai vfe to fpeik) confeffit yame to hef bene afore. For na man is of ony iugement, quha markis nocht yair fchaimles confufioun, quhen yai wald thraw ye exempill, of ye converfioun of S. Paull to be a trim cloke and excuis of yair euerfioun. For S. Paull at yat tyme wes ignorant of Chrifte, of his word and facramentis, and blindit be feruent zele towart ye Mofaical law, perfeuit ye membris of Chrifte in mirk ignorance firmilie, albeit maift wranguflie perfuadit, yat all yat he did wes a thing maift ple-

*1. Tim. 1.*

*Sen infameit perfones may nocht be witnessis in manis caufe: quhow fall yai be iugeis in ye caufe of god.*

fand to God : and yairfor, fayis he, *Mifericordiam confecutus fum, quia ignorans feci in incredulitate.* Bot yai contrarie confeffit yame felfis to hef techeit and wrocht contrare yair knawlege and confcience, and willinglie and wittinglie to hef borne fals witnes, nocht contrar man nor manly biffines, bot contrar God and his eternal veritie. And zit becaufe fum of yame wes efchamit, to teftifie fa planelie yair gret vngodlines : bot allegeit yat yai had obtenit mair illuminatioun of ye haly gaift, and greatear knawlege of ye veritie : I conferrit with me felf, quhow yat micht be, yat Chriftiane men profeffing, techeing, and preching Chrifte and his word fa mony

*a subdane change to be in ye faythfull. an. 1559. A grete occasioun quhareby ye auctour wes first moueit to wryte.*

zeris, in ane monethis fpace or yairby, fuld be changeit fa proudly in fa mony hiech materis in ye plat contrar men. At pafche and certane foundays efter, yai techeit with grete appering zele, and miniftrate ye facramentis til ws on ye catholik manere : and be witfonday yai change yair ftandart in our plane contrare. And fa iugeit I, yat it neceffarlie behuifit thame, othir to hef bene afore werray finzeit hypocritis, and temperizaris with ye tyme contrare yair confcience, or to hef bene reuiffit be fum mychty fpirit. And yairfor thocht I it a thing nocht only profitable at yat tyme, bot werray neceffar, to obey ye counfell of ye Apoftill: yat is

*1. Io. 4.*
*1. Pet. 3.*

to try and examin ye fpiritis, gif yai war of God. Heirfor fen all men fuld be reddy, to geve compt of yat faith and hoip in him, yat I, being a Preift, fuld notht hef bene iugeit be ye waik, to yair fclander (to quhome

*Apoc. 3.*

my conuerfatioun afore wes knawin) faithles and feble, nother hait nor cauld : I intendit, be godis grace, to declare me planelie in yis dangerus

feditioun an vnfeinzeit Chriftiane, yat is, ftoutlie to gainftand all abufe, negligence, licentius leuing, and pharifaicall hypocrifie to me knawin, other
of ye former aige, or of it now prefent: and ficlyke to fchaw me a manifeft aduerfar, efter my fmall leirning and knawlege, to all fchifme feditioun, errour, and herefie. And albeit I wes nocht fa weill exerceit in
ye fcripturis, as become me of my aige and vocatioun, nor zit guidlie micht
fua be, fen I had fpent my maift flurifling zowtheid apt to yat ftudie, in
techeing of cheldring: zit I rememberit yat I fuld nocht be an hypocrite,
nor applaud to ye warld contrar my confcience, to beleue ane thing in ye Eccl. 1.
law of God, and fay ye contrar: nor zit for ye feir or fauour of man, Ro. 14.
fulechelie to appreue or condemne in Godis caufe ony thing to me Eccle. 5
wnknawin. And yairfor yat ye waik fuld nocht hef bene offendit be my
filence, and yat I micht hef knawin my aduerfaris ftrenthe, gif ony had
bene for yair nouationis, collectit I yan in fynceritie of confcience, fum of
yai heidis, quhilkis I iugeit ye foirfaidis perfones to hef techeit erroneouflie, and wrait to yame familiarlie in a plefand manere, forzetand all former
iniuris done to me, or to wtheris my faithfull brethir. To ye quhilkis
heidis my new king kinloquhy, in findry writtingis woid of all humanitie
and compatience, and taiftand nocht only of contentioun, bot of contempt,
maid findry promiffis of an anffuer, with grete boifting of ye victorie to
him, and triumphe alrady in hand: bot as zit, yat we mot knaw his invart
religioun, be his fidelitie (I will nocht fay be his leis) in externe materis,
we heir na thing of his promis fulfillit. That delay fuythfie of his anffuer, The se-
fra yat I efter fa mony oblifingis had avytit vij. or viij. monethis yairupon, sioun to
moueit me efter yat I had conferrit with fum weill leirnit catholikis, and largelie to
with fum ftrang Caluinianis alfo, and had red fum controuerfeis and ref- Iohne
foning yairupon on baith fydis, to collect almaift ye haill fumme of yai Knox.
thingis, quharein I wes offendit, in ye doctrine, ordour, and maneris, now
auctorizit, contrar all auctoritie. Quhilkis fa collectit I prefentit to my
catholik afflictit brethir, layt men and wtheris, in quhome apperit to me ye
fpirit of knawlege and godly feir. Quha anffuerit in ane mynd yame all,
fpecialie to be moueit be ye famin reffonis and auctoriteis, nocht to affift
to ye new impietie, callit be fum ye reformatioun of ye proteftantis. Bot
zit yai defyrit yir queftionis mair trimlie and ftrenthelie to be fet furth,

with ma large auctoriteis, and to be writtin agane: and yairefter to be deliuerit to ye principall precheouris of ye new factioun. For I had collectit yame schortlie wanting buiks, quhen I wes in travell, as yai come in my memorie of former reiding, and of conferring with wtheris at yat tyme be ye way: as sum honorable personis knawis. This I eik, baith for ye trewth, yat gif ony thing negligentlie, and nocht sufficientlie strenthit be set furth in yis werk, it suld be impute to my haist and seruour, and to nane wtheris iniustlie: and to signifie also, yat gif ye lauchfull pastouris, and wtheris bettir leirnit of ye catholik syde, did yair diligence in yir materis, and spak frelie without feir, yat sik proud, sulege phantaseis, pyntit leis, brutall irreligiositie, and damnable errouris, as now regnis, in ye place of syncere veritie, and trew catholik religioun, defenceit only be finzeit eloquence, iesting, and mockrie, wald nocht haif sa lang reinzeis, nor ye existimatioun amangis ye peple, as yai haif presentlie, allace. Bot to ye purpose: I nocht yan haifing opportunitie, and werray desyrus to hef wtterit my religioun, to avoid all occasioun of sclander till wtheris, and to hef reduceit, sa fer as lay in me, ye wildsum wandering vnto ye richt way agane: or to hef bene assuirit be ye licht of Godis word (quhilk our aduersaris boistit yame to hef hald) yat we had bene furth of yat way in ony poynt, incontinent deliuerit yame writtin on yis ruid manere folloving to Iohne Knox, as to him, quha wes haldin in ya partis principal Patriark of ye Caluiniane court. And yat be ressoun, yat ye ane of my former competitouris keipit na promis, and ye wther maid na anssuer: hoipand mair fidelitie in yis renounit man, gif it had plesit him to promitt anssuer yairto in speciall, as he afore did generalie sindry tymes in ye pulpet, oblising him self to sik ressoning in word or writt: oftymes obiecting to the catholikis (quhome he callis papistis) yat nane of yame durst impugne ane propositioun of his doctrine: albeit ye contrar wes knavin to be trew. For quhais anssuere yairefter oftymes publiclie and priuatlie promissit be him, we hef awaytit almaist keiping silence sen the xx. of Februar, or yairby: quhill now laitlie within yir fews days is cum to my hand a ressoning anentis ye mayst blissit, seirfull, and haly sacrifice of the mes, haldin about a zere bypast betuix my Lord of Croceraguel and Iohne Knox, a werk in beginning decorit with a pece of an epistil, als bali, as is ye

*wharein ye wrytetar is to be repreuit.*

*quhy wes yis buik deliueret to Ione Knox.*

*An. 1561. Of ye tractate set furth anentis ye ressoning betuix my Lord of Croceraguel and Iohne Knox.*

## TO YE CHRISTIANE REIDAR. 57

auctour yairof, and I warrane zow, cunninglie gloiffit be fum weill leirnit and difcrete man, god wate, in ye mergin: quharein Iohne Knox of his pregnant ingyne and accuftomit craft of rayling and bairding, attributis to me a new ftyle, calling me procutour for ye Papiftis, and yair oblifis him of new, to geve anffuer to our queftioun tueching his lauchful vocatioun, and as we can collect yairof and of his former promis, he intendis to anffuer lykewayis to ye reft folloving in yis buke. Of ye quhilk twa poyntis I wes fingularlie reiofeit: firft yat God maid me worthy to be mockit for my fmal labouris in defence of his catholik kirk, fra ye fals accufatioun of hir aduerfaris, and to be reknit be yame in tyme of perfecutioun, in nummir of ye faythfull, quhome yai in yair iefting callis Papiftis. For in defence of yat thing only procuir I, quhilk ye honorable and haly Papiftis, ye haly Bifchope and Martyr of Chrifte S. Cypriane with ye wtheris renounit martyris in ye primitiue Kirk, and quhilk ye renounit Papiftis and excellent Doctouris S. Auguftine, Hierome, and Ambrofe, zea breuelie, ye haill Kirk of God fen ye Apoftolis days, in an vniformitie of doctrine maift clerlie appreuis. And na thing difaggreing yairfra procuir I: nocht adhering to ye priuate iugement or obfcuir fayngis of ony ane man, (as is ye commoun practik of our aduerfaris, to mak of obfcuir mirknes, a commentare to ye cleir licht) bot to ye plane and vniforme confeffioun of all, or at ye leift, to ye aggreable confent of ye maift part of ye beft lernit, euir be ye kirk of God auctorizit. And fua, godly Reidar, quhattin a Papist I am in yis famin ruid buik of queftionis (be ye infallible and inconfutable treuth of ye quhilk my aduerfar is offendit) I tak on hand to preue, on perrell of my lyfe, ye maift haly martyris, ye beft leirnit confeffouris afore reherfeit, and wtheris mony may bayth of ye Greik and of ye Latin kirk, togiddir with generall counfelis to hef bene ye famin Papiftis. O happy heirfor and happy agane think I yis day to me, quhen ye grete guidnes of God, of his mere mercy has præferuit me in yis maift ftormy tyme, fra ye rolkis of fchifme, errour, and hærefie: zea, fra manifeft rebellioun raigeing at yis præfent aganis Godis plane word, his kirk vniuerfal, his ordinance, his Princis, and his Prelatis: and befydis yat alfo hes lent me of his fpirit, to confes my faith to his gloir, quhill ye erroueous affault me be tanting, and mockrie, quhen yai

*Of twa poyntis yairin concerning yis mater.*

*For quhat mater procuiris ye wrytear.*

*Note ye trew catholik doctrine. For of ye trewth of ye scriptuir we contend nocht, bot of ye trew sense yairof approuin be Godis haly kirk vniuersal.*

*Reioising in God.*

may naways be veritie. For quhat veritie culd Iohne Knox fchaw for his lauchfull vocatioun (quhilk ane article fpecialie, he chefeit out of fa mony, to confute and confund in ye pulpet, to augment his gloir) I think it is nocht vnknawin to Scotland: and is nocht in my defalt, bot in defalt of my fmall freind Dame Cunzey, bot it fuld hef bene layng or now, as it fal be, God willing, fchortlie, to ye mein leirnit always (for ye godly cunning neidis nane of our labouris yairto) mair notifiit in Scotland, and in vther Chriftiane cuntreis: in quhat wickit apoftafie, he and all vtheris preiftis, munkis, and freris of his fect ar fallin in, in yat yai renunce as rennigatis, yair preiftheid gevin yame, be ye facrament of ordour: and quhow yai ftill remane preiftis be ye famin facrament (lat yame renunce it, as yai pleis) ay quhil yai de: albeit to yair mair feueir punifment æternalie, except yai (quhilk ye guidnes of God mot grant yame) in tyme repent yair fall: and fiklike in quhat proud arrogance and damnabil facrilege is he fpecialie, and ye vtheris his fallowis in yair degre, fliddin: vsurping ye auctoritie of godly bifchopes and vtheris paftouris and preiftis in ye kirk, aluterlie aganis all lauchful pover onyway gevin be man to ony minifterie, yat tha vfe in ye kirk, except only be yat titill, quhilk tha efteme nochtis: yat is, infafer as tha ar preiftis: and yat tha ar nocht fend as trew prophetis be God, it falbe, God willing, mair cleir yan ye day licht, be mony euident demonftrationis at lenthe. Bot now quhen all his blunt boultis and pithles artelzerie ar fchot, to infirm and adnull his awin caufe, rather yan to ftrenthe ye famin, yat be his lang filence efter fa mony promiffis he fchawis him felf conuict in confcience, haifand na appering reffoun for ye defence of his vocatioun, except we admitt him to be a new S. Iohne ye Baptift, or a new prophet Amos, hes he nocht win ye hoifs worthelie, in forgeing a mok to me mony mylis fra him, calling me procutar for ye Papiftis? Gif ony man, gentil Reidar, fall think yis my procuratioun in yir articulis to be wngodly, lat him remember, quhat he menis be yat article in his creid, *The haly Kirk vniuerfal.* For only quhat yis kirk (quhilk my aduerfar infinuatis to be it, quhilk he callis papiftical) hes euir defendit, and now defendis, intend I, be Godis grace, efter all my fmal pover and fpirit, euir to defend, and na thing difaggreing yairfra. Bot as to ye terme Papift, albeit faithful Chriftianis, of guid reffoun reiofeis in na new ftylis, concerning religioun: zit yat yai fuld be gretunlie offendit be ye terme Papift, obiectit to yame be yair aduerfaris, I can naways vnderftand: fen by it fpecialie may be bot vnderftandit, a man yat dois knaw ye lauchfull auctoritie of his bifchopes, quhome almychty God hes commandit be his expres word to fauour, luve, and humelie obey: and fpecialie to ye fucceffour of Petir now commonlie callit Papa: albeit Papa be a terme efter ye myndis of ye aunciant fatheris, commoun to ony Bifchope, as efter in yis buik is fchawin. Quha feis nocht yis day, yat gif Kingis ande Quenes buir nocht a fuord, quhilk our aduerfaris ferit mair, yan ye fpirituall fuord of ye Pape and vtheris bifchoipis, bot yai wald mok ws on lyke manere, and call ws Kingiftis and Queneiftis, or fiklyke name of yair commoun craft of mockrie, for our humil and dew obædience vnto our lauchful Souerane? And yis mekle concerning ye procutar for ye Papiftis. As to ye fecund poynt yat he promiffis in his buke to mak anffuere, as be word he did afore oftymes oppinlie, I am reiofeit yat he intendit yan to keip his firft promis: albeit as zit in dede efter ane haill zeris aduifement, we heir nocht yairof. Nochtyeles yat he is fa layng making anffuer, I hoip only guid yairthrow yat efter fa lang confultatioun, he fal, be Godis grace, præfer ye knavin veritie and his faluatioun to all wane gloir or plefuir of man. Bot failzeing yairof (quhilk God forbid) and gif alfo perchanfe, he keip na promis heirin: he dois bot yan, as becumis his new profeffioun and according to ye commoun trade of yat part of ye realme be him and his, præfentlie corruptit: quha declaris expreflie, quhatkin a faith yai haif in God, be ye faith and promis, yai vfe now commonlie to keip to man. Bot always becaufe in ye mein tyme we ar offendit be his layngfum delay, and ar ftoppit be ye tyrannie of fum, to put furth our mynd in prent at hame: and vnderftandis ye copiis of our quæftionis and vtheris tractatis corruptit be vnleirnit writtaris, to ye fclander of ye trevth and to our fchame we fett furth yis iuft copie, without altering or eiking ony thing, fa fer as we can remember: except onlie yat in place of yis epiftill wes fum Latin to ye cunning reidar, exhorting him nocht to haif refpect to our ruid ftyle, bot to ye trew catholik fentence: fen we controuertit nocht with our aduerfaris for trim talk, bot for ye trying of ye trewth: nocht for deckit vanitie, bot for ye æternall veritie.

Deut. 17.
Heb. 13.
Matth. 10.
Luc. 10.
Io. 13. 21.
Note.

The fecund poynt.

The caufe of ye prenting of yir quæstionis.

## TO YE CHRISTIANE REIDAR.

*Quhy ar yir quæstiounis now, nocht maid mair strenthy.*

Quhilk thing we requeift the, gentill Reidar, zit anis agane, and to purge yi copie according to yis præfent: willing ye to be perfuadit, yat gif it pleifit ws at ȝis tyme and place, to alter or eik yis tractate, yat with litill labouris, it micht be maid tueching ye ftyle mair plefing and perfuading, and in fentence fer mair ftrenthy and difficill to our aduerfaris to mak anffuer yairto. Zit nochtyeles becaufe Iohne Knox apperis to fchaw yat with his fallowis he labouris to fulfill his oblifing, we will eik nor alter na thing heirin, except fum illuftratioun in ye mergin, yat ye Reidar, gif ony anffuer beis maid may fyncerlie confer ye ane with ye wthir: and in ye mein tyme yat ye fempill beleuear may haif fufficient licht, to efchew ye diffaitful fnairis of ye erroneous. As to ye phrafe and dictioun heirof, guid it war to remember, yat ye plane and fempill trewth of all thingis requiris only amangis ye lautefull and faithfull peple, plane, familiar, and na curius nor affectat fpeche: as ye defence of fraud and falfet neceffarlie requeris a cloke of finzeit eloquence, be ye quhilk ye incircumfpect and licht of iugement oftymes ar diffauit. And as tueching ye mater, as we ar informeit, yat Iohne Knox efter aduifement wes efchameit to fet furth an anffuer, quhilk wes be certane of his grete fcoleris about a zere and thre monethis paffit deuifeit heirto: fua we ar affuirit, yat na leirnit of yame without prik of confcience (fa grete is ye guidnes of God to knok at ye breift of man) without ye ftudie, I fay, of fchifme and diuifioun, and without rebellioun and wilfull malingning aganis ye knawin veritie, fall tak pen in hand in our contrare, zea, contrare ye waik membris of Chrifte, an hundreth ways inuadit maift feircelie to leve yat haly religioun, quhilk yai maift godly profeffit at yair baptifm: For quhais defence fpecialie yir quæftiounis ar fet furth: yat ye vnleirnit mot haif fum defence aganis ye erroneous and contentious pleidaris: quha with yair continuall altercatioun, blafphemeis, and mockrie of all godlines, ithanlie labouris to fubuert ye fillie femple anis. Thir thingis I fpek in na fulege confidence of my eruditioun, bot in fynceritie of confcience, and godlie fortitude in ye defence of ye vndoutit veritie, techeit be ye haly Kirk vniuerfal, quhome only efter my knaulege and confcience, I follow as ye pillar and ftabilifment of veritie, as ye fpous of Chrifte our Lord, be ye illuminatioun of his fpirit induceit according to his promis in all richteufnes, haifand ye

*Of ye fpeche of veritie, and of diffait.*

Apocal. 3.

1. Timo. 3.
Cant. 6.

Io. 14. 16.

famin haly fpirit at all tymes hir doctour, gyde, comfortar, and aduocate  Act. 1.
Matt. vlt.
to hir promift, gevin, and to ye warldis end with hir remaning. Bot gif
ony falbe fa feble in faith and negligent of his faluatioun to maling contrar his confcience and inftinct of ye haly fpirit, for plefuir of his forlorne
brethir, and for a fchaddow of gloir to him felf: lat him be perfuadit, yat
ye almichty God, qua is ye defence and fuir protectioun of all yame, quha  Prouer. 2.
walkis in fimplicitie, fall fteir wp in his contrare ftrangar kempis and per-
fytear procutaris, yan I am, to oppin out and mak manifeft ye hyprocrifie
of ye fule, and of al his mainteimaris: according to it, yat is writtin of ye
leing maifteris, quha in ye latter days be ye yair fuete flattering eloquence  Ro. 16.
ar to feduce ye hertis of ye innocent, and be fiklyke iouglarie ar to gane-  1. Tim. 4.
Exod. 7.
ftand ye manifeft veritie: as Iannes and Mambres be yair leing deuilrie
and incantatiouns gainftuid Moyfes in ye præfence of Pharao: *Infipien-*  1. Tim. 4.
*tia eorum,* fays ye Apoftill *manifefta erit omnibus, ficut et illorum fuit:*
yat is ye fulegenes of yame falbe maid manifeft to all men, as wes ye
fulegenes of Iannes and Mambres. This mekle, Chriftiane Reidar, thocht
I expedient to be notifiit: quhareby my firft motioun to yir materis, and
caufe of ferther proceding, with my hoip of ye end heirof mot be knawin.
For as a Theologe I profes me to be nane, nor zit of ye nummir of ye hie
leirnit: fua nocht to confes me a faithfull Chriftiane, fpecialie quhen be
baneifing fra my tender freindis, I am almaift compellit yairto, I am effrayt
in ye præfence of God, and efchameit afore angell and man. And as it
is knawin nocht to be ye kirk rentis, nor roytous lyfe yairby, yat moueis
me to profes my name in yis debait and tentatioun, fen of ye kirk rentis
I had neuir my leuing, quhilk now I micht haif abundantlie, gif I præferrit my belly to guid confcience. fua I wald it war to nane vnknauin,
me euir to be an humil fone of ye haly kirk vniuerfal. For as fra vitious
leuing, abufe, fuperftitioun, and idolatrie, I (to God be gloir) aluterlie
dois abhorre: fua neuir fra my barneaige intendit I to fik proud arrogance, as to be a fchifmatik, nor zit to fik obftinat wilfulnes, as to be an
hæretik. And fa I hoip yat ye grete guidnes of yat lord maift bliffit, quha
of his mere mercy gaue me ye former mynd, fall corroborat and ftrenthe
alfo my præfent intentioun: quhilk is, nocht to be fa feble and fleit, for
na trible of tyme, nor tyrannie of man, yat I be a temperizar in Godis

caufe contrar my confcience: and fer les heirfor a plane rebell yairto. The famingift wifhe I to the beneuolent Reidar, yat of cheritie and for yi awin faluatioun yow wald affift till ws, as a faithful and conftant Chriftiane, in ye manifeft veritie : and yat without refpect of perrel, in feir of yat Lord, quha only knawis and fall iuge, zea, ye fecretis of ye confcience of man. Quha mot mak the with ws and all profeffing ye name of his only fone our Lord Iefus, of ane mynd, and of ane fpirit, humill and obœdient fones to all treuth and auctoritie, in his haly catholik Kirk. Amen.

Of Louane ye VII. day of October. M.D.LXIII.

The faythfull Sones of ye haly catholik Kirk in Scotland, of ye inferiour ordour of clergy and laytmen, humill fubditis to yare Souerane Lady Marie, and obœdient to yare lauchful Bifchopes and Paftouris, depofit of yare offices, incarcerat, exilit, or violentlie eiectit fra yair iuft poffeffionis and native citeis, for nocht affenting to ye prætendit reformatioun at yis præfent in religioun, to Iohne Knox and his complices prætending and allegeing yame to haif ye lauchful auctoritie and ordinatioun of trew Bifchopes, and wtheris Paftouris of ye Kirk within ye faid Realme wifhis helth, and illuminatioun of ye haly gaift.

WE perfaueand zour feruent diligence, to alluir all men to ye embraiffing of zour prætendit religioun, and zour feueir punifment alfo, and rigorus indignatioun agains, yame quha reffaues nocht ye famin : and confydering fiklyke, and alfo firmlie beleving yat yair is bot ane fayth of Chriftis Ephes. 4. deirbelovit fpous his haly Kirk, out of ye quhilk yair is na faluatioun nor Luc. 22. remiffioun of finnis : ye quhilk fuppofe be tribulit, fall nocht decay aluter- Matt. 28. lie conforme to our faluiouris promitt al ye dais of yis warlde : hes had confideratioun partlie of zour prechingis, and partlie of ye iugement of ye aunciant Doctouris and Martyris of ye primitiue Kirk, declarand fumtymes incidentlie ye fcriptuiris and ordour in ye materis of controuerfie now being in religioun : to ye intent we mot be inftructit in ye trewth yairof : and to abhorre and fle, be Godis grace, fra all kynd of idolatrie, fuperftitioun, fchifme, and herefie : and to be at ane alfo in ane Godlie vnitie with all yais, quha profeffis fyncerlie ye trew doctrine of Chrifte Iefus. Expending ye matur fua, and confidering fiklyke, quhat perrel it is Ephes. 4. to be cariit about with euery wind of doctrine, we ar be ye grace of God (to quhome be all gloir) perfuadit to yat conftancie, yat for na feir of trible, with help of ye hieaft, we wil affirm in diffimulatioun, yat thing to be trew in religioun afoir man, quhilk ye haly gaift hes nocht perfuadit

## TO THE CALUINIANE PRECHEOURIS.

<small>Ro. 14.
Matt. 10.
Luc. 12.</small>

ws to be trew afoir God. And yat fpecialie becaus we haif in rememberance yat all thing quhilk is nocht of fayth, is fin: and yat quha thinkis fchame of ye veritie, quhilk is Chrifte, afoir man : ye Sone of God fal be efchamit of him afoir ye angelis of his fader in heuin. Seing alfo yat ye Bifchoipis and wtheris Paftouris of yis Realme for ye maift part, hes nocht us zit, yat fpirit of fortitude to confes and affirm bauldelie on athir fyde without feir, yat thing quhilk yair confcience and fayth inwartlie dytis

<small>Exod. 22.
Act. 23.
Iud. 1.</small>

yame to be trew : we can nocht contrare ye word of God detrect yame, nor railze difpitfullie contrare yame : bot committis ye amendiment yairof to ye mercy of ye hieaft. For we ar certifiit be haly Scripturis, yat hypocritis and wikit perfones (bot of wices we accuis nane at yis præfent) als

<small>Iob. 34.
3. Reg. 22.
Ose. 9.
Ro. 14.
1. Pet. 2.
Galae. 6.
2 Cor. 5.
Hebr. 11.</small>

weill of ye Ecclefiaftical ftate, as of ye ciuill Magiftratis (to quome nocht yeles we aucht dew obædience with reuerence in all thingis nocht repugnand to ye will of God) hes fumtymes reull abone ye peple for yare iniquitie : of ye quhilk we knaw our felfis nocht giltles nor innocent. Zit fen euery man fall beir his awin burding at ye leift, and fall geue compt of his awin doingis, and yat without fayth it is impoffible to pleis God : neid is till ws to labour for ye faifgarde of ye trew fayth for our awin part. Heirfor we defyre zou of zour humanitie, gif ze wald yat we war iunit in religioun with zou, to anfuer till ws in writt zour opinioun and auctoritie yairfor, concerning ye articlis fubfequent : in ye quhilkis maift cheiflie ze

<small>Iud. 1.</small>

appere to hef fegregat zour felfis fra ws, infafer as we zit vnderftand of zour doctrine in yame. For in word, or preching only, we can nocht fa firmlie iuge yairin, tweching zour faid doctrine, yat we dar bauldlie without prik of confcience, embrafe ye famin as ye indoutit veritie. And zit defyris maift feruentlie, as we hef fchawin afoir, and as God knauis : all contentioun and difcord being trampit doun, all errour and abufe being cuttit away, to leue at quietnes, fa fer as is in ws, in all godlie vnitie, with all yais, quha vnfenzetlie luuis Chrifte Iefus, his eternall word, haly law, and immutable will, and covatis to duell in his grete houfs, quilk is his haly Kirk, in ane godly band of luve, without ftryfe and contentioun. Thir

<small>ye speciall caus of ye moving of yir quæstionis.</small>

thingis folloving we demand zow, as God knawis, of na malice contentioun, or oftentation of ony fcience, yat is in ws : quhilk we mifknaw nocht to be werray fmal, in refpect of mony wtheris : bot fpecialie for

## TO THE CALUINIANE PRECHEOURIS.

depreſſioun of errour, illuſtratioun and magnifiing of ye veritie, libertie of our conſcience according to Godis will : and yat ye waik and infirm be nocht ſclanderit be our vngodly ſilence in tyme of perſequutioun. And ſecundlie for twa cauſſis, of ye quhilkis ane is : forſamekle as we ar ſa tribulit be zow, and (as we wnderſtand) iniuſtlie perſuitit, with ſa grete rigour, as we war heretikis or apoſtatis, vnworthy ye cumpanie of trew Chriſtianis : and yat only for nocht aſſenting generalie to zour prætendit reformatioun : quhilk contrare our conſcience, led (as we ar perſuadit) be na wilfull ignorance, bot be ye trew wnderſtanding of Godis word, we dar naways attempt : fering gif we ſua do, ye offence of ye lord our God, and yairthrow our iuſt damnatioun. The wther is, yat ze ſa bauldlie exhortis all men to impugne zour doctrine planelie, gif yai may iuſtlie : or wthir ways in ſa fer as yai ar doutſum, to deſyre reſſoning with zou, in word or writt, in ony controuerſie affirmit be zou, quhare with yai be offendit : promitting zou to vndertak yai panis glaidly, and pleſandly to ſatiſie yame, according to zour doctrine, of ye expres word of God, gif yai be deſyrus of ye treuth yairof : of ye quhilk we confes ws maiſt deſyrus. Of yis ſamin promis cheiflie, we ingere ws bauldlie, nocht ſuſpectand zour offence yairby, to propone yir quæſtionis folloving : teſtiſiing to zow afoir God, yat we aluterlie of conſcience abhorris fra ye vnderſtanding yairof, according to zour, doctrine inſafer as we zit vnderſtand it : deſyring heirfor effectuuſlie, and requiring zour anſſuer yairof in writt conforme, to zour ſaid promis : and yat ſynceirlie without ſophiſtical contentioun of wordis, as ze will geif compt to him, quha miſknawis nane of al our thochtis : deſyring ſiklyke, and alſo maiſt hertlie and humbly praying ye nobilis and wtheris of zour congregatioun, to conſider attentlie, and treulie iuge, our former cauſſis to proceid of na hatrent, nor intent to moue diabolical ſeditioun (quhilk we ſpeik vnſenzetlie in Godis præſence) bot only of ye trew fontane of ſyncere luue : yat God and his æternal veritie mot be treulie acknaulegeit : and we, and al profeſſing ye name of our Saluiour Chriſte, bot ſpecialie our nobilis and wtheris our countreymen (to quhome beſydis ye profeſſioun of Chriſte, we ar in mony greis of luue naturalie coniuuit) mot be in vniforme ordour of religioun, of ane ſpirit, of ane mynd, and ane in all godlines in ye ſamin Chriſte Ieſus our only Saluiour and media-

*wtheris .ij. cauſſis.*

*Hebr. 4.*

tour. To the end heirfor, yat we may fa be, we exhort zour modeftie, gif ony thing in yis tractat be obiectit to zow, of ye quhilk ze fall peradventure pleis to fchaw zour felfis innocent, yat ze purge zou yairof, without cauillatioun in ane word: and impute yat to ye imbecillitie of our iugement, nocht throuchlie vnderftanding zour doctrine: Or (gif ze pleis) to our ignorance. For we had leiur be callit be zou our countreymen ignorantis, nor wit zou to be eftemit be al faythful nationes, in grete fchame of our natioun, wilfull and erroneous: certefeing zou of our confcience and alfo geuing be yir præfentis to zou our iuramentum (as yai cal it) calumniæ, yat we oppone na thing to zou heir, except only yat apperis till ws manifeft errour, or ellis curious, new, indiftinct, and confufit doctrine, of ye quhilk manifeft errour and præfumptioun vpryffis: or quhare miffordour, and maneris ar vngodlie be zou approuin, eftir our iugement. Or yat, quhilk ze calumniuflie (as we think) in diffimulatioun afcriuis to ye name of Papiftrie, nochtwitftanding ye famin be in deid (as we dout nocht zour felfis ye famin thing nocht to mifknaw) othir ye euident confent in doctrine of ye primitiue Kirk, expreffit till ws be ye writtingis of ye Doctouris within four hundreth zeris till Chrifte: or determinationis eftabiliffit be general Counfelis, according to ye haly fcriptuiris. We fufpect na thing of zour prudence, to putt in dout, quhat part of euery quæftioun, is obiectit to zou as erroneous: and quhat part fiklyke yairof is beleuit and appreuit be ws, as ye treuth. Forfamekle as it may chanfe, yat fum of our quæftiouns may appere to zour iugement mair prolixt, yan becumis eftir ye common confuetude, to fik materis: beleue heirfor ws, to hef tane willinglie ye mair labouris on ws at yis præfent, corroboring our iugement with fufficient defenfis, and fumtyme anffuering to zour maift ftrang obiectionis, to ye intent, yat eftir yis mair efalie without ftryfe, we mot togidder embrafe ye knauin veritie. Ferther ye fpirit of Chrifte promittit and geuin to ye Apoftolis to teche and perfuade yame all veritie, mot conuoy and confirm zou and ws, in ye perfyte beleue, and fyncere knaulege of Godis will, and continual obœdience to ye famin. Amen.

*Quhat materis ar proponit in yis tractat.*

## ¶ THE FIRST QUÆSTIOUN OR ARTICLE.

1. *Of ye trew vnderſtanding of ye Kirk, and be quhome ſpecialie expreſſit.*

SEN ye haly catholik Kirk is without controuerſie, to all profeſſing ye ſcripturis of God, ye pillar and firmament (or eſtabiliſing) of veritie, indoutitlie haifand ye trew vnderſtanding of ye ſyncere word of God, be ye inſpiration of ye haly gaiſt, conforme to our ſaluiouris promitt: quhidder beleue ze ye iugement of yis ſaid haly Kirk, mair treulie ſetfurth and expreſſit till ws, tueching ye trew vnderſtanding forſaid, and ſpecialie in materis of controuerſie being at yis præſent, be ye Martyris and wtheris aunciant Doctouris of ye primitiue Kirk: as Dionyſius, Clement, Martialis, Ignatius, Iuſtinus, Tertulliane, Cypriane, Irenæus, and Origene: and efter be Hierome his maiſter Nazianze, Ambroſe, Auguſtine, Athanaſius, Baſill, Hilarius, Chryſoſtome and Cyrillus with mony wthiris in yair days aborit .xjC. zeris paſſit at the leiſt: togiddir with general counſelis writand in ane conſent and vnitie of doctrine, ſpecialie quhare yai tueche incidentlie ony mater of religioun now controuertit: or be Iohne Caluin and his complices in yir our days? And to quhilk of yair conſentis and iugementis dar ze maiſt bauldlie aſſiſt in zour conſcience afoire God?

*[marginal notes: 1. Tim. 3. Io. 16. Becauſe nane ſectare can anſuer heir without manifeſt confuſioun of his errour: you Chriſtiane reid Vincenti lirinen, neulie putt in Scottis: quba Godly and cunninglie diſcuſſis yis queſtioun about a .xjC. zeris paſſit.]*

2. *Of ye calumnious allegeing of Papiſtrie.*

GIF ze præfer in zour conſcience afoir God the iugementis of the ſaidis aunciant fatheris and counſelis to Caluin and his forenemmit (quhilk we beleue ze dar nocht planelie deny afoir man, except ze wald be iugeit ſchameles) quhy depres ye in diſſimulance and obſcuiris in zour doctrine, be the name of Papiſtrie, as be ane terme, to mony maiſt odious the ſaidis fatheris and counſelis vniforme conſent in ſindry controuerſiis being at yis tyme: and follouis in zour techement the priuat opinioun of Caluin, and his complices rather yan yame?

*[marginal notes: Note yair ſimulatioun and diſſimutioun. And yat in all ye materis heir follouing. Reid for yis queſtioun ye ſext buik of Optat putt in Scotis with wtheris tractatis for yis porpoſe.]*

### 3. *That ye catholikis defendis na new doctrine.*

<small>quia pleiss to reid Tertulliane de præscrip. aduers. here. new lie putt in Scottis, quha wrait about .xuij C. zeris passit. sall knaw quha is now a catholik, and quha is an heretik.</small>

SEN all hæresie yat euir hes bene in ye kirk (except sum in few countreis knawin) had sum cheif Archiheretik inuentour yairof: of quhome yat hæresie and ye defendaris of ye famin maist specialie had ye name: as of Marcion, Arrius, Manes, and Pelagius: gif ze heirfor haldis ws catholikis to be hæretikis: quhy schau ze notht quhois hæresie we follow? For we (to ye intent we may haif godly vnitie) makis our purgatioun to zou, and also oblising, yat we sall nocht adhere to ane iot in religioun, except we schaw ye samin expressit in scriptuir, appreuit be general counselis, or be the best leirnit fatheris Greik and Latin, writtand in ane consent abone ane thousand zeris passit. Heirfoir gif we sua do (as we do in deid) quhy condemne ze nocht yai scriptuiris, auncient Doctouris and Counselis, quhois iugement in ane consent as deducit, or aggreing with ye scriptuir of God we follow, and nocht ws efter ye religioun estabilissit sa mony zeris?

### 4. *Of certane articlis of our beleif, and first of yat,* he descendit to the hellis.

<small>* Psal. 15. Act. 2. Psal. 48. Aug. epist. 57. Ambr. de p[?]. lib. 3. Irinæ. contra hæres. lib. 5. Cyprian. in symb. Basil. in Psal. 18.</small>

QVHY diminiss ze or takis away at the leist ye trew and propir sentence fra ws, of yis part of our catholik beleif: to wit, yat Christe descendit * to the hellis, and makis in that part, ane Idoll of Caluin, adherand to hes priuat opinioun, but ony apperand scriptuiris, or consent of the kirk afoir zow, bot platt contrare bayth: quhen ze affirm be yai wordis to be signifiit, the dolour and anguis, quhilk Christe sufferit! Will ze yat our Saluiour sufferit panis, eftir yat he wes deid, and buriit?

### 5. *Of ye haly catholik Kirk.*

<small>Psal. 2.</small>

QVHY spulze, and deunde ze ws, of yis part of our catholik beleif: to wit, The haly catholik kirk ye communioun of sanctis? Quhilk ye do, quhen ze abſtract ws fra the vniforme conſent of all kirkis, in all cuntreis and aiges ſen the days of the Apoſtolis: and bindis and aſtrictis ws only to ye doctrine and ordour laitlie ſet furth at Geneua: and litil eſtemis, or erar deſpiſeis the communioun of doctrine and ordour in religioun, of al ye ſanctis of God, ſen Chriſtis aſcenſioun. *Quhen yai cleik fra ws, twa coupounis of our crede: tyme is to ſpeik.*

### 6. *Gif our new prechouris and yare ſcoleris be ye catholik kirk.*

QVHIDIR affirm ze zour ſelfis only, with zour ſcoleris to be the ſaid haly catholik Kirk, and zour determinationis in controuerſiis neuir afoir yis determinat according to zour doctrine (bot erar be the beſt leirnit declarit in zour contrare) to haif ye ſtrenthe of the decreis of a general counſell, or nocht? Gif ze ſua do (as ze appere till ws) ze ſchaw zour arrogance only but mair confutatioun, to be lachin and geſtit at. Gif ze do nocht: quhy determinat ze ſa proudlie in hiech materis weill obſcuir in ſcriptuir: as ye glorius virgine ye mothir, to hef bene pollutit, nocht only with original, bot als actual ſin? Sen ye ſamin virgine wes præſerwit, (as we may godly but arrogance ſua vnderſtand) be the merciful prouidence of God, as apperis till ws, be the ſcripturis Geneſ. 3. afoir Eua for hir ſin, wes be God accurſit: and be yis alſo writtin, that the Lord hes ſanctifiit his tabernacle: and that in hir lyfe, ſcho wes pronunceit be the Angel to hef bene full of grace, ſua that na place culd be left to ſin: ſen S. Auguſtine alſo ſpeikand of ſinnaris, dar nocht moue quæſtioun yairin, of the ſaid bliſſit virgine, for the honour of Ieſus our Lord, hir ſone? we ſpeik yis mair largelie, becaus we heir ſum of zour ſcoleris affirm, yat eftir hir bliſſit birthe ſcho turnit to ye commoun effairis of Mariage: *Et alia magis abſurda, quæ clariùs promere, nobis religio eſt.* And ſiklyke quhare ze neulie concluid in zour doctrine of Baptim, the infantis to be ſaiſit but ye ſamin: the ſaid S. Auguſtine inhibitis to promit ſaluatioun in yat caſe to yame, ye quhilk ye ſcriptuir of God (ſays he) to all manly inginis tobe preferrit promittis nocht. We mein ſiklyke yat ze affirm ye ſaulis of ye faythful to hef paſſit to heuinlie gloir afoir Chriſtis aſcenſioun: yat the perſones ſeparat for fornicatioun may mary agane with wtheris perſones, athir of ye partiis being on liue, by ye practiſe nocht only of ye catholikis, bot *Pſal. 45. Luc. 1. Auguſt. de nat. et grat. ca. 36. Auguſt. de peccat. meriſ. et reſ. miſ. multis in locis.*

by in Scottis and in Inglis toung is nocht ane.

alſo of Ingland, Denmark, Saxone, and mony wthiris cuntreis (as we ar informit) prætending reformatioun: yat ſum men and women profeſſing monaſtik lyfe, and wouing virginitie, may efter mary but brik of conſcience, with mony wtheris thingis, as eſtir ſall follow. To the quhilkis zour determinatiouns, ze wald aſtrict our conſcience, as to the expres word of God, and trew wnderſtanding yairof pronunceit till ws be a generall counſel: ſen we man othir embraiſs zour doctrine, or be baniſſit. Gif we

Tit. 1.

beleif ſuirlie ye articulis of our commoun fayth togiddir wyth the ſcriptuiris of God tobe trew: may we nocht in ſobir ſimplicitie, miſknaw mony thingis of obſcuir and dirk places in ſcriptuir, albeit treulie declarit be particular men, but perrell of our ſaluatioun: committand ye iugement yairof to the haly catholik kirk? And contrarie may we ſuleſchelie embrais, and profes ony new interpretatioun in ye ſcripturis, albeit nocht erroneous bot to ws always doutſum, pronunceit be zow (zea ſuppoſe ze war lauchful miniſteris, of the quhilk we ar nocht zit aſſuirit) except we incurre the ſamin perrell?

### 7. *Gif fayth may be in a man but cheritie, and of ye perrell of yat general doctrine.*

Eftir ſa lang diſputatioun of faith, quhy concluid ze yat faith can naways be in a man but cheritie? Sen S. Paull planelie diſtinctis the office, and

1. Cor. 13.

præſence alſo of the ane fra ye wthir tobe poſſible (we mein nocht that cheritie may be ſeparatit fra fayth) ſayand: gif I hald all fayth and nocht cheritie: I am maid lyke ſoundand metell, or ane tincland cimbal? And

1. Cor. 9.

in ane wthir place ſchawis himſelf albeit prechand to wtheris (quhilk he culd nocht do but faith) to feir and be ſoliſt, that be the inlake of cheritie

Matth. 7.

throw diſobedience, he ſuld be maid reprobat. Mairouer our Saluiour ſchawis, that he ſall miſknaw and repell fra him at the latter day all wirkaris of iniquitie, euin yame quha had propheciit, wrocht wounderis,

Iac. 2.

and caſſin out deuilis in his name: quhilkis thingis yai culd nocht without fayth. S. Iames corroboratis the ſamin ſentence. And S. Petir af-

Iac. 2.
1. Pet. 4.

firmis that the iugement ſall begin at the hous of God, quhilk is the faythful. Albeit we mifknau nocht, yat ye perfyte, quik fayth, be ye quhilk we apprehend ye grace of God, conqueft till ws be Iefus Chrifte, throw exercife of his facramentis and wtheris his ordinance, be ye quhilk we ar iuftifiit, can naways be feparat fra cheritie: for quha ar moueit be Chriftis fpirit, ar ye fones of God: and quhare is cheritie, yair is God: zit be quhat reffoun, can ze affirm generalie, fayth naways tobe in ony but cheritie. Perfuade ze nocht be yis zour new determinatioun, manifeft præfumptioun and vngodlie fecuritie of confcience, to ye wickit, to think it fufficient to bable yair beleif, and to haif na regaird quhou yai leue? Or wil ze, yat quhou oft a man finnis, fa oft he be denudit and fpulzeit of all fayth: fen quha euir offendis God and his nichtbour iniuftlie, throw fin, wantis cheritie? Galat. 5.<br>Ro. 8.<br><br>Heir neidis na anssuer, mair yan ye commoun practik of leis and dissait, etc. yis day in Scotland. Esa. 59. Sap. 1.

### 8. *Of ye diſtinctioun of actual ſin.*

QUHY mak ze na diftinctioun nor difference of actual finnes? Sen S. Iames diftinctis ye famin fayand: Concupifcence quhen it confauis, generis fin: and fin quhen it is confummat, perfytit, or endit, generis deid: diftinctand ye fin, quhilk ftandis with grace callit be Theologis venial, and ye wthir, quhilk feparatis ws fra God, callit mortall. Sen ye iuft man finnis feuin tymes on ye day, and ryffis agane: and as S. Iohne writtis, nane of ws ar but fin? Will ze haif ws be yis kynd of fin, euir in ye ftate of damnatioun? and na difference of ye lycht imperfectioun callit fin, zea, in ye regenerat be Godis fpirit, and ye fin of ye wickit? Sen ye former kynd of finnaris ar manifeftlie callit iuft, as wes Iob, Zacharias, and Elizabeth. And maift trew it is, yat na damnatioun is to yame, quha ar in Chrifte Iefu, and walkis nocht eftir ye flefche. Ar we nocht commandit nocht tobe defauit, bot beleue yat ye rychteous man is rychteous, as Chrifte his heid is rychteous? Bot of ye wthir kynd it is writtin: Quha ar nocht iuft, ar nocht of God. Quha ar nocht moueit of Chriftis fpirit, ar nocht his. Departe fra me (fall Chrifte fay to ye wane bragaris of fayth) all ze wirkaris of iniquitie. Perfuade ze nocht, for nocht diftincting yis generalitie of fin (as we faid afoir of fayth,) ye wickit to præfumptioun? Iacob. 1.<br>1. Io. 5.<br><br>Prouer. 24.<br>1. Io. 1.<br><br>Prouer. 20.<br>3. Reg. 8.<br><br>Iob. 1.<br>Luc. 1.<br>Ro. 8.<br><br>1. Io. 3.<br><br>Ro. 8.<br>Matt. 7.<br><br>werk beiris wisnes.

## 9. *Of calumnious alleging of Papistrie, and lesum simplicitie.*

Qvhy saw ze sa planelie manifest seditioun in Godis kirk, euir clockand zour apperand malice, and peruersitie be ye name of Papistrie, nocht only escriuing in mony controuersiis ye vniforme doctrine of ye Martyris and wtheris Fatheris, aggreing with Godis word, to ye said Papistrie: bot also allegeing impudentlie and calumniuslie, yat thing to yame, quhome ze cal Papistis, quhilk neuir ane of yame (sa fer as we can collect) thocht anis in mynd? As yat our Saluiour descendit to ye hellis in his body: that men ar saifit be yair workis and nocht be fayth in Christe, and wtheris siklyke: and also imputing to ye vniuersal consent of Godis Kirk callit be zow Papistis, yat thing quhilk euery man in his priuat opinioun hes writtin within thir few zeris, sen we addict our selfis to ye doctrine of na man, of quhateuir leirning and auctoritie he be, except in sa fer as it manifestlie aggreis with ye catholik doctrine, planelie declarit till ws, be ye maist aunciant writtaris, abone ane thousand zeris passit, to hef bene beleuit and obseruit afore yame, fra ye Apostolis days and keipit in dayly practyse to yis præsent in Godis Kirk. Mairouer as we knaw yat our Saluiour and his Apostolis did and spak mony thingis, quhilkis ar nocht expreslie writtin: and yairfor of na necessitie iniunit ws to beleue, except yai be of yai traditionis vniuersalie beleuit and obseruit. Zit sen mony thingis ar writtin in historiis and keipit fra tyme to tyme in ye memorie of man aggreing with ye scriptuiris and apperand tobe trew: as yat knycht quha peirsit our Lordis syde with ye speir, to hef bene callit Longinus: and to hef obtenit at yat tyme nocht only the cleir sycht of his corporal, bot also of his inwart Eis, and to hef bene saisit throw ye plentuesnes of mercy, with ye theif yat hang on ye rycht hand. This grossis exemple we propone apperand trew, and to ye gloir of Christis grete mercy schawin to his inimeis, bot amangis ws of na existimatioun, in ye rebuk of cheif arrogantis, intending be yis and wtheris siklyke to saw, and nureis discord, amang ye membris of Christe Iesu, be ye name of Papistrie. Siklyke yat ye croce and pillar quhareat oure Saluiour sufferit wyth his cote, and siklyke tobe keipit zit amangis Christianis: yat ye Apostolis and Martyris bodyis be zit lyand in sik places, as sum men affirmis yame tobe. Quhat perell, or er-

rour is it to beleue in fimplicitie of mynd, yir thingis and fiklyke, fua yai be nocht abufit in idolatrie nor fuperftitioun, bot in ane moderat reuerence: nor zit iniunit to ony man to beleue ye famin as neceffar to his faluatioun? Gif ye think na perrel yairin, quhilk ze behuis to do, on ye maner forfaid, except ze be maift mad and vnkynd to Chrift: quhy attempt ze fik diuifioun yairthrow, cryand Papiftis, Papiftis: makand ye femplie and humill membris of Chriftis body as ane geftingftok, ane fable or bable to lach at, and yat be ye name of Papiftis? Gif ze for our fimplicitie in godlines, humill iugement and fubmiffioun of our felfis to ye iugement of ye haly catholik Kirk in all controuerfiis, keipand fuirlie ye articulis of our beleif, and leueand as we may be Godis grace (quhilk we intend) in ye feir and luue of our God and nychtbour, quhilk thing is ye end of all ye law: haif we na mair iuft caus to reiofe tobe callit Papiftis (be ye quhilk name we vnderftand catholikis, fones of ye haly catholik kirk) yan ze haif in ye name of proteftantis, or Caluinianis? For fiklyke with ws reiofit ye haly Prophet Dauid, to be callit ye fone of Godis damicell, quhilk is ye haly kirk: fayand, I Lord, I yi feruand and ye fone of yi Damicel. And in an wthir place: Lor faif yi feruand, and the fone of yi Damicel. 1. Tim. 1.
Pſal. 115.
Pſal. 85.
Sep. 9.

### 10. *Of the firſt four general counſelis efter ye Apoſtolis.*

Sen na hæretik that euir wes in yir our lattir days, or afoir, denyit the firſt four general counſelis eftir ye Apoſtolis (we mein of Nicænum Epheſinum Conſtantinopolitanum and Chalchedonenſe) except yai hæretikis or yair ſcoleris, contrare ye quhilkis ya counſelis wes haldin, tweching ye cheif articulis of our beleif, to wit, the haly trinitie, and incarnatioun of our Saluiour: (quhy hef ze left out in zour confeſſioun, laitlie ſetfurth at Geneua in Ingliſ, the counſel of Conſtantinople: confeſſing zou to condemne al hærefiis condemnit in the wthir thre, makand na mentioun of it? Will ze nocht grant with ye ſaid counſel contrare the hæretik Macedonius condemnit yair, yat the haly gaiſt is wery God? And gif ze confes the famin, as we dout nocht bot ze wil do: Quhy geif ze iuſt occaſioun to the infirm tobe in yat part ſclanderit be zow? Or quhat wthir thing appreuis yat counſell, yat ze dar impreue? And zit to thir thre principal counſelis, quhilkis yai in yair buikis approue, in yair doctrine yai ar contrarius: tueching ye oblatioun in ye mes, ye real preſence of Chriſtis body yair, in ye mariage of yair munkis and nunnis, and in yair vſurpit auctoritie.

## 74   TO THE CALUINIANE PRECHEOURIS.

### 11. *Of ye terme facrament and numbre yairof.*

SEN ze admitt na thing in religioun, except yai thingis, quhilkis ar expreſlie contenit in fcriptuir : Quhy mak ze fik brag tumult and diuifioun for the
terme facrament, cryand fa oft tobe twa facramentis in Chriſtis kirk, and
na ma? quhilk terme is nocht peculiarlie appropriat in fcriptuir to ony of
yai feuin callit be ye kirk facramentis, except to Matrimonie allane, quhilk

<small>Ephes. 5.
Io. 3.
1. Cor. 11.
Act. 8. 19.
Act. 13.
1. Tim. 4.
Matth. 16.
Io. 20.
Ephes. 5.
Iacob. 5.
Mar. 6.
Luc. 8.
Matth. 13.</small>

ze contrare the fcriptuir, denyis tobe a facrament? Quhy vfe ze nocht ye
famin feuin be fik names, as yai ar expreſſit in fcriptuir but feryair contentioun, as Baptifm, ye Lordis fupper, ye impofitioun of handis, in confirmatioun and ordinatioun of minifteris, ye keis for abfolutioun to ye
pœnitent, matrimonie, ye prayer on ye feik with vnƈting of oill? Or
quhy cal ze nocht ye famin myfteriis conforme to ye Euangell but mair
brag? And fuppofe ze contemne ye terme facrament to all ye feuin fua
haldin : quhy contemne ze ye vfe and exercife in zour congregatioun of
ane grete part of ye faidis feuin, contrare ye expres fcriptuir ? Quhy vfe
ze yis terme communioun for ye Lordis fupper nocht contenit in fcriptuir
in yat fignificatioun, and famekle abhorris fra ye terme Miſſa expreſlie con-

<small>Deut. 16.</small>

tenit in ye original Hebrew text for an oblatioun : fen na Chriſtiane of ye
former aige, and few of the proteſtantis at yis præfent in Alemannie and
wthiris cuntreis, denyis ye rycht vfe and praƈtife of ye Lordis fupper, tobe
callit ane facrifice or oblatioun.

### 12. *Of ye twa facramentis and na ma.*

QVHAT haif ze for zou, that in Chriſtis kirk yai ar bot twa facramentis,

<small>Cal. in in-
ſtitut. de
sacram. in
genere. et de
ordine Ec-
clesiast.
Melan. in
loc. com.</small>

and na ma : fpecialie fen zour grete Maifter Caluine denyis nocht tobe
thre : Melanchton and wtheris four : wthiris fiue, and fum fex? For
fcriptuir haif ze nane, nor zit as we ar informit, aunciant fatheris, nor general counfelis : nor zit (that fuld moue zou mair) vniforme confent of
zour awin writtaris.

### 13. *Gif ye sacramentis be signis only of saluatioun.*

Qvhy make yir twa sacramentis signis only of saluatioun, quharby we fuld be assuirit (as ze teche) of Godis grace? and nocht erar meanis of efficacitie, quharby God workis his grace in ws? sen it is writtin, yat God makis ws sauff be ye lawar of regeneratioun. And S. Petir hes yir wordis: that baptim onlyke maner makis ws saif. And S. Iames hes, yat ye prayar of fayth sall saif ye patient. S. Paull writtis yat Timothe had grace, be impositioun of his handis. Tit. 3.
1. Pet. 3.
Iacob. 5.

### 14. *Gif ye infantis be saifit but Baptim.*

Qvhat haif ze for zou, yat ye infantis of ye faythful ar saifit alrady but Baptim? Sen ye scriptuir techis, yat we ar borne the sones of wrayth: and, except we be borne agane of ye watter and ye spirit: we sal nocht entir in ye kingdome of heuin. And S. Auguftine affirmis yis his sayngis in mony wthiris places, Trow nocht, say nocht, nor teche nocht (says he) gif yaw wale be a catholik, yat ye infantis or yai be Baptizit cumis to remissioun of sinnis, gif yai be præneutit be deth but Baptim? Bot quhow can ye promiss maid to Abraham and his seid, preue zour intent in yis mater? sen efter ye promis maid to Abraham in yat samin place, it follouis yat ye maill barne nocht circuncidit ye auchtin day, fuld perifs fra his peple. Bot ze affirm circuncifioun and Baptim tobe of ane strenth and efficacitie.* Or zit quhou may yat place of S. Paull allegeit be zou, confirm zour sentence, Wthirways zour sones var vnclene, bot now yai ar haly? Except yat ze wald an indurat Iow, and an vnfaythful Ethnik be the fayth of an wthir tobe saifit. Ephes. 2.
Io. 3.
August. ad Vincent. de fid. lib. 3. cap. 9.

Genes. 17.
1. Cor. 7.
* For yair it is writin ye vnfaythful man tobe sanctifiit be ye faythful woman, &c. Of sanctificatioun tharefor yai ar diuers maneris.

### 15. *Of the contempt of Baptim to ye ministeris perel.*

Gif ze affirm with Caluin Baptim tobe sa necessar, that it sald nocht be contemnit gif occasioun and tyme serue yair to (as we grant also that the guidnes of God astrictis nocht wthirways in the persones of adult aige his grace to the Sacramentis) quhy refuse ze to baptize the barnis, quhen yai ar brocht to zou, except it be zour appoinctit day yairto? And quhy allege ze it tobe na perel to zour felfis always, contrare zour doctrine (to wit that the Sacramentis fuld nocht be contemnit) gif the barnis deceiffs but Baptim, throw zour necligence, or erar contempt and lichtliing of Godis ordinance? Or quhy refufe ze to baptize the barne præfentit to zou, be faythful men, for the iniquitie of ye father, fen it is writtin, yat ye fone fall nocht beir the fatheris iniquitie: and fen a Chriftiane is nocht faythles, albeit he be fallin wthirways in fin? Infafer as ye wald punifs fin, we diffent nocht fra zou: bot gif ze lat the barne perifs, quhou fal we nocht diffent fra zow? Or quhou can ze excuis zour crueltie yairin?

*Note.*

*Ezech.* 18.

### 16. *Of ye ceremoneis at Baptim.*

*Iuft. in quaest.*
*Basil. de spiritu sanct.*
*Tert. de corro mili.*
*Origen. in num.*
*Aug. de Ecclesias. dog.* and in mony places ma. Quhen yai cry out Papistis on ws yai think mair ewil on the bail martyris of Christe, ye doctouris, &c. quhome in ane confent we folow heir.

Sen the maift aunciant Martyris and Doctouris of the primitiue Kirk, as Iuftinus, Cypriane, Tertulliane, Origene, Bafill, Auguftine and wthiris, witneffs mekle ordour tobe obferuit at Baptim nocht expreflie writtin in fcripturis: and alfo mony of yai ceremones vfeit be the kirk of God in yir our days at Baptim, to hef bene traditionis vniuerfalie obferuit, and throw that caufs nocht tobe neclectit, nor contemnit: quhilkis ar fpecialie exorcizatioun, the figne of the croce, with ye rycht hand on the forret tobe maid, to renunce the deuil and all his werkis, the vncting with oyll and Chrifme, the baptizit tobe coueirt with a quhyte clayth, callit ye cuid, tobe thryifs dippit in ye wattir: Quhy accuis ze ws of idolatrie, fuperftitioun, or papiftrie, as ze call it, for ye vfenig yairof? And wil nocht condemne planelie, as ze think (quhilk thocht efalie may be confiderit) ye faidis Martyris, Doctouris, and all kirkis of Chrifte afoir yir oure days, as an idolatricall and fuperftitius kirk, pollutit with the faidis filthy wices?

Note heir yai ar compellit to blaspheme ye sanctis of God, and imagein a kirk inuisibil.
*Luc.* 22. *Matt.* 28.

### 17. *Of Godis kirk.*

Gif ze condemne ye faid kirk of ye martyris (quhome the reft hes euir follouit to our days in yat part) of fuperftitioun, and Idolatrie: quhare fall ze find yis kirk of God promittit in the Euangel, quhois fayth fuld nocht failze?

## 18. *Of ye ceremoneis, amang ye new reformaris.*

GIF ze will admitt in zour kirk na ceremonie, except expreſſie commandit in ſcriptuir: quhy will ze ye nocht baptize ye barne except ye father yair- of, hald it in his airmis afoir zour pulpet: and nocht contentit with wtheris gentlemen, except yai bring yair bairnis throw ye ſtretis in yair awin airmis? And quhy baptize ze in ye kirk, and in ony prophane baſin, and nocht in ye plane feildis, and in ye reuar or fluid: as did S. Iohne ye Baptiſt, Philip and ye reſt of ye Apoſtolis? Quhy haif ze God fatheris and God motheris: fen ye haill congregatioun yair præſent may be witneſs? Quhy hald ze godmotheris in ye beginning, and now repellis ye famin? Quhy baptize ze nocht except ze geif euiry barne ane name at yat tyme? Of ye quhilk albeit ze haif exemple of S. Iohne ye Baptiſt at his circuncifioun, and of our Saluiour, zit quhat expres command haif ze yairto? Quhy couer ze zour table with a quhyte clayth at zour communioun? Quhy caus ze wthiris, yan ye miniſter partlie to diſtribut zour breid and wyne at zour communioun? fen our Saluiour (quhois place ye lauchful miniſter occupiis) gaif his ſacrament himſelf to his diſciplis, commanding yame as his lauchful miniſteris to do ye famin. Quhy mak ze zour communioun afoir dennar, fen our Saluiour inſtitutit his haly ſacrament efter ſuppare? Quhy vſe ze at zour communioun now four, now thre coupis, and mony breidis: nothir keipand ye ceremonie expreſſit in ye Euangel, nor confeſſing ye treuth of ye myſterie with ws? fen our Saluiour vſeit ane breid and ane coupe. Gif ze nothir affirm Chriſte realie yair præſent, (quhilk ane indiuidit ye trew heuinly breid till ws promittit, euiry Chriſtiane of ws at our haly communioun moſt aſſuritlie, throw Chriſtis omnipotent word reſſauis) nor zet keipis ye ceremonie in ye vſenig of ane breid and ane coup: quhou vndirſtand ze yat is writtin be S. Paull, we ar mony ane breid and ane body, all yat ar parctakaris of ane breid and ane coup? And quhy will ze nocht folemnize zour band of matrimonie, except yai be proclamit thre bannis afoir? Quhy caus ze at mariage ye perſones yan mariit, to tak wthiris be ye hand: and in fum places, a ring tobe geuin? Thir thingis we ſpeir nocht yat we repreue yame all, bot to knaw, quhou ze eſtabiliſs zour doctrine, to ye quhilk ze

*Heir be yair awin doingis ye ground of yair doctrine fallis in the myre.*
Matth. 3.
Io. 3.
Act. 8.

Matth. 26.

Note

1. Cor. 10.

will yat we aftrict our felfis : fen ze teche na thing tobe vfeit at ye facramentis or in religioun, except yai be expreflie commandit in fcripturis, albeit ze vfe the contrare zour felfis.

19. *Gif all ye Sacramentis of auld and new teftamentis ar of alyke ftrenthe and efficacitie.*

SEN the Sacramentis of the Euangell exhibitis in deid and veritie, yai graces figurat only and hoipit for in the auld Teftament : as largelie exponis the Doctouris, as Ambrofe writtand on the 73. Pfalme, The facramentis (fays he) of ye auld and new Teftament ar nocht alyke : for ye ane promittis the Saluiour, and the wtheris wirkis faluatioun. Quhy teche ze yat yai ar al indifferentlie of ane efficacitie, and actual ftrenthe ? Say ze yat manna in ye defert wes ye famin thing in effect, that the Sacrament of Chriftis body, fen the ane wes the figure, and the wthir the veritie ? Or hald ze manna of greitar excellencie yan the wthir ? quhilk ze do, gif ze confes breid and wyne allanerlie yair præfent : fen manna defcendit frome the heuin be miracle, and breid and wyne afcendis frome the erd be natuir. Quhiddir affirm ze herfor the figure and the veritie tobe ane thing, or nocht ? Or the figure and the fchaddow of mair excellencie, yan the wthir, or nocht ?

Note.

20. *Of the real præfence of Chriftis body in the Sacrament, bepouer of the wordis of Chrifte omnipotent.*

QVHAT haif ze for zour defence to affirm in the Sacrament of our Lordis body to remane breid and wyne with (I wate nocht quhat) fum fpiritual imaginatioun ? and mair erroneouflie alfo contrare ye Lutheranis, and all kirkis afoir zou, that yair is nocht yair bot breid and wyne only ? fen the wordis of our Saluiour (quha is werray God, omnipotent in pouer) ar fa expreflie fpokin, This is my body : This is my bluid. And S. Paull exponing the famin writtis that the man quha eitis yairof vnuorthelie, eitis his damnatioun, nocht decerning (fays he) the Lordis body. And fiklyke all the aunciant fatheris and counfelis, nocht allanerlie that hes bein laitlie,

Luc. 22.
1. Cor. 11.

bot quha hes writtin fra the beginning, quhare yai tweche that mater, writtis contrare zour doctrine: as ane sufficient teſtimonie yairof, may be the firſt counſel haldin at Epheſus: to the quhilk ze aftrict zow in zour beleif ſet out in zour confeſſioun at Geneua. Bot gif ze allege that ſum of yame callis that Sacrament a figure: we ar certifiet be euident demonſtrationis of yair writtingis, yat quhare yai call it anis a figure, yai call it an hundreth tymes Chriſtis warray body and bluid. Quhareby yai ſchaw yame ſelfis planelie, that yai call the ſenſible ſignis of that Sacrament, a figure or figne of ye thingis præſent inuiſibilie, and nocht abſent: that nane ſuld haif that carnal and groſs iugement of the Capernaitis. Note.

### 21. *Of certane argumentis tweching ye premiſſs.*

Ze takand zour argument contrare ye real præſence of Chriſtis body in ye ſacrament, vſeis to reſſoun of ye natural propirteis of a manis werray body, to ye quhilk ye body of our Saluiour wes alyke (bot zit nocht æquall) in all thingis tueching ane werray man, except ſin and ignorance, as ze godly in yat caſe, confentis with ws. Bot we demand gif our Saluiour in this lyfe enduit nocht his mortall and paſſible body with ye propirteis and giftis of an immortall and impaſſible body? Gif ze ſay na, Ze deny ye ſcripturis: as quhen he paſſit vpon ye ſee, quhen he tranſfigurat his body afoir his paſſioun, quhen he paſſit throw ye middiſs of ye thik peple to euade yair furie: and fiklyke eftir his refurrectioun, by ye propirteis of a body gloriſiit, and yan immortall, eit with his diſcipulis ye fuid of mortalitie: and als by ye propirteis of a werray body enterit in, ye duiris being cloſit, zea, as Godis Kirk declaris till ws, throw ye cloſit duiris. We demand zou heirfor, gif ze beleue yat our Saluiour did yir thingis veralie and in deid, or be ane certane Iouglarie craft? Gif ze grant with ws (as we hoip ze ſall) yat he did yir thingis truelie and in deid, becaus it is ſa writtin, albeit agains all naturall iugement, and by ye propirteis of a werray body: quhy beleue ze nocht ye wthir alſua? Sen zour grete maiſter Caluin confeſſis yis ſacrament tobe a myſterie mair hie, yan he can ſchau be toung, think in mynd, or onyways can defcend in his hert, and an wthir matir yan to trow only. And ſen Chryſoſtome maiſt erneſtlie

Io. 6.<br>Matt. 14.<br>Ibidé. 17.<br>Luc. 24.<br>Io. 8. 10.<br>Luc. vlt.<br>Act. 1.<br>Act. 20.<br>Io. 20.

Cal. *in inſtitut. de cœna domini.*

*Homel.* 83. *in Matth.*

forbidis, to attend to our natural fenfis, and manlie reffoun in yat mater: bot to geue credit to ye expres word of God, albeit it appere contrare our wittis and fenfis. Bot fen Chrifte hes fpokin (fays he) This is my body: Lat ws geif credit, and repugne nocht to God? Ze mifknaw nocht, findry of zour maift leirnit Precheouris within yir twa zeris and ane half, to hef affirmit with ws planelie: and zit hes fchawin na expres fcriptuir in ye contrare. Quhy wald ze heirfor thral ws, as ze war ye catholik Kirk ye pillar of veritie, yat can nocht erre?* Quhare ze allege yat Chrifte afcendit to ye heuin, and fittis at ye richt hand of ye father, ze wil nocht haif him fa bund in heuin yat ye may naways be in erd. For eftir his afcenfioun he apperit to S. Paull in ye way. Be ye quhilk S. Paul prouis his werray refurrectioun .1. Cor. 15. And to fit at ye rycht hand of ye father confirmis mair our purpofe, fen be yat is fignifiit his omnipotent pouer.

* we ar nocht affuirit gif yis wes in Iohne Knoxis copie. bot zit yair is na diuerfitie heirin fra ye reft. Act. 9. 1. Cor. 15.

### 22. Gif ye dew celebratioun of ye faid facrament be a facrifice.

Qvhy abhorre ze to affirm and cal ye rycht vfe always of ye celebratioun and fanctifiing of ye faid facrament of our Lordis body, ane facrifice or oblatioun, fen our Saluiour maid facrifice at his laft fupper, eftir ye ordour of Melchifedech: quhilk famin felf thing he commandit tobe done in remembrance of him: and fen ye laft of ye twelf Prophetis Malachias, to quhome aggreis Dauid, forefpak expreflie of ye abolitioun of ye auld facrifices and oblationis, and vpfetting of ane clene new oblatioun, tobe offerit in ye new law to ye name of God in all places: mening of ye vnbluidy facrifice of ye Kirk, in ye body and bluid of Chrifte: as witneffis haly Martialis S. Petiris difciple, Iuftinus, Irinæus, with Auguftine, Eufebius, and wtheris Doctouris? Bot fen ze efteme Auguftine gretumlie (and nocht without caufe amangis the refte of the Doctouris) intend nocht in yis caufe to thraw him (as fum of zour new writtaris dois) to mein in yis mater of ane wthir facrifice of louing allanerly. For we aduertis zow as tender freindis, yat ze wilbe efchamit yairin, he is fa plane in fa mony places in zour contrare.

Cyp. epi. 3. li. 2.
Matt. 26.
Malach. 1.
Pfal. 49.

Marti. ad Buthg. cap. 3.
Iusti. in dialogo cum Iudæo.
Irinæ. lib. 4. ca, cа. 32.
Aug. de trinit, lib. 3. cap. 4.
Euseb. demonst. euang. cap. vlt.

### 23. *Of the numbre of the communicantis, and wtheris ceremonies.*

As we grant it lauchful and godly yat mony wald cum daylie to ye Mefs, and refaue the haly facrament of the altar (we fpeik on yis maneir with Auguftine) togidder with the Preift: fua can we nocht vnderftand zour fcrupulofitie and wane ceremonie, quhilk is, yat ane faithful man haueand na wthir impediment, bot wantand cumpanie to communicat with him facramentalie, may nocht refaue yat facrament him allane, without errour, or idolatrie. Quhou can he be him allane, fa lang as he is a membre of Chriftis Kirk? Heirfoir we demand zou gif our Saluiour at ye inftitutioun of yis facrament, præfcriuit ane law till ws of all ye ceremoneis vfeit at yat tyme, as of ye place, quhilk wes ane hall: of ye tyme, quhilk wes eftir fuppare: of ye numbre of ye communicantis, of ye quhilkis we reid only twelf? Gif ze affirm yat he did fua: ze failze zour felfis, quhilkis keipis nocht ane iot of all thre. And quhy wald ze heirfor thral ws to ane ceremonie, nocht expreflie commandit, contrare zour awin doctrine in wtheris places?

<small>Aug. *serm.* *de sanct.* 19.</small>

<small>Of place, tyme, nor numbrir of the communicantis is na expres command in scriptuir.</small>

### 24. *Quhy yis facrament is nocht vfeit, tobe miniftrat to the feik.*

QVHY neclect ze to miniftrat yis haly facrament to ye feik, afoir yair departing of this lyfe, by ye laudable vfe and canounis of ye primitiue Kirk, in tyme of ye glorious Martyris? Gif ze fay, that ze may nocht deliuir it to ane allane? Quhy nocht now als weil as ye tyme of ye Martyris be ye exemple of ye haly penitent man Serapion: quha in ye tyme of ye refauing yairof wes illuminat be ye fpirit of prophetie? Gif ze excuis zou be yir wordis of our Saluiour, fayand: Drink ze al of yis, and yairthrow ane man can nocht refaue it him allane, gif ye minifter or wtheris be nocht rady to communicat: quhow can yat preue zour intent: fen al Chriftianis at ane tyme and ane place can nocht keip yat commande, and ze interpet it fua?

<small>Euseb. *Eccls. hist.* ll. 6. cap. 34.</small>

<small>A grete absurditie following yair doctrine heir.</small>

## 25. Of ye wordis of sanctificatioun.

ZE confeſſing oftymes treulie with ws, eftir ye techement of S. Auguſtine, yat a ſacrament in Chriſtis Kirk, conſiſtis nocht only of a ſigne, bot of ye word of God innit yairto at his command : quhy teche ze, and ſettis furth in zour catechis, yat ye wordis of ſanctificatioun of ye ſacrament of our Lordis body and bluid, ar nocht tobe pronunceit to ye end, yat yair ſuld be ony tranſubſtantiatioun yairby, or be ye intent of ye ſacrificear : bot to aduertis the peple communicant, quhou yai ſuld behaif yame in ye mein tyme ? Quhou can ze appropriat yir wordis : This is my body : this is my bluid : to teche ye peple, quhou yai ſuld behaif yame, except only to ye intent, yat yai ſuld beleue ye ſamin tobe trew, yat is ſpokin be God, and commandit to be ſpokin be the miniſter in his name, quho may nocht lie ? Or be quhat temeritie and fuilhardines dar ze miniſtrat a Sacrament, nocht pronunceand ye wordis of Chriſte, to ye intent yat it ſuld be a Sacrament : ſen ze teche in wtheris places rycht treulie, yat without ye wordis of God commandand and promittand grace yairto na ſacrament can be maid ? Or quhou ſuld ye miniſter nocht haif intent to performe and perfyte that thing, yat he wirkis in ye name, and at ye command of God ?

*Note yair wriſting and wrying of the expres word of God.*

*And nocht to teche ye peple geſtuiris, quhow thai suld behaif yame.*

## 26. Of ye names Sacrifice, Preiſt, and Altar.

ALBEIT to ws Chriſtianis be properlie ane God allane, ane King, and ane Lord : quha only be nature and eſſential ſubſtance, is guid, ryhteous, trew, and merciful, zit ye inexplicable benignitie of ye ſamin our God diſtributis and appropriatis in his ſcriptuir, ye ſamin names to his reularis and wtheris membris of Chriſtis myſtical body in erd, calling yame Godis, Kingis, Lordis, iuſt, guid. &c. And ſiklyke oure Saluiour Chriſte Ieſus being only our hie Preiſt, and only yat ſacrifice, quhilk fra ye fall of Adam, to ye day of iugement, takis away ye ſinnis of ye warld : And only ſiklyke yat Altar, vpon the quhilk the prayaris of all acceptit and hard be our heuinly Father, ar offerit. Zit ze miſknaw nocht yat ye ſamin names war appropriat to the Preiſtis, ſacrifice, and altar, in the law of Moyſes, præ-

*Matth. 19.*
*Luc. 18.*
*Mar. 10.*
*Ro. 3.*
*Exod. 7.*
*1. Cor. 8.*
*Io. 10.*
*Psal. 81.*
*Io. 1.*
*Apocal. 8.*

*Passim in Exod. and Leuit.*

figuring only Chrifte Iefus yan tocum. The quhilk names Preift, facrifice, and altar the Kirk of God hes vfeit, fen the Apoftolis days, for the minifter offering, at Chriftis command, ye vnbluidy facrifice of ye body and bluid of Chrifte, vpon the table of the Lord: quhilk thing ze mifknaw nocht: albeit ze wink at the famin applauding to the tyme. Albeit we may bring intellable teftimoneis theirof: zit for fchortnes, we will adduce, bot a certane to zour memorie.

*Dum altaria dæmonum in puluerem redigerentur, aram ignoti Dei ad confecrationem referuari iuffimus, &c. Sacrificium Deo creatori in ara offertur, non homini, nec Angelo.* Martialis D. Petri difcipulus ad Burdegalen. ca. 3.

*Ego omni die facrifico, non thuris fumum &c. fed immaculatum agnum quotidie, in altare crucis facrifico.* Philal. de B. And. in eius vita.

*Ecclefiæ oblatio, quam docuit Dominus offerri in vniuerfo mundo, purum facrificium reputatum eft illi.* Irinæus li. 4. c. 34.

*Noui teftamenti nouam docuit oblationem, quam Ecclefia ab Apoftolis accipiens, in vniuerfo mundo iam offert Deo.* Ibid. ca. 32.

*Nam fi Iefus Chriftus Dominus et Deus nofter, ipfe eft fummus Sacerdos Dei Patris, et facrificium Deo Patri ipfe primus obtulit, et hoc fieri in fui commemorationem præcepit. Vtiq; facerdos ille vice Chrifti verè fungitur, fi id quod Chriftus fecit imitatur. Et facrificium verum et plenum tunc offert (facerdos) in Ecclefia Deo Patri, fi fic incipiat offerre, fecundum quod ipfum Chriftum videat obtuliffe.* Cyprianus li. 2. epist. 3. M. George hay fy haist zow to recant. Loquitur de calice vino et aqua miscendo.

*Chriftus de corpore et fanguine fuo inftituit facrificium fecundum ordinem Melchifedech.* Aug. in Psal. 33.

*Vouentur omnia quæ offeruntur Deo, maximè fancta altaris oblatio.* Idem epi. 59.

*Cùm Melchifedech Abrahæ benediceret, ibi primùm apparuit facrificium: quod nunc à Chriftianis offertur Deo, toto terrarum orbe.* Idem de ciuit. dei, lib. 16. cap. 22.

*Sacerdos ad altare Dei ftans, exhortatur populum orare pro incredulis.* Idem ep. 107.

*In altari conftituitur panis et calix.* Amb. li. 5. c. 1. de sacr.

*Sacerdos altari affiftens pro vniuerfo orbe terrarum, pro abfentibus. &c. facrificio illo propofito, gratias Deo iubet offerre.* Chryfos. in Mat. ho. 26.

Siklyke we dout nocht yat ze mifknaw the famin Fatheris, and all ye reft maift aunciant, commonlie to hef vfeit the famin termes in all aiges,

# TO THE CALUINIANE PRECHEOURIS.

*Note.* as the Kirk dois at this præſent. And the Apoſtolis ſiklyke to hef abſtenit commonlie in yair writtingis fra thir termes in this ſignificatioun, for the abolitioun of the Preiſtheid, ſacrifice, and altar in the auld law, and diſ- tinċting the ſamin in the law of grace fra the wthir.

As the vſeing of the ſamin names in al aiges ſen yair days in vniforme conſent manifeſtlie to ws perſuadis. Quhy cal ze ws heirfor, for the vſe- ing of the ſamin Papiſtis, and ſparis in yat part, the haill kirk afoir ws?

### 27. *Of ye ornamentis of ye Altaris, and ye Preiſtis.*

Gif the law of natuir ingraftit in our hertis reioſs in al cumlie and decent ordour, and ye ſamin nocht being aboliſſit, bot confirmit be the Euangel : 1. Cor. 14. And ſen S. Paull alſo commandis al thingis tobe done honeſtlie and eſtir ordour in the kirk of God : quhat haif ze for zow, to affirm all the veſti- mentis and ornamentis in the houſs of God, ſpecialie on the Altaris and miniſteris, in tyme of the diuine offices, tobe ſuperſtitious and idolatrical? Specialie ſen we may preue in the primitiue kirk ſiklyke ornamentis to hef Prouerb. 1. bene vſeit, nocht commandit in ye new teſtament. Salamon alſo com- and. 6. manding ws naways to dimit the law of our mother, quhilk is the kirk (ſen be it na thing is promulgat, bot aggreing with Godis word, and prof- fetable to the out ſetting of the ſamin) na mair, yan we ſuld nocht heir the præceptis of our fathir, quhilk is, God.

### 28. *Gif it be leſum to vſe ony prophane coupis at yis ſacrament.*

Sen ye weſchelis and ornamentis appropriat to ye ſeruice of God, ſuld nocht be prophanit in wthir commoun vſeis : as the feirfull exemple of Daniel. 5. Balthazar preuis maiſt planelie : Quhy hef ze wappit doun al ye affixit A ſacri- lege. tabellis of ye Lord, be al aunciant fatheris afoir our dayis callit altaris, to- giddir with ye font of Baptim, and vſeis zour tabillis baiſſinis, and coupis, A pro- furth of ony prophane taueroun? Wil ze haif ye ſacramentis of grace in phane im- pietie. ye new law, of les dignitie and honour, yan yais war in the auld : for ye abuſing of the weſchelis of ye quhilkis, the grete King Balthazar wes ſa ſeueirlie puniſſit?

*29. Euiry guid Chriſtiane man is a king, and a preiſt, and quhat is meanit thairby.*

ALBIT we acknawlege be the fcriptuir of God, yat al iuft man in ye kirk of God, quha fubdeuis his concupifcence and luftis to the diuine law, is a victorious king, and preift alfo fpitualie : Nochtyeles we demand zou, gif be that titill euiry man (albeit he haif wit, and piffance yairto) may iuftlie be a king to miniftrat iuftice ? Gif ze fay, Na : quhy allow ze, and prouokis alfo, the proueftis and ballies of euiry burgh (quhome we can nocht call Magiftratis propirlie, as ze do : fen yai ar nocht principalis in a fre citie, as wes Rome, to mak lawis bot fuld be Subitis to our Souerane Lady) to baneis Chriftianis and trew Scottifmen fra yair roumes and poffeffiones, confifk yair guidis, put yame to the horne, and condemne yame to the dethe: for breking only of yair actis and decreis vnknauin to our Souerane Lady, or hir Maief. prædeceffouris ! fen yai haif only pouer to punifs yair awin comburgeffs in an.viij.fs vnlaw or fiklyke. <small>Apoc. 1. 1. Petr. 2. Quhow yai prouoke yair acoleris to vsurpe auctoritie.</small>

*30. Gif ye ſubditis may violentlie compel yair Princes to religioun.*

GIF the peple of Ifrael vnder ye Idolatrical kingis in Babylone, wes nocht commandit be God, to refift ye faidis Idolatouris, or be ony violence to remuif yame fra yair errour, bot to obey yame, fuffer yame, pray for yame, and ferue God in yair awin religiuon : And Dauid being vnctit king of Ifrael, wald do na violence to king Saull yan being repellit and reprobat of God, and perfuitand ye faid Dauid iniuftlie to ye deth : bot fufferit him to rage in his furie, fleing onlie fra his violence, for the honour yat he wes a king. Alfo we reid nocht yat the Apoftolis or ony of the catholik religioun euir puniffit in body or geris the infidelis, quha had nocht reffauit the religioun of Chrifte, albeit yai chaftifit the apoftatis relapfit fra ye trew fayth anis reffauit. Bot quhou the trew Chriftianis wes fcharpelie perfuitit and iniuftlie puniffit and oppreffit be ye Arrianis and wthiris heretikis and apoftatis the exemplis ar ouer patent. Quhat auctoritie heirfor haif ze for zou to comptrol our Souerane Lady, and compel hir Maief. to reffaue zour priuat opinioun of materis in religioun vnknauin to the haill <small>Hiere. 27. Baruch. 1. 1. Reg. at lenthe. 1. Tim. 1. Reid Athanas. and Nicephor.</small>

Chriftiane kirk afoir yir days : and as zit nocht reffauit be ony Chriftiane King at yis præfent? For zour felfis knauis Ingland, Denmark, and Alemannie except fum Caluiniftis and wtheris ftrange fectis, prætending reformatioun alfua by the Romane kirk, to diffent in mony heidis fra zour doctrine.

### 31. *Of obedience to our natiue Souerane Marie.*

THINK ze nocht our maift noble, humane and gentil Souerane hes fchawin hir felf mair yan king Dauidis trew dochtir, quha in that cafe diffenting fra the counfel of maift Chriftiane princis, wald fle all occafioun of trible tobe done be violence of men of weir and ftrangeris, nocht to a king, quha fumtymes wes hir maifter, as wes Saull to Dauid, bot to hir awin fubiectis, vfurping (as Chriftiane Princis hir G. nerreft freindis thocht) hir Hienes auctorite in prætending fa to reforme religioun in hir abfence : wald aduenture hir Hienes awin perfoun, by counfell and exhortatioun of maift noble princis hir G. neir coufingis, and vndoutit freindis, in the ftormie feis, throu euident perellis of vnfreindis, and præfent hir felf to yis Realme maift humblie, nocht as a Souerane, bot as a fubiect, or erar hertlie mother, haifand compaffioun of hir tribulit fones : obiecting hir Maief. to maift extreme perelis, to ye intent, yat hir fones maift deirbelouit fuld hef bene deliuirit frome all perel : albeit yai had maift fulefchelie in ane furius rage, obiectit yame to ye famin : and in ye mein tyme nocht intendand to ye punifment of ony cryme with rigour, committit be zouris, in hir Hienes abfence : bot labouris maift diligentlie for Godlie concord in the realme, and dew obedience to the auctorite, but the quhilk ye wthir may no ftand : committand alfo libertie of confcience to zouris in religioun (quhilk only in the beginning of ye tumult yai defyrit) and yat by ye confuetude of al Chriftiane princis vfeit to yare fubditis, quhill ordour be tane yairin, be ye thre eftatis of the realme. Think ze nocht yat yis grete humilitie, gentrice, and fingular humanitie iunit with wifdume of fik excellent zour natiue Souerane, fuld mollifie to humill obedience, ye hert of ane trew Scot, albeit it war forgeit of irne or fteill? Gif ze think fua with ws (as is zour dewtie but dout to do) quhy exhort ze the fubiectis fa

*O humane, hertly, gentle, and wyse Souerane.*

*The commoun prouerb is ouer trew, Lat ye sow put in ane fute, &c. Thair for faythful man, resist the auld serpent, yat he enter nocht his heid.*

feruentlie to rebellioun againft hir G. except fche leue the ordour and catholik opinoun in the Sacramentis of Chrifte Iefus vniuerfalie reffauit,
and mak a monftruous Idoll of zour Maifter Caluin : adheirand only to his
priuat opinioun, vnknawin to the warld afoir yis præfent? Gif ze can
nocht preue zour doctrine in the controuerfiis now præfent amangis ws,
tobe vniuerfalie reffauit: quhow can ze but fchame bable in zour beleif,
*The haly Kirk vniuerfal?* 'Or quhat proffettis zow yat part of zour be- Note Rei-<br>dar.
leif: fen ze ar as bund Slauis, addictit to zour awin priuat opinions iugement, contrare the mynd and auctorite of the famin kirk ?

## 32. *Gif in the Mefs be ony Idolatrie.*

AND gif it fall pleis our maift excellent Souerane, to ye intent to faif
zouris fra vter ruine (as yair is na dout of hir G. guid mynd yairto) to Thair is na<br>dout bot al<br>trew Chris-<br>tiane will<br>do all that<br>may stand<br>with Godis<br>plesuir for<br>an vnitie in<br>ye kirk.
permit zou fafer as Godis æternall word fufferis in the Mefs, aganis the
quhilk ze fchaw zour felfis fa coniurit inimeis: as for exemple yat yai be
na preift nor minifter admittit yairto, bot fik, that may inftruct the peple be
hale and fyncer doctrine, and guid exemple of haly lyfe : and that yai be
daylie mony to communicat with the preift facramentalie, gif yai may be
had, and that vndir bayth the kyndes, gif it fall pleis the vniuerfall kirk,
to keip that vniformitie : fua ze condemne nocht of fuperftitioun, or Idolatrie, a Chriftiane man, minifter or wthir, quhen he may haif na communicantis with him to reffaue the famin Sacrament him allane, be exemple
of Serapion in the tyme of the martyris, and the haill kirk in our days. Euseb.<br>eccl. hist.<br>lib. 6. cap.<br>34.
Quhat haif ze for zow, to hald the Mefs idolatrie, or yairin ony fuperfti-
tioun ? Gif ze deny Chriftis humanitie be reffoun of ye infeparable coniunctioun yairof with his diuinitie, tobe adurnit : ze ar alrady confundit
be the exemple of the thre kingis, quha adurnit him in the crib : and be
exemple of wthiris alfo in the Euangel. Gif ze deny the real præfence of Luc. 2.<br>Mar. 15.<br>Ioan. 9.
Chriftis body maift bliffit in ye Sacrament: ze diffent fra the fcripturis,
and haly kirk vniuerfall, and als fra the fegregatioun of all hæretikis afoir
zow and zour maifteris, to wit, Oecolampadius, Zuinglius and Caluin :
except Berangarius and his, as ze knaw præfentlie ye Lutheranis in yat
part, tobe zour manifeft aduerfaris. Gif ze deny Chrifte tobe adurnit in

ye Sacrament. (fen we adurne na vifible nor fenfible figne yairof) Quhy condemne ze nocht ᵃS. Auguftine for an heretik and ᵇChryfoftome fiklyke with wthiris of yair aige, quha erneftlie accuiffs ws of fin, gif we adurn nocht Chriftis maift haly body in the Sacrament?

<small>ᵃ in Ps. 98.<br>ᵇ .1. cor. 10.<br>Ambros. *de spir. Sancto* li. 3. ca. 12.</small>

### 33. *Gif Iohne Knox be lauchful minifter.*

<small>Ro. 10.<br>Heb. 5.<br>As Moyses and ye apostolis.<br>Luce. 1.<br>Ioan. 1.<br>Esa. 40.<br>* At yis place weil obscuir (as God bade) Io. K. maid a fel farde, to his gloir ze wate. Act. 13.</small>

SEN we reid, that nane fuld tak the honour of miniftratioun of Godis word, and Sacramentis on him, except he be lauchfullie callit yairto, othir be God immediatlie, or be man haifand pouer to promote him yairto: and fen we reid nane callit be God only, except fik as fchew yair pouer geuin yame be him, be pouer * of the fpirit, or in fignis and wonderis. Heirfor gif zow, Iohne Knox we fay, be callit immediatlie be God: quhare ar zour merwelis wrocht be the haly fpirit? for ye merwelis of woltering of Realmes to vngodly feditioun and difcord, we adnumbre nocht tobe of his giftis. Bot gif ze be callit be man, ze moft fcaw yame to haif lauchfull pouer yairto: as the Apoftolis ordinat S. Paull and Barnabas, albeit

<small>1. Tim. 4.<br>2. Tim. 1.</small>

chofin be God afoir, and ya fiklyke wthiris in ye fourtein of ye Actis: and as S. Paull ordinat Timothe and Tite, geueand yame pouer and command to ordour wthiris: quarein apperis the lauchful ordinatioun of minifteris. Zour lauchful ordinatioun be ane of yir twa wayis, we defyre zou to fchaw: fen ze renunce * and eftemis yat ordinatioun null, or erar wickit, be ye quhilk fumtyme ze war callit Schir Iohne.

<small>* And yat to zour grete schame brother.</small>

### 34. *Gif Iohne Knox be nocht lauchful Bifchope, quhow can yai be lauchful ordinatit be him.*

<small>Tit. 1.</small>

GIF he can nocht fchaw him felf a lauchful ordinat Bifchope (nocht only a Preift or inferiour minifter) quhow can ze fuperintendentis, or wthir inferiour Precheouris, electit and ordinat be him, nocht haifand pouer thairto, iuge zour felfis tobe lauchful minifteris in ye Kirk of God?

## 35. Quhy ar nocht ye Lordis and wtheris, lauchful miniſteris, as Iohne Knox, and his complices.

Gif Iohne Knox and ze affirmis zour felfis lauchful be reſſoun of zour ſcience, and that ze ar permittit always, gif ze be nocht admittit be yais Kirkis, quhome ze ſerue. Quhy hef ze prechit manifeſtlie a gret errour and ſchiſme in zour congregatioun, contending with twith and nail (as is ye prouerb) ſum Lordis and Gentilmen to hef gretumlie failzeit, miniſtrand zour communioun in tymes bypaſt to thair awin houſhald ſeruandis and tenentis? Sen ye Lordis and Gentilmen being men of ſcience, be thair awin iugement, in yat caſe wes permittit be thair ſaidis ſeruandis, to that office: quha affirmis yame felfis tobe a Kirk of God. *Heir Ioh. Knox be his awin ſentence aganis wtheris, is faſt tedderit in ye girn.*

## 36. Gif ye ordinatioun of miniſteris be a ſacrament.

Qvhy deny ze ye ordinatioun of miniſteris to be a Sacrament in Chriſtis Kirk? Sen zour grete Maiſter Caluin grantis in zour contrare, with mony wtheris new writtaris in Alemannie. Quhidder hes it ye viſible ſigne, videlicet, ye impoſitioun of handes, the promiſſis of God with the command (quhilkis thre only ze think neceſſare to a Sacrament) expreſſit in ſcriptuir or nocht? *Cal. in inſtit. de Sacrament. Ibidem de ordine eccleſiaſt. There is na thing mair plane.*

## 37. Of vnqualifeit miniſteris.

Ze allegand zour felfis, to reduce ye ordour in religioun according to the puritie of the writtin word: and nocht miſknawing alſo, yat ye grete decay of ye ſyncere religioun is, ye electioun and admiſſioun of ye vnqualifeit and vnable miniſteris, as we confes with zou, yat yis lang tyme ye maiſt part to hef bene admittit, mair throw auarice, ambitioun, or wthir carnal affectioun (and yat in puniſment of the peple, yat God ſa ſuffereit) nor for godly leirning, or wtheris guid propirteis requirit in a miniſter: and yairthrow ſpecialie all miſordour or abuſe, yat iuſtlie can be allegeit maiſt cheiflie to hef ſprung. Quhy admit ze tobe zour Precheouris and miniſteris in findry places zoung childring, of na eruditioun, except ye reiding *A dum paſtour or a wicious, is a ſair ſcurge on the peple: as is ye fals prechour.*

of Inglis and fmall entreflis in grammar, of na experience, nor zit haifand præeminence by wtheris of godly leuing: except ze call yat godly, to couet a fair wyfe, and ane fatt penfioun, by ye lawis of ye monaftik lyfe, quhilk findry of yame hes profeflit? Sen S. Paull techis, yat men in this vocatioun, by mony wthir godly propirteis, fuld nocht be zoung of leirning, and godly exercife always: bot potent to exhort and teche in helthful doctrine and potent to repreue and conuict ye gainfayaris of ye famin.

1. Tim. 3.

Tit. 1.

### 38. *Of a new ordour of eldaris.*

SIKLYKE fen be ye name of eldaris in ye new teftament expreflie is meanit Bifchoipis and Preiftis, quhilkis laft names ye Apoftolis vfeit nocht (apperantlie to ye intent yat yai fuld nocht be eftemit of yai fort of Preiftis and Bifchoipis of ye auld law) quhois office is expres to preche and miniftrat ye facramentis. Quhy inuent ze in zour Kirk a new ordour of Eldaris, quhome ze difcharge to vfe ony of the offices forfaidis? Silklyke quhy committ ze to ye faidis eldaris yat office, of ye quhilk ze haif na pouer: to wit ye office of a ciuill magiftrat, quhilk pertenis only to an Emperour, or King, or lyke public perfones, or to quhome yai cheis conforme to our Saluiour fayngis: Geue to Cæfar, yat pertenis to Cæfar, and fiklyke faying to Pylat: Yow wald haif na pouer ouer me, except it war geuin ye frome abuif, quho bald his pouer of the Empriour. Quhy fua tak ze fra ye eldaris: quhilk is yair dewtie and office, and geuis yame, quhilk pertenis nocht to yame, nor zit ze haif pouer to geue yame?

1. Pet. 5.
1. Tim. 5.

Note.

A confufioun of ordour and auctoritie.

### 39. *Of ye Pape, and gif a fuperior fuld be amangis ye Bifchopes.*

SEN naturalie be Godis prouidence amangis fowlis, fifcheis, and beiftis, in euery cumpanie is ane principal, as it war fuperiour: and fiklyke amangis men in euery Realme, is nocht only ane King or Quene, to quhome all obeys: bot alfo in euery prouince, fchyre, citie, and hous, is ane principal or fuperior, as yair is in euery craft almaift, ane decane. Quhy fuld it nocht be fua in ye Ecclefiaftical ftate, amangis ye Bifchopes, wtheris Paftouris, and minifteris? Sen in ye law of Moyfes God prouidit ane hie

Deut. 17.

Bischope, quhois sentence in controuersie of religioun, the peple suld follow vnder the pane of dethe? We can nocht be assuirit of na scriptuir, yat ze allege, bot S. Petir had ye famin pouer geuin figularlie and feueralie to him by ye rest, and aboue ye rest of ye Apostolis: as we ar at yis præsent persuadit, be yir wordis of oure Saluiour. *Simon Iona diligis* Io. vlt. *me plus his? &c. Pasce oues meas, &c.* And that all the rest of the Apostolis wes numerat amang the famin oues, it apperis till ws in yir wordis: *Omnes vos scandalum patiemini in me in nocte ista: quia* Matt. 26. *scriptum est, Percutiam pastorem, et dispergentur oues gregis.* And in an wthir place Petirs actorite aboue yame: *Ego rogaui pro te Petre, vt non deficiat fides tua: Tu verò conuersus confirma fratres tuos.* Quhilk pouer he apperis planelie to hef exerceit amang ye Apostolis takand ye Act.1.2.3. speche on him specialie in all conuentionis: albeit he sufferit S. Iames Act. 15. Bischope of Hierusalem, to pronunce a fentence at his awin Kirk, in his præfence. And gif ony be superiour: quhy suld nocht ye successour of Petir? Knaw ze nocht yat all ye aunciant Fatheris attributis mekle to ye Kirk of Rome by wtheris Kirkis: and also ye general counselis quhilk ze appreue? As for exemple ze knaw yat S. Augustine confirmis his doc- Epist. 165. trine specialie contrare ye Donatistis: yat neuir ane of ye Bischopes of Rome till his days (citand thair names to ye numbre aboue .xxxvj.) trowit wthirways nor he did, contrare ye faidis heretikis. Gif ze affirm ye Pape tobe ye Antichriste: will ze nocht schaw of quhat Pape ze mein, Of ye name gif ze speik of ye Romane Pape? or quhidder vnderstand ze be ye Pape, Pape. all Bischopes? for be yat name we reid ony Bischope to hef bene decorit: as S. Hierome writtis to S. Augustine Bischope: *Hieronymus Presbyter beatissimo Papæ Augustino S.* Gif ze had ye Bischopes of Rome Antichristis be ressoun of ony wice (quhilk we intend nocht to defend) quhilk of zow is but wice, cast ye first stane at yame. Gif it be for ony doctrine contrare Christe, schaw it in speciall (we pray zou) yat we may fle frome it.

### 40. *Of ye sacrament of pennance.*

Qvay deny ze the Sacrament of pennance? and quhy neclect ze to vse at ye leift ye abfolutioun of ye minifter afoir zour communioun always? Sen ye Apoftolis wes inftitut be our Saluiour with fick folennitie in that part of thair office, yat eftir his refurrectioun, he blew in yame, fayand: Re-

Io. 20.

faue ye haly gaift. Quhois finnis ze forgeue, yai ar forgeuin: and quhois finnis ze retene, yai ar retenit. And quhy diffent ze frome ye maift part of Allemannie in yat part?

### 41. *Of contritioun, confeffioun, and fatisfactioun.*

QVHY affirm ze yat contritioun, confeffioun, and fatisfactioun, ar Papifticall inuentionis, and callis ws Papiftis for ye vfeing yairof: and callis nocht Cypriane and ye Kirk fen his days Papiftis: quhois doctrine in yat cafe we follow, as collectit and euidentlie deducit of fcriptuiris?

### 42. *Of confeffioun.*

Io. 20.

Cyp. *serm.*
*de lap.*

GIF ze condemne confeffioun to be maid to ye Preift of fpecial faltis: quhow can he abfolue, conforme to the word of God, fum of thair finnis, and retene wthir nocht abfoluit, gif he fall mifknaw the fin? Or quhy call ze it Papiftrie, fen ye faid Martyr Cypriane witneffis it to haif bene in ye Kirk of God in his days: and wtheris fiklyke aunciant Fatheris eftir him?

### 43. *Of contritioun.*

Lu. 13.

OR quhy call ze contritioun Papiftrie? fen na man can haif forgeueance of his finnis, except he repent with intentioun of amendiment of lyfe, as our Saluiour techis: Except ze do repentance, ze fall all perifs?

### 44. *Of fatisfactioun to God.*

Serm. de
laps. et
passim.

QVHY hald ze fatisfactioun Papiftrie? fen Cypriane with mony aunciant Doctouris oft inculcatis yis terme in yair writtingis, to the fentence vfeit and refauit at this præfent in ye Kirk? Mifknew yai trew ze, ye fatif-

factioun and redemptioun conqueſt till ws be Ieſus Chriſte, as ye full
ranſoun to the Father, for the finnis of all the warld? Bot yis we think Note.
ze wil not ſay: for miſknawand yat thing only: quhou culd yai be Martyris of Chriſte, yat is witneſſis of ye veritie? And zit yai ſpeik and yat
be euident ſcriptuirin, of a ſatisfactioun requirit of our obœdience: as to
turn to God in murning, faſting, prayar, and almus deid, with ſiklyke
worthy fruitis of pennance, ſa oft inculcat be our Saluiour and ye Apoſtolis
to ye Iowis, with ſik dolour and hauines quharof S. Paull ſpeikis, 2.
Cor. 7. Gif ze admit nocht ſatisfactioun on yis maner tobe maid to God,
and nocht to man only: quhou vnderſtand ze yir ſcriptuiris, Cheritie 1. Pet. 4.
coueris the multitude of finnis: Turn to me in all zour hert in faſting, Ioel. 2.
ſobing and greting: Geue almus, and all ſalbe clene to zou: And yat Luc. 11.
Daniel says to Nabuchodonoſor, Redeme thi finnis with almus deid. with Daniel. 4.
mony ſiklyke places?

### 45. Of ſatisfactioun to men.

We deſyre zou to ſchaw, gif ze think it neceſſar to a pœnitent, to the end
he get remiſſioun of his finnis fra God, yat he mak ſatisfactioun to his
brothir at ye leiſt, inſafer as he hes offendit and rubbit him of his geris or
honouris: gif it be in his pouer? Gif ze diſſent fra ws, ſayand, Na: the
ſcriptuiris ar ful of teſtimonies in zour contrare, as thir:

    Quha luuis nocht, remanis in dethe.      1. Ioan. 3.
    Quha is nocht iuſt, is nocht of God.      Matt. 7.
    Departe fra me all ze wirkaris of iniquitie.      and 5.

Quhen thow offeris yi gift at ye altar, and remembiris yat yi brother hes
ocht aganis the, leif yi gift afoir the Altar: and pas and be reconcilit with
yi brother: and ſyne cum and offir yi gift. Quha luuis nocht his brother,
quhome he ſeis: quhow ſall he luue God, quhome he ſeis nocht? Can a
man luue his brother, ſa layng as he nocht only, nocht helpis him in his
miſtar, bot contrarie opreſſis him be violence and fraud: quhilkis all to
our purpoſe S. Auguſtine concluidis in yir wordis, Sin is nocht forgeuin
(ſays he) except it quhilk is tane away, be inſtorit? Gif ze grant with ws
yat it is neceſſare: quhy miniſtrat ze zour communion to ſik perſones,

quhome ze knew perfytlie to hef intromittit violentlie, with wthiris mennis poffeffionis, and als rubberie of the kirk guidis : nocht only of monafteriis, quhilkis ze imaginat to hef bene idolatrical, bot alfo of Bifchopis faitis and paroche kirkis, but ony repentance, fatisfactioun, or intentioun of amendiment : quhilk thing ze man othir grant tobe intromiffioun with idolatrical geris, and fua yame and it tobe burnt togiddir, be ze law of God, as efter fal follow : or ellis tobe facrilege war, yan commoun thift. Of ye quhilkis it follouis confequentie, yat yai hef failzeit hauelie cumand to ye communioun, but reftitutioun of wrangous geris, or intentioun to yat ilk : and ze fer hauiar, quha miniftrat ye Sacrament (gif we may fua call it with zou) to ye vnuorthy : knawand yame in yat eftate.

Iosue. 7.

### 46. *Of twa partis of pennance, neulie fetfurth.*

Joel. 2.
Luc. 11. 6.
2. Cor. 7.
Luc. 3.
Matth. 5.

THAIR being fa mony thingis requirit, to trew pennance or repentance : as fobing, mourning and teris, walking, fafting, prayair and almus deid : with abftinence for a tyme fra mony thingis wthirwayis lefum, hawy dolour for the foremer offenffs, with firm intent of reneuing of lyfe yairftir with witheris worthy fruitis of pennance : and fpecialie fatisfactioun to all men quhome we hef offendit : quhy hef ze fetfurth the faid pennance fa obfcuirlie, appuntting yairto twa partis only, quhilkis ar fayth and reneuing of lyfe, callit be zou refipifcentia : fen fayth is na mair a part of pennance, yan it is of ony wthir vertew, it being ye grund of al vertew : and be ye wthir name ye forefaidis propirteis of pennance ar ouer obfcuirlie declarit. Perfuade ze nocht heirby to mony vngodly proud præfumptioun, and vnfuir fecuritie of confcience ?

Na word to geue ye kow agane: nor trew dolour for ye sin committit, &c.

### 47. *Gif præfumptioun vpfpringis of the præmiffs or nocht.*

WE defyre zow to maturelie confider, and anffuer till ws, quhiddir it cumis of zour licentious doctrine in neclecting and contemning yir thre partis of pennance abone fpecifiit (as it apperis planelie till ws to cum) or wthirwyis : yat findry at yis præfent ar defcendit to fik beiftlie ruidnes, and præfumptuous fecuritie of confcience, and fchamelis præfumptioun,

yat yai ar nocht efchame it, nocht to fatifie yair inferiouris or brethir, in
yair deuitie of dettis or fiklyke : bot to mak mony maift large promiffis
and obliffingis, knit with word, writt, walx and feil, als weill to fuperiour Note, and efchew.
poueris (quhare yai dar) as to æquall and inferiouris : and nothir keipis
nor intendis to keip ye famin : by ye noble and faythfull conftancie of our
noble Progenitouris, to ye blafphemie of Godis law, and to maift vile
fchame of our countre. Think ze nocht yat yis maift barber ruidnes, and
maift beiftlie impietie of vnfaythfulnes to man, wald be fpittit at be a Iow
or an Ethnik, ze be the ftarkaft theif in Riddifdale ? Or think ze fik perfones tobe of Godis elect, quha aucht to perfuade yame felfis be certitude of
fayth (as ze teche neceffar to beleue) tobe of the prædeftinat fones of God ?

### 48. *Gif concupifcence in the regenerat, be damnable fin.*

SEN it is writtin, yat quha ar borne of God or regenerat, finnis nocht : 1. Io. 3. 5.
and yat we ar wefchin fra our finnis, fanctifiit and iuftifiit : and alfo yat 1. Cor. 6.
Chrifte clengeis his kirk (of ye quhilk we ar membris) be the lawar of Ephes. 5.
regeneratioun in the word of lyfe : Quhy teche ze yat ye concupifcence
left in ws eftir regeneratioun, for our humiliatioun and exercife, is damnable fin ?

### 49. *Of Confirmatioun.*

SEN ze fee ye Sacrament of confirmatioun fa expreflie vfeit be ye Apoftolis. Act. 8. 19.
And affirmit be Hierome and wthiris Doctouris, yat it fuld be miniftrat
be the Bifchoipis only : quhy efteme ze it a thing of na importance : and
bot a Papiftical fuperftitioun ?

### 50. *Of extreme vnctioun.*

SEN yat ye Preiftis of ye kirk fuld cum to ye feik, vnct yame with oill,
and pray for yame : As our Saluiour techis tobe his Godly will, be the
mouth of S. Iames : quhy put ze it out of the vfe of Chriftianis, and nocht Iacob. 5.
only depriuis it of ye name of a Sacrament ?

### 51. *Of Matrimonie.*

QVHY put ze Matrimonie furth of ye numbre of Sacramentis: fen it is
callit in ye fcriptuir a Sacrament. Will ze hald ye communioun tranfla-
tioun fals becaus ye Greik text hes μυστήριον? Will ze nocht grant yat yai
twa Sacramentis, quhilkis ze fua cal, ar μυστήρια. Mairouer is nocht Sacra-
mentum in the Latin text, of als large fignificatioun, as ye wthir is in ye
Greik? And al fua quhiddir gif Matrimonie hes ya thre propirteis, requirit be zow to a Sacrament or nocht?

*Ephes. 5.*
*Daniel. 2.*
*Ephes.1.3.*
*Collos. 1.*
*1. Tim. 3.*

### 52. *Gif ye perfones feparat for fornicatioun may mary wthiris perfones agane, ye athir being on lyue.*

QVHAT haif ze for zow, that a mariit man or woman leuand ye wthir for
caus of fornicatioun, conforme to ye fcripturis, may mary an wthir perfoun, ye firft party being on lyue? Sen S. Paull, techis yat a woman is
fubdewit to ye law, fa lang as hir hufband leuis: and alfo he geuis ane
expres command to ye innocent woman dimittand hir * hufband, to remane vnmariit, or tobe reconcilit to hir hufband?

*Ro. 7.*
* Zea, be-
ing an adul-
terar.
*1. Cor. 7.*

### 53. *Gif ye harlotis, for quhais caufs matrimonie is violatit, or adnullit: may mary wthiris.*

ZE knawand haly matrimonie being fa erneftlie commandit, indiffobublie
tobe keipit, except for caus * of fornicatioun: quhat apperand reffoun haif
ze for zow (we appele to zour confcience) to admitt it a Godly law to
fuffir an harlot in his wyfes tyme lyand with an wthir harlot: or a * preift,
or vnmariit man, lyand with an wthir manis wyfe, for yat caufs the matrimonie tobe diffoluit: and the twa harlotis tobe zokit vp in a prætendit
band of matrimonie maift honorable: as it is practifit be zow, of fum of
our rennigatt preiftis, and wthiris as ze knaw?

*Mat. 19. 7.*
*Mar. 10.*
* and yat
fra bed and
buird only.
* In Glas-
gow.
O abomi-
nable prac-
tife.

#### 54. *Of twa contrare lawis tweching mariage.*

MAIROVER quhow deliuer ze zour felfis of the perplexitie of yir twa contrarious lawis? to wit, yat an adulterar feparat fra his wyfe for fornicatioun, hes na pouer be Godis law to mary agane, his former wyfe being on lyue: and on the wthir fyde ze permitt a man or woman, yat may * nocht leif chaft, to mary? Alfo quhiddir gif a man or woman being lang abfent fra yair party, or haifand yair party impotent throw feiknes, or throw obftinat mynd nocht focial, and zit may nocht, as ze teche, leif chaft, may mary an wthir in ye mein tyme? Gif ze fay na, be reffoun of yair former promife and luue to yair party: quhy will nocht ze Chanounis, Munkis, Freris, Preiftis, Nunnis keip the famin reull, for ye luue of Chrifte zour fpous, and promifs maid to him?

* na wther excufis hes munkis,&c. to violate yair wow and promis to God. Nane is sa ignorant, quha seis nocht thame heir fetterit.

#### 55. *Gif Preiftis may mary efter yare promotioun.*

WE nocht ignorant in that part, of the fcriptuiris and hiftoriis, yat in ye 1. Tim. 3. primitiue kirk, of honorable men haifand ane wyfe, wes oftymes promotit tobe Bifcopes, Preiftis, and Diaconis: of ye quhilkis mony yairefter turnit yair wyfes in yare fifteris. And heirfor think we ye famin lefum as zit, with an vniforme confent. Bot quhare reid ze euir in the primitiue kirk, Note. yat men wantand wyfes, ye tyme of yair promotioun to yai offices, and eftir mariit but repreif and punifment of ye kirk? Shaw ane exemple gif ze can?

#### 56. *Gif ye Preiftis in ye new law fuld be als beutifull, as yai in the auld.*

AND fiklyke S. Paull counfelit ye layt man and woman, to abftene fra yat vfe of yair bodyis till wthiris requirit in matrimonie, for a tyme, that thai 1. Cor. 7. mot waik on prayar: quhat tyme is it, we pray zow, yat a guid Bifchope, or wthir Paftour, fuld nocht waik on prayar, ftudie, or preching: and yat he fuld nocht be rady to miniftrat ye Sacramentis? And gif ye Preiftis in ye law of Moyfes (quha in yat tyme behuifit to haif wyfes, for continuatioun of yair tribe of Leui: quha only of yair natioun wes appointit tobe

Preiſtis) abſtenit fra yair wyfes all ye tyme of yair obſeruance in the temple, and certane days afoir. Will ze yan, yat ye Preiſtis, and miniſteris of Chriſtis Euangel, and Sacramentis yairof, quharein is miniſtrat realie yai graces, præfigurat in ye auld law, quha continualie and dayly ſuld waik vpone yair miniſtratioun: tobe les beutiful, and of les cleinnes of lyfe, yan wes ye wthiris? And knaw ze nocht yat Ambroſe, Origine, and wthiris pronunces planelie vpone yis ſimilitude and conferrence, yat the Preiſtis in the law of grace ſuld leue in continual chaſtitie, ſen yai ſuld waik continualie vpon yair prayar, miniſtratioun of the Sacramentis and ſiklyke? Ze knaw yat Achimelech wald nocht geue ye ſchew breid to Dauid and his ſſuandis, quhil he knew yat yai war clene fra al women thre days afoir. Gif ſik honour wes hald to ye figuir! quhat ſuld be hald to ye veritie, quhilk is Chriſtis body, and bluid, daylie tobe reſauit, or miniſtrat in ye Sacrament be godly paſtouris?

<small>Quhy ye preiſtis under ye law had wyfes.</small>

<small>Ambros. in .1. Timoth. 3. Orig. in Num. homil. 23. Hierome contra Iouin. lib. 1. cap. 19.</small>

### 57. Of ye wow of chaſtitie.

QVHIDER gif it be leſum or nocht, yat men of perfite aige, haifand na lauchful impediment, to wow chaſtitie? And yat wow being complete, gif it be leſum yaireſtir to mary, conforme to ye law of God, or nocht? Gif ze think yat yai may: quhow vnderſtand ze yat place of S. Paul ſpeikand of ye zoung wedowis, quha had wowit continence, yat yai had yair damnatioun for only willing to mary: becaus yai brak yair former promiſs. And yis being trew of women: quhou can ze religious men abone ſpecifiit, mary: and eſchew alſo ye famin ſentence? Gif ze allege yat ze wowit nocht: Of quhat mynd enterit ze in zour religioun? Or quhou ſal ze defend zour ſelfis nocht tobe hypocritis, gif ze aſtriƈtit nocht zour ſelfis afoir God, to yat thing: quhilk mony ways ze profeſſit afoir man?

<small>Note. 1. Timot.5.</small>

### 58. Of ye ſaulis departit afoir Chriſtes aſcenſioun, and ſen ſyne.

SEN ſum of zour religioun affirmis ye ſaulis of ye fatheris, quha deceiſſit in fayth afoir Chriſtis aſcenſioun, to hef entirit yan to the gloir æternal, as

## TO THE CALUINIANE PRECHEOURIS. 99

the Martyris and wtheris iuft hes done fen fyne: and wtheris of zou A grete techeis yat nothir afoir, nor fen fyne, quhill ye day of ye generall refur- schisme in rectioun of thair bodyis, fall afcend thair: quhy cry ze nocht out ye ane bunde. fyde contrare ye wthir: or conuenis amangis zour felfis on ye ane fyde, and fchawis zour determinatioun in the mater corroborat be euident fcriptuiris? For of manly coniecturis or fcriptuiris thrawin by ye refauit vnderftanding yairof, to nothir of zour partis may we decline.

### 59. Of Princis and Nobilis fepulturis.

SEN ye Prophetis and Patriarkis in ye auld teftament had fik cuir for yair Genes. 24. honorable fepulturis: and commandit yat eftir yair deth, yair banis tobe Exod. 13. cariit furth of ye cuntre of ftrangearis: And in ye new teftament fiklyke Matth. 27. we reid nocht only of oure Saluiouris maift honorable and magnifik Act. 8. buriing, bot alfo of S. Iohne ye Baptift, and S. Steuin, with wtheris. And all this wes done, we ar affurit for ye honour of ye bodyis, in hoip of ye refurrectioun. We will nocht fpeir in aduentuir ze be crabit, gif ze beleue firmlie ye refurrectioun with ws? Bot fen ze aggre with ws in yat beleif: quhy hef ze difhonorit fua ye bodyis and fepulturis of the Princis Na low, of Scotland, and wtheris our noble Progenitouris, and wappit yair banis wald hef fchamefullie furth of yair fepulturis: and maid alfo a filthy ftable of beiftis playt yis to ftrangearis vpone our maift excellent Kingis body, quha laft deceffit? to yair el-
Gif ze allege ony occafioun of Idolatrie at ye faidis fepulturis: yat trifle is na excuis to zou, except ze grant zour felfis mair ruid and barber, yan euir wes natioun vnder heuin, ta tak occafioun of idolatrie, quhare nane is.

### 60. Gif ye Kirk geris wes Idolatrical, and of ye intromiffioun yairwith.

WE effectuouflie demand zow, gif ye veftimentis, chaliffis, and wtheris ornamentis in ye Kirkis of Scotland wes Idolatrical, or nocht? Gif yai war nocht, quhy techit ze yame fua tobe, and burnt fum of yame in teftimonie of zour doctrine? Gif yai var pollutit in idolatrie: quhy referuit ze ye beft part yairof, vnburnt? Quhou can ze excufe zou nocht tobe puniffit with Saull, quha fparit Agag with certane of his beft guidis contrare Godis command? Quhow will ze defend certane of ye Nobilis and Gentlemen in Scotland, quha intromittit with ye faidis Idolatricall guidis, nocht tobe tane with ye famin geris togiddir with yair fones, dochtiris, horfs, cattell, and all thair infprayth, and tobe burnt in puldre, be exemple of Achan: quha committit only ye famin cryme (gif ye faidis geris wes Idolatrical, and fuld hef bene burnt, as ze hef techit) and yat mair lychtlie yan yai, fen he committit his cryme quietlie? Bot God forbid, gif it be his pleſour, yat ze be the caus of fa feueir iugement aganis our Nobilis. Quhow deliuer ze zow heirfor, of yis perplexitie: bot othir ze man confes zour ignorance and errour, or fik feueritie tobe exerceit, as faid is?

*1. Reg. 13.*

*Iosue. 7.*

*O schiris recant, and saif: ze ar bot men; it is na schame for sa grete a cause.*

### 61. *Of ye beft geris tane away and fauld, and ye werft referuit.*

THE faid Achan being fa puniffit, for ye beft geris intromittit be him: quhy iuge ze ye goldin and filuir chaliffis, and wtheris thingis of gold and filuir: welwot, filkis, and wtheris fyne clathis: bellis, fepulturis, of brace, leid, and fiklyke, yat geuis money: to hef bene pullutit with Idolatrie, and yairfor tobe deftroyt, and nocht ye auld and reuin ornamentis, fklate, thak, and grof ftanis, rottin tymmir and fiklyke? Gif ze allege ye intromiffioun and difpofitioun of ye faidis guidis, to hef bene contrare zour will: quhy techit ze nocht vnfentzetlie, contrare fik manifeft facrilege, and impietie? Or quhy admittit ze fic oppin finnaris, without repentance, and fatisfaćtioun, to zour communioun?

*Zca, ye caillwyfe seis zow heir, bund fute and band.*

### 62. *Gif thingis dedicat to God, fuld be prophanit in wtheris vfeis.*

GIF thingis anis dedicat and fanćtifiit to God, fuld nocht be tranflatit and appropriat in wtheris prophane vfeis, as the forfaid hiftorie of Balthazar preuis: bot gif yai be dedicat vngodly to God, aucht to be fanćtifiit in a mair Godly vfe: be exemple of the incenfuris of Dathan and Abiron: quhidder cumis it be zour* exhortatioun, or nocht? yat mony defyris ye Kirk landis anis dedicat to God, for fuftentatioun of godly minifteris, puir ftudentis, and feble, and waik indigentis, tobe appropriat to ye croun, or to ye firft fundatouris pofteritie? Gif ze exhort yame nocht yairto: *

*Leuit. vlt.*
*Daniel. 5.*
*Num. 16.*
*\* Ouer trew.*
*\* Because zour awin belliis forbiddis zou, and inwy agains sum.*

quhy cry ze nocht out vpone yair wickit confait, and als manifeſt ſacrilege of wtheris: and aduertiffis yat ye Prophet incallis ye wrayth of God on yame: 'quha ſays, Lat ws poffeid be hæretage ye ſanctuarie of God? *Pſal. 82.*

### 63. *Of traditionis vnwrittin: and firſt exemple of certane ſolennit days.*

SEN ye Apoſtill S. Paull commandit in ſindry places his traditionis tobe keipit, als weil ye vnwrittin, as ye writtin. And S. Auguſtine ſiklyke af- firmis that to diſpute of thai thingis vniuerſalie obſeruit, gif yai ſuld be keipit, or nocht: tobe maiſt inſolent madnes. Exemple he geuis of the zerly celebratioun of the Paſche day, of our Saluiour aſcenſioun, and doun cuming of the haly gaiſt, onlyke manere zerlie tobe celebratit. Quhy abo- liſe ze ye ſolenniteis of ye ſaidis days with ſiklyke, and all wthir ordour of that ſort vniuerſalie obſeruit: as zuil day, Circumciſioun, Epiphanie, Lentren. *2. Theſ. 2. 1. Cor. 11. Aug. ad Ianua. et ad Caſula. epiſt. 86. he is blind, yat ſeis yame nocht heir, re- bellis to Godis kirk.*

### 64. *Of ye mixing of ye Lordis coup with wattir and wyne afoir ye ſanctificatioun.*

ZE knawand yat our Saluiour ſched wattir and bluid in ye myſterie of our redemptioun, and yat ye Lordis coup with wattir and wyne tobe ſanctifiit in ye Sacrament is præfigurat in the auld teſtament in mony places, as Cypriane preuis maiſt largelie and erneſtlie: quho affirmis alſo that ye Lord commandit ws to mixt ye ſamin. Quhy detrect ze and rebukis ws catholikis for ye obſeruatioun yairof. And will nocht blaw out zour in- dignatioun vpone ye Martyris, Cypriane, Irinæus, Fabiane, Euariſtus, Al- exander, Auguſtine, and mony wtheris Doctouris, quhome as witneſſis of the veritie we follow in this parte? Bot ſen ze do nocht ſa: appere ze nocht to ſchuit out zour malice contrare ws, and nocht contrare that quhilk ze had an errour? And ar ze nocht contrare ye ſcriptuir, acceptouris of perſones? *Epis. 3. li. 2. Quhow ſchameful- lie puttis M. George Hay yis ſentence of Cyprian. eftir ye titill of his buik.*

### 65. *Of the Sounday.*

GIF ze admit na traditioun vnwrittin: quhy ar ze ſa bauld contrare zour

Be yir vj. quæstiounis follouing al ye ground of yare doctrine is doung in ye dirt: and yame selfis conuict of errour agains yair awin doctrine. For al yir thingis nocht expreslie, writin yai appreue, for a tyme always with ws. Bot take tent to yair taill.

doctrine, and manifest scriptuiris apperinglie also, to celebrat zour Sabbaoth day, with ws catholikis, on ye Sounday: and nocht with ye Iowis, on ye Saterday?

### 66. *Of ye names, persones, and trinitie.*

MAIROUER gif ze will appreue na thing bot expreslie writtin, quhou will ze anssuer contrare an hæretik denyand wickitlie ye Father, ye Sone, and ye haly Gaist, tobe callit godly and dewly, thre persones, and ye haly trinitie? Alsua quhidder admitt ze and appreuis the samin names, or nocht? And gif ze appreue yame: quhou estabilise ze zour doctrine, sen yai names ar nocht writtin expreslie in scriptuiris?

### 67. *Of ye forme Gloir to ye Father. etc. in end of euery Psalme.*

QVHY vse ze to sing with ws Catholikis at ye end of euery Psalme: Gloir to ye Father, to ye Sone, and to ye haly Gaist. As it wes in. &c. sen yat godly forme wes only commandit tobe soung, in yat place, be ye Pape Damasus: in ye rebuke of heretikis?

### 68. *That infantis suld be baptizit contrare the Anabaptistis.*

Orig. in caput. 6. ad Rom. Aug. lib. 1. de origine atæ. ca. 23.

SIKLYKE quhat hef ze for zou expreslie writtin, to conuict ye Anabaptistis errour, denying that bairnis in thair infancie suld be baptizit? For Origene, Augustine, and also the Lutheranis lenis in this mater rycht wechty, to the Apostolik traditioun, and vniuersal obseruatioun of the haly catholik Kirk.

### 69. *Of sa mony Euangelis, Epistolis. &c. in ye new testament.*

Contra epist. Fund. cap. 5.

ALSUA quhat scriptuir hef ze for zou, to resaue sa mony Euangelis, and Epistolis in the new testament, as ze do: and nane ma? Gif ze allege ye vniuersall consent of all aiges sen Christe, and ye auctoritie of Godis Kirk, to appreue ye veritie yairof: as S. Augustine dois planelie in ye samin mater. Quhy refaue ye nocht the vniuerfal interpretatioun of the faid Kirk fen Chriftis afcenfioun, in all materis of controuerfie, and ordour tobe obferuit in vnitie and peace?

70. My copie heir wantis ane quæftioun in yis place, anentis ye figne of ye croce: quhilk ye Reidar may haif in ye writtin copiis at hem.

### 71. *Of quhat traditionis we fpeik.*

WE fpeikand of traditionis meanis nocht to compell ony man to refaue ony thing contrare ye fcriptuiris, nor zit yai ritis vfeit in diueris kirkis, albeit aggreing with ye fcriptuir: fer les heirfor fuperftitioun, or ony abuiffis onyways croppin in religioun: bot meanis be traditionis, the trew vnderftanding of the word of God: and thai thingis vniuerfalie taucht and obferuit, be all catholikis, fen the days of the Apoftolis. Bot giue ze appreue nocht ye famin with ws, bot inuentis a new fenfe yairof contrare the former mynd of our fatheris: and ftudijs fiklyke to abrogat, and abolife ye vniforme ordour in religioun, als weill of ye facramentis, as of wthir godly ritis, albeit maift cleirly aggreing with the haly fcriptuiris: and fpecialie yais vniuerfalie obferuit, be all catholikis, to yis our aige: quhow can ze excuifs zour felfis of ye impietie of fchifme and diuifioun, and fra manifeft defectioun fra the Kirk of God, and nocht tobe ye werray Sones of the Antichrift, fawand fchifme and diuifioun in Godis Kirk, and contrare ye manifeft Scriptuir and promifs of our Saluiour: denyand, euir to hef bene an haly Kirk afoir zow? And gif ze præfer zour awin witt and iugement to all wtheris (quhilk God forbid) feikand thairby a glorious titill, by the gloir of God: quha promittit to fend his Prophetis, Doctouris, and Euangeliftis to the confummatioun of his Sanctis: quhow fall ze nocht iuftlie be reputit (quhilk gratious God in zow mot ftay) ye childering of arrogance, and ye warray Sones of Belial?

*Note diligentlie Christiane Reidar.*
1. Tim. 6. it is writtin, *Depofitum cuftodi.*

### 72. *Of ye inuifible Kirk.*

Gif ze appreue na kirk, to ye quhilk ze may affent, except an imaginat inuifible kirk (quhilk ze hef begit fra Luther) quhilk wantis Eris to heir: quhow fall ze fchaw zour compliant to the kirk, conforme to our Saluiour command? And gif it wantis toungis to fpeik, and handis to writt (as it man want of neceffitie, gif it be inuifible) quhow can it be, as S. Paull techis it tobe, ye pillar and firmament of veritie? Albeit ye elect of God ar knawin to him only: zit quhow can yai be inuifible to men: fen it behuifis yame tobe techit be men, refaue the Sacramentis be men? or wthirways quhou can yai be of Godis kirk? Quhy inuent ze fik a terme as inuifible, nothir expreffit in fcriptuir, nor refauit be aunciant fatheris: and fettis ye famin furth as an article of zour beleif? Will ze nocht confes, yat in ye kirk of God ar bayth guid and euill, expreffit in the Euangell, be ye fimilitude of quheit and fitcheis, guid fifchis and euill in ane nett: fua yat ye guid in the battell throw tentatioun may fall, and ye euil throw trew pennance, may ryfe agane to grace? Or quhiddir imaginat ze zour kirk tobe inuifible, to mair efalie perfuade yairthrow an vnitie in all godlinefs? Or (as mony fupponis) to ye end yat ze and zour priuat opinioun be nocht iugeit be men of fuperiour poueris? Gif ze perfuade ony Godlines or vnitie yairby: be quhat meanis, or maner we pray zow? And quhow can ze yairthrow, onyways efchew, nocht tobe iugeit of fuperiouris of ye kirk? fen ze neid obey yame in all Godlines: albeit yai in thame felfis, be wickit: fen na pouer is bot of God. Ferther gif God prouidit amangis the Iowis an vndoutit ordinance, yat all dout and controuerfie in religioun amangis yame mot be decidit: hes he les cuir of ws, quhome he hes bocht alrady with ye precious bluid of his only Sone, fa feruentlie commendand ws peace and concord, yan of yame: yat it may be lefum to euery ane of ws, to adhere to his awin imaginatioun and phantafie, but ony iugement or punifment of our fuperioris?

### 73. *Gif a woman may heir fuperioritie of a Realme, Prouince, &c.*

Ze nocht mifknawand yat we all ar maift ftrytlie commandit in ye fcriptuiris, tobe fubmittit and obedient to ye hie poueris: of ye quhilkis we beleue our lauchful King, or Quene tobe Principal in ye ciuill eftate, as ye cheif Bifchope in the Ecclefiaftical gouernment: Quhy affent ze to ye furthfetting of certane feditious buikis : quharein is denyit, that a woman may beir auctorite of ony Realme, Prouince, or citie? Sen we reid maift Iudic. 4. godly women to hef had fik auctorite: as the prophetife Debora. We reid ye Quene of ye South, be our Saluiour gretumlie commendit, for ye Luc. 11. vifiing of Salomon. We reid fiklyke of ye Quene of Candace, quhois Act. 8. Eunuch' wes baptizit be Philip. Quhare for flew ye wyckit Quene Athalia ye Kingis pofteritie, and it had nocht bene ye law, yat a woman micht 4. Reg. 11. beir auctorite: as fcho regnit feuin zeris? Gif ze affirm yat a woman may nocht fucceid to hir fatheris hæretable landis: Moyfes pronunceis planelie in zour contrare: admittand, and commandand alfua ye dochtiris of Salphaad, to eniofe but impediment yare fatheris hæretage in Iudæa. Num. 27. And quhat is ony Realme, or Prouince in Chriftianitie, bot as a part of Iudæa, be ye quhilk is fignifiit, ye haill kirk of God: profeffing trewlie Note. Chrifte Iesus, fubdeuit to ane God, ane King, ane Lord, and ane Law? Quhare mentioun is maid in ye fcriptuir, yat a woman may nocht haif do- 1. Cor.14. minioun aboue man: is nocht yat meanit only, of a mariit woman, and 1. Tim. 2. hir huifband: except ze will euiry Lady in ye land, tobe fubdeuit to hir awin cuik, or horfboy? Gif ze deny zow to affent to the faidis prophane buikis: quhy cry ze nocht out in zour prechingis, aganis fa manifeft impietie, treffonable feditioun, quhilk alrady intendis extreme deftructioun of yis Realme?

### 74. *Quhat cumis of the misknawing of the Souerane, and Bifchopos.*

GIF ze can nothir affuir ws of zour lauchfull Bifchopis and wthiris mini- Note yis, fteris, nor zit knawis zour lauchful Souerane, quhome ze aucht nixt God *O gens sine capite.* maift humelie obey: quhow can ze affirm zou to haif a kirk: or defend zour conuenticulis fra a Babilonical confufioun, and Diabolical mifordour forefpokin be the Prophetis, to the wickit peple reprobat of God on yis manieir, *Sedebunt multos dies fine Rege, fine Lege, fine Principe, fine* Ose. 3. *Sacerdote et Doctore, fine Sacrificio et Altari, &c.* 2. Paral. 15.

### 75. *Gif the bodyis salbe all alyke glorifiit.*

<small>Ha, ha, bald yair. wald ze confound also ye ordour in heuin?</small>  IT being sa expreslie schawin to ws in scriptuiris, that euery man sall resaue rewarde of God, conforme to his wirking in his body heir: quhy teche ze yat euery body of the Iust in the resurrectioun salbe alyke beutifull and glorifiit! sen the guidnes of God sall reward the hail man, in
<small>2. Cor. 5.
2. Cor. 9.</small> body and saul: and in nocht in saull only. The difference of the reuarde is mair expressit, yan we neid to proue the samin. As, quha sawis scairslie, sall cheir schairslie: and as a sterne differis fra an wthir sterne
<small>1. Cor. 15.</small> in brychtnes: sua salbe, says S. Paul, ye resurrectioun of ye deid.

### 76. *Gif all kynd of images and similitudes, be forbiddin be the secund command.*

GIF ze vnderstand be ye secund præcept, as ze distinct yame, na image nor similitude of ony thing, tobe maid absolutlie: quhy permitt ze but repreif, the nobilis, and gentlemen of zour congregatioun, to haif images or figuris, of beistis and siklyke, in yair armi? And quhy beir ze zour selfis gold, and siluer in zour purss quhareupon ar images and figures? And gif ze allege siklyze tobe lesum, bot nocht tobe put vp in ye temple of
<small>3. Reg. 8. 6. and 7. Reid that place, and be nocht sclanderit: nor zit wickitlie impute a falt to ye kirk of God. 4. Re. 18.</small> God: quhow wnderstand ze that part of the Scriptuir, quhar Salomon is gretumlie commendit, for the biging of the temple of Ierusalem: quharein he gart mak sindry images and similitudis: as of the Angelis, Cherubin, of lyonis, oxin, and wthiris thingis? Will ze haif the hail kirk of God of les auctorite, yan wes Salomon him allane: quha bayth set vp images in the temple of God, without the expres writtin word of God? Gif ze ansfuer heirin tweching the abuiss, quhilkis we wald glaidlie war put away, be exemple of ye brasin serpent cassin doun be Ezechias: quow can zour anssuer be of strenthe, or to purpose? or quou can ze, be ressoun, condemne of Idolatrie all our elderis, for the vpsetting of images of Christe crucifiit, of his martyris and of ye rest, mair yan Salomon? Sen nothir of bayth intendit ony abuss eftir tocum yairof? And gif ze abolise all thing yat is abusit: quhat thing sal ze leue nocht abolissit? nocht ye haly scriptuiris self: quhilk heretikis hes euir abusit, thrawing ye

famin in defence of yair fals opinionis: as did ye deuil and ye Iowis, con- <sub>Matt. 4.</sub><br>
trare Chrifte. <sub>Io. 19.</sub>

### 77. *Gif we may incal ye fanctis to pray, for ws but Idolatrie.*

ZE confeffing with ws, as we ar informit, yat all the membris of Chriftis myftical body, quhilk is his haly kirk: ar defyrous and glaid alfo of ye helthe and profperitie of wtheris: and prayis to our heuinly father for ye famin to ye indigent yairof: als weill ye Angelis and Sanctis in heuin for ws on erd in yis battell, as ye godly on lyue for wtheris: bot ze deny yat we may incal the Angelis, and Sanctis in heuin to yat effect, but ye cryme of Idolatrie: ane pronunceis vs manifeft Idolatouris gif we fua do: quhy condemne ze nocht of Idolatrie fiklyke Origene, Chryfoftome, Hierome, Auguftine, Bafill with mony wthiris, quhome ze knaw to hef incallit ye fanctis afoir yame departit, as we do at yis præfent? And gif ze allege yat the fanctis heiris ws nocht: be quhat fcriptuir preue ze zour allegeance? Knaw ze nocht yat ye Angelis ar blythe for ye weilfair of man in erthe? And knaw ze nocht yat our Saluiour pronunces planelie yat ye fanctis depertit heirfra, falbe *alyke and æqual to ye Angelis? Or quhow may ze affirm the Angelis and Sanctis, tobe of les knaulege yan the deuilis, quhome ze grant to knaw our doingis?

<sub>Orig. in Job li. 2. Chrys. ad populum Antiochie. Homel. 66. et in l. Tes. 1. Hieron. in Epitap. Paul. August. de cognitione vera vita, cap. 39. Basilius in 40. mart. *Mar. 12. Luc. 20.</sub>

### 78. *Gif ony temporall pane, remanis to a penitent refauit to mercy, and of prayer for yame departit.*

MAIROUER quhat fcriptuir haif ze for zow, to affirm fa bauldlie: yat quhow fone as a finnar is refauit in ye fauour of God to mercy, yat all temporall pane is alfo dimittit to him: for ye quhilk caus ye faulis of ye Chriftianis, fay ze, yat ar departit in grace: neidis nane of our prayaris, or wthir fupport. For othir yai depart in grace, and fua immediatlie to ye heuin: or ellis in ye wrayth of God, and fua (as we grant with zow in yat cafe) paffis to ye hell. Bot quow wnderftand ze it, yat is writtin Num. 14. I haif forgeuin yame according to yi word, fays God to Moyfes prayand for ye peple. Nochtyeles it follouis of ye grete punifment temporall, yat nane

<sub>Awa with ye, Communioun of sanctis, meane yai: nother ws frome heuin be angel nor sainct: nor in erd, be wit of our forefatheris: nor ye departit be ws, wil yai hef helpit.</sub>

<small>Num. 14.
2. Reg. 12.
13. 15.</small> of ye peple yat paſſit furth of Ægipt abone .xx. zeris auld, ſuld entir in ye land of promiſſioun, except Ioſue and Caleb? Quhow wnderſtand ze ye grete tribulatioun and ſcurge yat come to Dauid and his houſs, for his ſinnis eſtir he wes reſſauit to mercy? Quhat meanis ye ſorrouful puniſ-
<small>4. Reg. 21.
23.
2. Paral. 33.
Hiere. 15.</small> ment of ye houſs of Manaſſes to ye fourt generatioun for his offences, eſtir he wes reſauit to mercy: nocht only in tyme of his wickit offspring: bot alſo in ye days of ye maiſt godly king Ioſias his oy, it is writtin: yat ye
<small>Note.</small> Lord wes nocht turnit fra his wrayth and indignatioun contrar Iuda for ye ſinnis of Manaſſes? Ze grantand alſo yat in baptim all ſinnis ar forgeuin, confes ze nocht yat the miſerie and ye dethe ſiklyke yat followis eſtir to ye infant, afoir ony actual ſin, is the temporal puniſment for ſin?
<small>Ro. 6.
Heb. 12.
Hiero. in
11. prouer.
Aug. in libro confess.
in Enchirid. in lib.
de civi. dei
et de verb.
Apost.
Amb. de
obit. Valent.
fratris, et
Theodos.
2. Mac. 12.</small> Sen S. Paull techis yat ye reuard of ſin, is dethe. Gif we heirfor aſſuirit be Godis word, yat he chaſtiſſs all ſone quhome he reſſauis, limitatis nor determinatis nocht ye wiſdum of God be our phantaſie: quhen, quhare, or quhoumekle, heir, or efter yis, as it pleſſs his godly fatherheid, iuſtlie to puneis ws temporalie: bot with Hierom, Ambroſe, and Auguſtine, with the reſt of Godis Kirk, prays, and delis almus deid for the ſaulis of the faythfull departit: quhy cal ze ws heirfor Papiſtis? ſpecialie, ſen it is writtin yat it is a haly and helthful thing, to pray for yame departeit, yat yai be ſaiſit fra yair ſinnis.

### 79. *Of faſting at certane tymes.*

<small>Exod. 24.
3. Reg. 19.
Ion. 3.
Matt. 3. 4.</small> FASTING in all aiges ſa gretumlie commendit be God, as it is patent of Moyſes, Helias, ye Niniuitis and alſo be S. Iohne Baptiſt and his diſciplis, practiſit alſo be our Saluiour ſelf (quhois doingis till ws ſuld be a reull of leuing, ſa fer as we may follow) be quhome it wes foreſpokin yat his diſ-
<small>Matt. 9.</small> ciplis ſuld faſt in yai days, quhen yair ſpous, quhilk wes him ſelf, ſuld be tane fra yame: Quhiddir gif the kirk of God heirfor, obſeruing, ȝerlie abſtinence fourty days in the lentrene, and oukly on the fryday quhen he ſufferit, and on wodinſday generalie in the Orient kirk, quhen he wes ſauld: as maiſt commonly on the ſaterday in the Occident: wes gilty of Idolatrie or ſuperſtitioun yairthrow? Quhiddir gif ye primitiue kirk obſeruit ye famin voluntarie, ſen ya war maiſt feruentlie geuin at yat tyme to al godly

exercife, or be command of yair Bifchopis: trewith it is yat yai faftit ye   Consider
famin maift ftrictlie, nocht only as it apperis, fra flefche, bot fra wynis and   ye historie of Spiridion
al weill nurifling meitis and drinkis: of ye quhilk fafting remanis now   obiectit to ws catoliks.
only, the memorial yairof to abftene fra flefche. Heirfor gif ye peple now   Trip. hift. li. 1. ca. 10.
being bent and prone to all licentious leuing, contemnis bayth ye les and
ye mair: quhy exhort ze yame to brek yat fmall memorie of abftinence
fra flefche, ye tymes forfaid? And nocht erar fpurris yame to ye ftrict abftinence maift godly of ye primitiue Kirk: nocht only for caufe of ye com-   O warldly wittit.
moun weil, as ze callit: bot for godly exercife: as ye Kirk vfcit ye famin
befoir? Siklyke fen ye peple fuld obey yair fuperiour in all lefum thingis:
quhy caufe ze difobedience to yame in yis mater? Sen Iofaphat, King
Saull, ye King of ye Niniuitis, with mony wtheris commandit fiklyke faft-   Ion. 3.
ing, and nane durft difobey: infamekle yat Saull wald hef flane his maift
deirbelouit Sone Ionathas for breking the famin command: nocht wil-   1. Reg. 14.
linglie nor wittinglie, bot in ignorance? Quhy obeyt ze nocht zour felfis,   Note.
ye laft lentrene tyme, zour Magiftratis commandand, at zour deuife and
counfel, abftinence fra flefche certane days? Gif ze allege in yis mater,
contrare ye fafting of ye Kirk, ye fayngis of S. Paull: All thingis ar
clene to ye clene. And quhare he propheciis of ye hæretikis, yat fuld for-   Tit. 1. 1. Tim. 4.
bid mariage and eiting of certane meteis. We think that abfurditie neidis
na confutatioun, bot ye exemplis abone fpecifiit: fen yai hæretikis ar al-   Nicholaitæ. Manichæi.
rady cummin in ye primitiue Kirk.   Tatiani.

### 80. *Of ye monaftik lyfe.*

NA man of mein reiding doutand ye Monaftik lyfe in ye primitiue Kirk
to hef bene in grete exiftimatioun: as findry werkis of Hierome, Auguftine, Chryfoftome, Bafill, and wtheris, in commendatioun thairof, may be
fufficient witneffing: quhy reiect ze, and difpyffis ye famin indifferentlie
as fuperftitious, or Idolatrical: fen it hes the grund and deip ruitis in ye
fcriptuir, be exemple of Helias, Helifæus, S. Johne ye Baptift, and yair   3 Reg. & 4.
difciplis: be exemple alfo of mony difciplis of Chrifte, quha fauld yair   Matth. 3.
geris and landis at his counfel, yat yai mot be perfyte and follow him:
and kaift ye prices yairof at ye difciplis feit. For ye defrauding of ye

110    TO THE CALUINIANE PRECHEOURIS.

Act. 4. 5.   quhilkis, Ananias and Saphira wes ſtrukin be ane word of Petir to ye
Note ze
apoſtatis.  deth. Feir ze nocht ſiklyke puniſment heir or hyne, tocum on ya religious perſones, quha now gredelie embraſſis ye warld agane, be libertie
of zour doctrine, quhilk afoir be Chriſtis counſel yai had refuſit? And
Mntth. 19.  that damnatioun alſo tocum on yame, (quhilk God auert throw his ſpirit
1. Timot. 5.
Note.       to repentance) quhilk S. Paull pronunceit vpone ye zoung wedowis, quha
eftir yair wow, wald only hef mariit? Sen ye ſpeciall pray, yat mony of
yame huntis for, is an huir (as we zit vnderſtand) cloikit be ye name of a
wyfe. Ze miſknaw nocht ye Monaſtik lyfe to hef ſtand ſpecialie in the
renunceing of the warld, and pleſouris of the body, nocht only fra vnlefum huirdum, bot fra mariage ſumtyme to yame leſum: to ye entent, yat
yai mycht yairby mair eſalie waik on prayar and godly ſtudy: nocht re-
fuſing honeſt corporal exerciſe, be exemple of S. Paul, to ſuſtentatioun of
yair bodyis: Zit nochtwithſtanding in our days ye famin wes abuſit
amang mony in idilnes and welthy lyfe, and cloikit with gliſtering ceremoneis of germountis and ſiklyke, mair yan in trew religioun: quhy hef
ze ſchorne away in this mater, the quheit togidder with the fitcheis?
Quhy hef ze wappit doun the Monaſteriis, and principal policie of this
Realme: and counſelis the rentis thairof, iniuſtlie tobe appropriat to
wtheris? Of the quhilkis Monaſteriis euery ane be a godly reformatioun,
befydes a cumpanie to waik on prayar, micht haif bene a college of godly
leirning, to the ſupport of puir ſtudentis: and that to ye grete and neceſ-
far commoditie of this Realme: quhare now apperis ſchortlie to cum extreme ignorance, and thairby, be reiding of erroneous Inglis buikis but
ferther knawlege, confuſioun of all erroruris. Gif ze allege the ſaidis monaſteriis to hef bene pollutit with Idolatrie, and thairfor ſuld haif bene de-
ſtroyit: quhy hef ze nocht deſtroyt alſo to the ground (as ze hef done in
a part) all Paroche kirkis, and Biſchopes ſaitis: in the quhilkis the famin
thingis wes vſeit, haldin be zou idolatrie? and quhat pouer haif ze to diſ-
pence mair in the ane, nor in the wthir?

81. *Of prayar at præſcriuit tymes in ye Kirk.*

EFTIR yat we ar be our Saluiour and his Apoſtolis, maiſt erneſtlie com-

mandit to walk continualie but intermiffioun, in prayar and thankifgeuing : Luc. 18.
Matt. 26.
and be exemple of our grete Lord forfaid techit, nocht only afoir and eftir 1. Thes. 5.
1. Pet. 4.
mete to thankfgeuing : bot to ye feruencie of prayar, knawing him to hef
prayt thryfe ye famin prayar, ye nycht he wes betrafit: and be Daniel Dan. 6.
alfo captiue in Babilone, turnand him to Ierufalem, and adurnand ye
leueand God thre tymes euery day : and techit fiklyke be ye haly Prophet Psal. 144.
and 118.
Dauid nocht only euery day, bot at mid nycht to ryfe, and euery day feuin
tymes to loue the famin Lord our God. Siklyke in the Apoftolis days we
reid that certane houris wes appointit, as quhen Petir and Iohne afcendit Act. 3.
to ye temple at ye nynte hour of prayar : we reid fiklyke of ye magnifik
ordour and multitude of findry minifteris in the temple of God appointit 1. Par. 24.
be Dauid : Heirfor, albeit euery man fuld pray willinglie : think ze nocht
yat ye Kirk of God inftitutit godly, yat prayaris, and louing fuld be foung
or red dayly feuin tymes, be able minifteris elect yairto ? quhilk thing, as
we vnderftand, ze can nocht be reffoun deny. Quharfor hef ze prætending bettir ordour in the Kirk than wes afoir, diftroyt ye formair ordour
and prays only be ane perfoun, in zour beft reformit Kirkis, anis only
euery day? and in mony places thryfe in ye oulk ? and in fer may nocht
anis in ye moneth ? we mein of the Kirkis pertening to the reformaris.
Gif ze allege in the formair ordour abufe or fuperftitioun throw ignorance
to hef aboundit (quhilk thing we excuis nocht) quhy trampit ze nocht thai
abufeis vnder fuit, and fet vp yat godly ordour to ye awin fyncere puritie,
bot hes brocht yat mater as fafting, and Monaftik lyfe, to the mair licentious libertie, yan afoir ?

## 82. *Of fre wil.*

Aug. de spi-
rit. et lit.
Qvhy hald ze ye catholik doctrine of fre wil of man, a Papifticall inuen- cap. 33.
Nemo ha-
tioun ? Sen all ye auld aunciant writtaris bayth Greik and Latin : affirmis bet in potestate quid
the famin tobe collectit maift euidentlie of the fcriptuir : and nocht only si veniat in
mentem: sed
yai, bot alfo zour awin writtaris : as Bullinger and Melanthon, appreuis consentire,
vel dissenti-
ye famin. Will ze heirfor a man tobe, as a ftane, hors, or mule ? Or mak re, propriæ
voluntatis
ze God the wirkar of all iniquitie : and to hef geuin his haly commandis est.

<small>Et ca. 4.
Sine libero
arbitrio nec
bene nec ma-
le ruitur.
Matth. 23.
Act. 7.</small>

to the intent, that man fuld be damnit thairby : gif ze allege all thingis tocum of neceffitie ? Gif man preuentit be ye grace of God, hes nocht yat
fredome of will to affent or diffent thairfra : quhow vnderftand ze yir
fcriptuiris, and fiklyke : Quhou oft wald I hef gadderit ye (fays our Saluiour to Ierufalem) and zow wald nocht? And fiklyke yat S. Steuin
fays to the Iowis, ze haif ay gainftand the haly fpirit? Gif man hes na
fredome, as faid is, to quhat effect gaif God his commandis to man, geuand
him terrouris of panis gif he tranfgreffit ye famin : and fa mony large pro-
miffisis for ye obferuing of ye famin ? Was yair euir ony of ws quhome
ze cal Papiftis, yat affirmit with ye Pelagianis, yat man eftir the fal of
Adam, mycht of ye pouer of his frewil, do ony guid plefand to God, without his fpecial grace and help ? Nochtyeles man we nocht grant with

<small>Ro. 7.</small>

Sant Paull, yat wil is adiacent till ws ?

### 83. *Of ye name Papiſtis.*

QVHIDDER call ze ws of ye haly catholik Kirk, Papiftis : be reffoun of ye
Bifchopes of Rome in ye primitiue Kirk, of ye quhilkis yai war .xx. and
may maift conftant Martyris of ye veritie, quhilk is Chrifte ? Or be ref-

<small>Note for
godly vni-
tie.</small>

foun of ye Bifchopes of Rome, quha has bene laitlie ? Gif ze cal ws Papiftis for caus of ony new doctrine, vnknawin to ye primitiue Kirk, bot
fet vp laitlie be ye Bifchopes of Rome or wtheris : we to ye intent, that
we may cum to an vnitie in all godlines, will, with Godis help, condefcend vnto zow, fa fer as we may but manifeft errour, and in na point adhere to ony doctrine in religioun, or ordour in ye Kirk, fetfurth be Papes,
Bifchopes, or Kingis, yir thoufand zeris laft bypaft : except it euidentlie
aggre with the exprefs word of God, ye trew vnderftanding yairof, vniuerfalie fetfurth afoir thai days : declarit till ws, be the vniforme confent of
the maift aunciant Doctouris, difcuffit and determinat be generall Counfelis, or vniuerfalie obferuit and practifit in Godis Kirk. Nor zit allege
Doctour, Greik, nor Latin, quha hes writtin within yir thoufand zeris for
the defence of ony thing now in controuerfie, except in fa fer as thai manifeftlie confent, wyth the doctrine of the former aige. Gif ze diffent fra

# TO THE CALUINIANE PRECHEOURIS.

the doctrine approuin vniuerfalie, and ordour fetfurth in ye faid former Kirk, fen the Kirk of God moft be perpetuall, and in na aige euir mair fyncere in religioun, fulfillit and exornatit in godly leirning and integritie of lyfe, yan in yai days: haif we nocht iuft caufe, to imploir ye grace of God, and help of all Chriftiane Princis, tobe deliuerit fra zour furious tyrannie, maift Ethnik, and arrogant impietie?

114        TO THE CALUINIANE PRECHEOURIS.

*An exhortatioun to mature and Godly deliberatioun in ye premiſſs.*

Note and obserue gif yow wald be a sone of ye haly kirk vniuersal.
Matt. 7.
Tit. 3.
1. Cor. 1.
Ephes. 4.
2. Thess. 2.

WE being diligentlie, and alfo ſtryitlie commandit be our Saluiour and his haly Apoſtolis, tobe war of fals Prophetis, to efchew the cumpanie of hæretikis, to fle fra all fchifme and diuifioun, to walk in vnitie of fpirit, in the band of peace : and to the end, that we mot mair efalie fua do : to keip that vniformitie of doctrine, of præceptis and traditionis geuin till ws, als weil be word and preching, as be writt : maiſt faithfullie promittis to zou to confent, and affiſt alfua, nocht only to ye tramping doun of Idolatrie, fuperſtitioun, and abuiſſs in religioun, infafer yai be til ws cleirly notifiit : bot alfo to ye cutting away of ye apperand occafioun yairof, croipin in the kirk onyways, be warldly wickit men, be the fpirit of auarice, ambitioun, or carnal affectioun. Gif ze fchuit only at yis famin mark, as ze allege zow to do, (quhilk to intend vnfenzetlie, we pray the almychty maiſt merciful to illuminat zour myndis) we exhort zow in the bowelis of Iefus Chriſte, to defcend in to zour felfis, and to hef confideratioun, yat as ze allege zou tobe men of leirning, and witt : yat fua zour fatheris afoir zou hes bein men haifand indoutitlie the famin giftis : and as ze iuge the famin our fatheris (we mein fpecialie of the Martyris and maiſt aunciant Doctouris, about fourhundreth zeris to Chriſtes afcenfioun) to hef bene men, and fa mycht hef errit : fua zour felfis, nocht tobe as zit, in that Angelicall perfectioun, that ze may nocht erre. * And zit as we grant it poffible, yat ony ane of yame, adherand to his awin iugement micht hef ſliddin in fum pointis : fua we affirm it tobe impoffible, and a thing blafphemous to Chriſte, to think, that thai al writtand of ane mater, and in ane mynd, euir to hef errit.* We exhort zou alfua, as ze knaw fcience tobe the gift of God, fua ze wald remembir it, tobe indifferent to guid or ewil : fua yat naturalie without the heit of cheritie, it makis men bowldin and heicht. Bot fen ze mifknaw nocht, that godly wifdum may nocht dwell in the bodyis of yame, quha ar fubdewit to fin (quhilk we fay nocht to accuifs zou præfentlie) we befeik zou to haif infpectioun inteirly, of zour awin lyues, and yaireftir iuge and confer the famin with the lyues of the haly Martyris, and wtheris aunciant Fatheris. Quhilk thing being

Note.

1. Cor. 8.

Sap. 1.

Note.

done, we appele to zour confcience to declare, gif ze think we faill to lein
erar to ye iugement, and vniforme confent of thai Eldaris, quhois lyfe and
leirning ar notifiit to the haill warld) to the grete gloir and prayfe of ye
maift mercifull Lord yair vndoutit gydear : or to sour priuat opinioun in
yir our days: zea, albeit ze hald the haill warld at yis præfent a lyue (except a few numbre of ws) on sour fyde, diffenting fra all aiges of men,
profeffing Chrifte in all ye warld, fen his afcenfioun, afoir yis our maift
wrechit aige. Mairouer forfamekle as ze ar offendit and gretumlie dif-
plefit, yat we embrafe nocht generalie zour new interpretationis on findry
places of the fcriptuir, zour determinationis and ordour, in the hie myfteriis and facramentis of our Chriftiane and catholik religioun: and yairfor callis ws indurat Papiftis : affirming zou to reduce all to ye puritie and
fyncere doctrine of Godis word, as it wes treulie vnderftandit in the primitiue Kirk, with ye vniforme ordour keipit than. We heirfor effectuouflie defyris zou and all Chriftianis, quho heiris of our controuerfie : to
pance, wey, and confider, gif ze haif iuft occafioun yairto. And to yat
effect, to knaw and remembir ye conftancie of ye primitiue Kirk, in ye In ye mein tyme quhen Scotland firft resauit ye fayth.
leift ceremonie in religioun, refauit fra yair eldaris. And for exemple to
haif in vigilant memorie, the tumult, and controuerfie, that hapnit in the
tyme of ye aunciant Martyr Irinæus, neirby .xiiijC. zeris paffit, betuix the
Kirk of Afia (quhilk as principal Bifchope in yai partis yan reulit Poly- Ecclesiast. hist. lib. 5. cap. 24. and Hist. Tri- pert. lib. 9. cap. 38.
crates) and ye Kirk of Rome with ye wtheris Kirkis, about ye celebra-
tioun of ye Pafche day: nocht that other of ye fydis denyit ye zerly cele-
bratioun thairof, nor intendit, as ze do at yis præfent (of quhat fpirit we Neuir wes hard amangis the catholikis a grete a controuer- fie: and zit for a cere- monie.
refer to Godis kirk to iuge) to abolife : the zerly celebratioun thairof, bot
only that the kirk of Afia celebratit the famin folennitie zerlie, nocht on
the famin fonday as the Romane kirk and all wtheris did yan, and now
dois: keipand in the mein tyme ye fafting of the lentren præcedand thair
day of the moneth: quha being exhortit maift feruentlie, be Victor yan Asia, Aphi- ca, and Eu- ropa, wes commo- ueit: quhat gif yai christianis war nou alyue?
Bifchope of Rome, to change yat ceremonie: and aggre thairin with the
reft of Chriftis kirkis: diffentit aluterlie fra his defyre, and yairfor wes be
him excommunicatit, as fchifmatikis nocht keipand ane vniformitie with
the reft. Zit nochtwithftanding ye faid excommunicatioun, thai perfeuerit
ftiflie: in yair purpofe, affirming it naways lefum to yame, to change fa

## TO THE CALUINIANE PRECHEOURIS.

litle a thing in thair religioun, fra the ordour eftir the traditioun quhilk yai had refauit (as yai allegeit fra thair eldaris the Apoſtolis and wthiris Biſchoipis in Aſia) and that with ſa grete perſeuerance on bayth the ſydis,

*Irinæus ye peace makear.* yat nocht without grete labouris the ſaid haly martyr Irinæus cumand furth of it, now callit France to Rome: and cauſand ye fornemmit Polycrates, to cum thare at his requeiſt furth of Aſia, for the reconciling and aggreing al kirkis in the premiſſis: aggreit with grete difficultie ye mater ſua: yat the kirk of Aſia ſuld be abſoluit fra the former cenſuris, and permittit to vſe yat ceremonie of yair accuſtomit day, as thai vſeit it afoir: Sen it wes nocht diſaggreing in effect, fra ye ordour of wtheris Kirkis.

*Note.* Haif we nocht, iuge ze, be yis hiſtorie and exemple controuertit in ye tyme abone ſpecifiit, iuſt cauſe and grete occaſioun, to pance diligentlie, obſerue, and conſider with auiſement (gif ze wald we war ſaiſit be our awin fayth erar than be zouris) gif zour doctrine in ſa many nouationis, be ſuirlie foundit and bigit on Godis word trewlie vnderſtand, or nocht. Sen ze nocht only differris fra ws, as ye Aſianis did fra wtheris Kirkis, tweching ye ſaid day of ye moneth: bot aluterlie with mekle mair aboliſſis as Idolatrical or Papiſtical, as ze call it, ye ſaid ſolennitie of Paſche, and alſo of ye Afcenſioun, Pentecoſte, ye Natiuitie of our Saluiour, and Circumciſioun, ye Epiphanie, ye faſting of ye lentrene, zerlie celebratit and obſeruit be al Kirkis ſen Chriſtis aſcenſioun. Heirfor tweching ye trew vnderſtanding of ye articulis præceding, quharein maiſt ſpecialie ze hef ſegregat zour ſelfis fra ws (inſafer as we zit vnderſtand of zour doctrine) we erneſtlie deſyris zou to ſchaw till ws in writ, conforme to zour promis, as we twechit in the beginning, zour doctrine and confirmatioun yairof,

*Fy on ye Apoſtate, yat refuiſeis yis conditioun.* prouin be ye word of God. As to our parte, to ye intent yat ze may be præſeruit fra all damnage, and apperand confuſioun, and leue with ws in a godlie vnitie: we permitt to zou maiſt faythfullie, to play ye trew parte of ye haly peacemaker Irinæus, abone ſpecifiit: yat is, to beir ſafer with zou in all thingis, as we may but manifeſt errour, and defectioun fra

*A guid hoip, quhilk God of his grete mercy perfyte.* Godis Kirk. This we promit maiſt frelie, nocht doutand bot ye godly mynde, ye feruent zele, and trew luue of our Souerane Lady towart zow hir G. ſubiectis, is maiſt bent to the ſamin end. And ſiklyke nocht doutand bot our Biſchoipis and wthiris Paſtouris, quha ar of leirning able to yair offices, fall reforme yair lyfes to the plefour of all godly man, and trewlie leue heireftir conforme to yair vocatioun, and glaidly fall affent to yis our mynd: hoipand alfo yat wtheris vnable, falbe moueit be Godis fpirit, to dimit willinglie yair places to the mair qualifeit: or wthirwayes, be a Godly counfeill that ordour falbe put yairto. Bot gif ze intend to eftabilifs amangis ws a new forme of religioun, tweching ye interpretatioun of fcriptuiris, ye furthfetting of Sacramentis, and ordour in the kirk vnknawin to all aiges of men, quhill yis præfent: and will adhere to ye iugement of na aige of Chriftianis, in the materis controuertit betuix ws, fen ye days of the Apoftolis, bot interpret the fcriptuir and fett a prætendit ordour, conforme to zour phantafie, imaginatioun, and priuat opinioun: we will ze perfuadit and certifiit: yat be ye help of ye omnipotent maift merciful, quha conforme to his promitt hes bein, is, and falbe with his faythfull, to the end of the warld: geueand yame at all aiges the diueris giftis of his haly fpirit: for na feir of zour multitude, albeit ze war .x. Thoufand contrare .x. of ws, yat we will nocht only, nocht iwne with zow generaile in religioun, as ze maift feuerlie hes intendit to thrall ws: nor beir with zow in mutuall finzeit focietie, in diffimulatioun, contrar the law of our God, bot aluterlie fle zour cumpanie as of Ethnikis and Rennigatis, nocht heirand Godis kirk, nothir præfent nor bypaft, keipand vniformitie fa mony zeris. Zit hoipand in the ineffable mercy of God till zow and ws, we fall nocht defift day nor nycht, to pray with maift humil myndis, our heuinly father (quha makis all his feruandis of ane Godly concord in his hows) yat for the meritis of Iefus Chrifte our only Saluiour, he wald fua illuminat zour hertis, with the fpirit, of humilitie, fobirnes, and trewth, yat ze nothir think afoir God, nor anffuer till ws in the premiffs arrogantlie, in ftryfe and diffentioun: bot only as afoir God, and of God, and in Chrifte according to his gloir and immutable will, to the Godly peace and vnitie of all yame, quha vnfenzetlie luuis IESVS; to quhome with ye father, and haly gaift, be all glore, pouer, vertew, and impire for euir. AMEN.

*Ad quod peruenimus, idem fentiamus, in eadem permaneamus regula.* Philip. 3.

Finis.

Quhasoeuir is a treu Chriſtiane; will cry yis ſentence on heicht without reſpect of perel.

Matth. vlt.

Pſal. 67.

2 Cor. 2.

¶ *To Iohne Knox. writtin .27. Oct.* 1568.

IT apperis to me, Brother, yat ze haif fum grete impediment, quhareby ze ar ftoppit, to keip promife tuecheing zour anffuering to yis our tractate, eftir fa lang aduifement. Gif ze perfaue zour fall : *quid tardas conuerti ad Dominum ?* Bot gif my hand writt peraduentuir hes nocht bene fa legible, as ze wald : pleis refaue fra yis beirar, ye famin mater now mair legible. Gif ze throw curiofitie of nouationis, hes forzet our auld plane Scottis, quhilk zour mother lerit zou : in tymes cuming I fall wryte to zou my mynd in Latin : for I am nocht acquyntit with zour Southeroun. The caufe that moueis me at yis tyme, to eik yis mekle to zow in al haift, is yis Beirar N. quha wald fane be haldin a piffant patroun of zour caufe: obliffing him to bring me zour anffuer, in ony thing I wald propone to zow. Bot fen I fe yat ze can find na outgait, in ye materis ellis to zou proponit : I will burding zou with na new thingis (hoiping in God to heir fchortlie of zour conuerfioun) except only with a new errour, quhilk yis beirar zour difciple affirmis bauldly : yat fen Chrifte fufferit for man, fays he, neuir man paffit to hell : quhome quhen I culd nocht diffuade to think ye contrare, and haueand commiferatioun of ye man, I faid yis : and now to moue zou to repentance repetis ye famin. Gif al Iohne Knoxis doctrine, fay I, be trew, to wit, that all thing quhilk he condemnis be ye name of Papiftrie, be damnable : all thing idolatrie and fuperftitioun, quhilk be fa callis : yat al ye Martyris of Chrifte with ye maift aunciant Doctouris, quha wrait afore a thoufand zeris paffit, togidder with all our eldaris in Scotland, ar alrady in hel. My propofitioun I preue be yis fyllogifme : All man defendand a damnable opinioun, agains the trew catholik fayth, and deand without repentance, togidder with all Idolatouris deing on lyke maner, but ftop gois to hell : ye Martyris and principall Doctouris of ye primitiue Kirk, quhais doctrine defendit euir our forebearis in Scotland without repentance, wes (gif ze teche treulie) ye famin men, ergo. &c. I refer ye confequence be ye blafphemous mowthis tobe pronunceit. The maior (as yai terme it) I think yat be zow nor zouris fal nocht be denyit. The minor, as I vnderftand, is in this tractat be mony heidis fuf-

*Fy man, other conforme thy doctrine to thiris, or deny ye bailwair.*

ficientlie prouin. Quharefor to zour fchame is my propofitioun neceffarlie inferrit. And becaufe ze hef bigit vp zour tour of Babel fa, yat nane vnderftandis wtheris, zour toungis being alrady confoundit, I chocht, I wald zit anis agane bid zou, hald zour hand. Obferue my caufe :. firft, ze zour felf, brother, of zour magnificence and liberal hand, hes oppinit ye zettis of heuin to ye faythful fatheris, a fore our Saluiour be his dethe, refurrectioun and glorious afcenfioun, had præparit yairto yis way to man. And wtheris zour fcoleris, ze knaw, mair cruelie hes in yare imaginatioun cloifit vp, flotit and neidnalit ye famin zettis of our hæretage (albeit nou alrady oppinit to ye iuft) quhil ye latter day of all. And now yis zour difciple, hes maift mercifullie faft fteikit ye zettis of hel : yat ye iuftice of God, do quhat ze lift, fal haif na place. Quhat fall we collect of yis zour confufit bauldnes, bot yat a part of zou nixt fal lay a fcharpear feige to heuin, and an wther parte to hel, and deny yat othir yair is a God in ye ane, or a deuil in ye vthir. For ze Apoftolis fentence is maift trew : *Mali homines et feductores proficient in peius. &c.* and yis apperis tobe neir the nixt ftep. Quharefor, my freind hald zit zour hand, and luke a little ypon zour werkmanfchip. To the quhilk the almichty mot illuminate zour eis. Amen.

*And salbe sein mair cleirlie.*

*Othir recant, or cause yir zour difcip. recant.*

*2. Tim. 3. Och for mair paper or pennyis.*

Of Antwerp. ye .27. of October .1563.
Ninianus Winzetus Prefbyter.

# VINCENTIVS LIRINENSIS

OF THE

## NATIOUN OF GALLIS,

FOR THE

### ANTIQUITIE AND VERITIE OF THE CATHOLIK FAYTH,

AGANIS YE PROPHANE NOUATIONIS OF AL HÆRESEIS,

A RICHT GOLDIN BUKE WRITTIN IN LATIN ABOUT .XLC. ZERIS PASSIT,
AND NEULIE TRANSLATIT IN SCOTTIS

BE NINIANE WINZET A CATHOLIK PREIST.

---

Vt ædificentur muri Ierusalem. *Psal.* 50.

---

ANTVERPIÆ
EX OFFICINA ÆGIDIJ DIEST, 1. DECEMB. 1563.
CUM GRATIA ET PRIUILEGIO.

TO YE MAIST CATHOLIK, NOBLE, AND GRATIOUS SOUERANE,
MARIE QUENE OF SCOTTIS, &c.

*Niniane Winzet a Catholik Preift, and hir G. humble Subiect, wifhis grace frome God our Father, conftance in ye trew catholik religioun in Chrifte our Saluiour, throw ye gouernance of ye haly gaift. Amen.*

---

<small>2. Efd. 1.
2. &c. vnto
ye end.</small>

AMANGIS ye mony comfortable exemplis of ye haly fcriptuir, maift excellent SOVERANE, ye notable hiftorie of ye wailzeant cheiftane of God and wpbigare of ye wallis of Ierufalem Nehemias, in yis tribulous and maift dangerous tyme of fchifme and diffenfioun, apperis weray mete tobe doung in ye eris of al faythful catholik, quhafoeuir preifis to haif ony Godly quietnes in vnitie and peace within our new Ierufalem ye citie of God, Chriftis haly kirk.

Forfamekle as Nehemias being prefoner (albeit gentlie intertineit) in a ftrange countrey, fra he wes aduertifit of the deftructioun of ye wallis of Ierufalem, fat doun, weipit and murnit mony days, faftit alfo and prayt for remiffioun of his finnis, of ye finnis of Ifrael, and of his forefatheris: quharethrw he and his cumpanie, war be God iuftlie fufferit tobe led and haldin in captiuitie amangis infidelis, and ye haly citie tobe fe ouirthrawin. And yis he dois hoiping in ye fuete promife of God maid to the faythful peple, conuertit to him in al thare hert. Be the quhilk meanis he apperis weil, to hef bene recouncelit vnto his fauour.

Quhilkis being done fra he had obtenit ony tolerance and opportunitie, makis he to without delay, be fik pouer as he micht, in a meruolous fortitude of fayth, without refpect of the micht, contempt or lichtliing, writtingis, boift or craft of his potent aduerfar Sanabalath and wtheris his Enimeis: without refpect of the murmuring and penuritie amangis his peple nocht regairding ye terrouris fpokin to him be fals prophetis: nocht regairding that his priuat counfel wes reuelit to Enimeis be his awin natiue familiaris: nocht finalie yat the principalis of ye peple, put nocht yair craigis in zok to the werk of the lord: and fa in a gret ftoutnes of fpirit biggis he wp in a fchort fpace, contrare al manis expectatioun, al the braid wallis of Ierufalem afore deftroyt: renewis and ftrenthis the portis thairof, fettis furth ye law of God fyncerlie to ye peple: and fa furth, quhilk al war lang to reherfe.

Bot zit naways fulefchlie attemptis he yir thingis, bot in al aduentuir airmis he his folkis with habirione, fuord, fpeir, bow and targe: yat in the tyme of thare labour, yai hald ye fpeir reddy in ye ane hand aganis ye force of Enimeis, and biggit wp ye wallis of Godis Citie with ye wther hand.

· Bot to expres Madame, vnto zour G. my porpofe conforme to yis mater, in few wordis: The wallis of our Ierufalem præfigurit be ye wther, I hald tobe vnitie amangis our felfis, in ye treu Catholik religioun, feruing God yairin treulie in feir and luue, euery man walking in a cumlie ordour according to his vocatioun.

Gif yis vnitie micht be conqueft amangis al the profeffouris of the bliffit name of our Lord Iefus: I think that our new citie of Ierufalem fuld be fa ftrang an hald: yat al the Enimeis thairof (as ar infidelis, hæretikis, and fchifmatikis) fuld nocht mak thame be force and plane violente to faét it, or onyways fubdew it. And zit gif ye trew citienaris thairof (that is the faythful catholikis, quha allane may clame ony hæretage in new Ierufalem) war recouncelit vnto our hie Empriour and Prince of our citie, the Lord of Sabaoth, be fik meanis as we fcheu Nehemias to hef bene: yai war na dout bot fik ftoutnes of fpirit with Nehemias we fuld refaue, and fik terrouris and draidour fuld be amangis our aduerfaris, yat our wallis fuld be biggit in continent in difpyte of Sathan and of al his minifteris.

Bot be reffoun yat grete controuerfie is, in findry wechty pointis quharein we fuld be recouncelit to him: ye wickit (as ye wyfeman wryttis) efteming ye wirfcheping of God tobe abominatioun, and crying in word to turn to God, and to big wp the wallis of Ierufalem: quhais labour zit is nocht ellis, bot to draw fra God, to diuyde his peple fra Godly vnitie, and finalie to fchuil doun thir wallis to the ground: neceffare it is heirfor tobe

Eccl. 1.

alſo aſſuirit of the trewth of yat controuerſie. And albeit I can nocht think me to hef wrocht ſik pennance, for yai thingis confeſſit be al man tobe ſin, as did Nehemias : zit for twa cauſeis I hoip tobe admittit ane of Godis airmie, amangis wtheris catholikis to yis werk. Firſt for his awin names ſaik, quhilk throw the trible of the catholikis in ſum partis at this præſent, is pollutit amangis our aduerſaris : as it wes ſumtyme be ye ſub- iectioun of the Iſraelitis amangis the Gentilis. And ſecundlie becauſe we hait with the Kirk of Epheſus, zea and with God himſelf ye father of peace, the doingis of the Nicolaitis of al forgearis and manteameris of ſchiſme and errour. And thairfor, Madame, ſen I intend be Godis grace, al my ingyne, wit and pouer tobe a faythful Souldiour to yis wailzeant cheiftane of God Nehemias, in ye wpbigging of yir haly wallis : and zit is in yat penuritie yat I may nocht furniſe to yis excellent werk euery kynd of neceſſar waippin and werklume, quhilk did Nehemias cumpanie : as habirione, ſcheild, ſuord, bow, ſpeir, ſpade, mattok and mell, &c. (yat is al neceſſar eruditioun to ſuppres al errour, and to ſett wp al trewth) I hef præparit to me ſelf, and to thais ſiklyke of zour G. faythful Subiectis, quha ar of ſmal leirning, or quha miſknawis the Latin toung a litle partie handſum inſtrument, yat may ſuffice ws in tyme of neid, bayth for a waippin and a werklume, for a ſpeir or a ſpade, a heumont or a hemmir or for ony wthir ſiklyke : and with yat alſo may ſted for a bricht lantern, quhareby we may cleirlie ſe, quhat way we ſuld happelie return and be recouncelit to our grete Empriour, or quhat way we hef vnhappelie turnit ws fra his maieſtie. Quhilk ſingular inſtrument I am aſſuirit, be the iuge- ment of ye maiſt godly experimentit, quhays ſentence in this mater I hef othir hard or red, tobe of ſik ſtrenth, yat be na force of Enimeis it may be brockin : of ſik ſcharpenes, yat na armour of thairis may reſiſt it : of ſik piſſance and aptitude, that with ane ſtrake it ſal bayth ding a faa deid to ye ground, and with yat alſo ſal help wp ye wallis of Ieruſalem : and beſydis al yir, ſal ſchaw ſik licht, as ſaid is.

This noble inſtrument is, yis litle tractate of yis cunning and anciant father Vincentius Lirinenſis, an haly man ſumtyme in ye Ile of Lire. The forcie and irrecouerable ſtrake, quhilk he richt michtelie oft doublis aganis al ſawaris of diſcord in our treu catholik fayth, is, yat al faithful

Chriftianis fuld hald firmlie and perpetualie in religioun yat thing, *Quod vbiq;, quod femper, et quod ab omnib. eſt creditum:* yat is, quhilk oueralquhar, quhilk at al tymes, quhilk be al (trew Chriftianis without dout) hes bene beleuit. This is, Madame, or I am begylit, an infallible, as it id a general reul to al richt, an ewin lyne of lawtay, a tweche ſtane of the treuth, a cleir licht to ſchaw ye way, and a neceſſar meanis at al tymes of debate, to tramp doun on al ſydis bayth errour and hærefie, abuſe and fuperſtitioun: and to ſett wp in ye awin fynceritie, our trew catholik religioun, quhareupon the inuincible wallis of vnitie, quhareof we now trete, ar maiſt ſuirlie and only biggit. For albeit maiſt trew it is yat ye ſcheip of Chriſtis flok heiris, and obeys his voce, and fleis frome ye voce of a Io. 10. Strangear: zit amangis ſa mony diſſaitful ſpiritis transfiguring thame ſelfis in angelis of licht, obſtinatlie allegeing ye haly ſcriptuir to mak for thare 2. Cor. 11. dremis, na man may fufficientlie ſchaw ye obſtinate conuict, and ditt ye mowthis of ye contentious, yath ony fentence in ye haly wreit is ye voce and mynd of Chriſte, or ye contrare ſenſe conſauit be ye wickit ye voce of ye Enimie: bot infafer as he may preue ye ane fentence *Oueralquhare, at al tymes, and be al Chriſtanis to hef bene beleuit,* and ye wther as to it planelie contrarious, to hef bene euir refufeit. Be yis reul it is expreſlie knawin, quha ar ſones of the haly kirk vniuerſal, in ye communioun of ye Sanctis of God: quhare as in ye houſe of God, quhilk is the pillar and 1. Tim. 3. eſtabiliſſing of veritie, ye vndoutit trewth without al dout is tobe focht.

This fentence of my auctour tobe maiſt trew, it is mair yan plane, be the mony diuerſe and contrarious ſectis, raigeing at this præſent amangis ye profeſſouris of Chriſtis name: raigeing I ſay, nocht only aganis our mother the haly catholik kirk, bot maiſt ſauagelie aganis thame ſelfis: euery ane of thame allegeing with Sathan thare maiſter the wordis of the ſcriptuir for thare defence: and zit neuir ane of thame (be ye teſtimonie zea, of euery fect aganis wthir) haifand ye word of God, yat is the trew ſenſe of ye ſcriptuir, for ye porpoſe yai allege it for aganis ws.

For wald ony of thame al lay to this lyne and ſquare reul, and preue yair doctrine amangis al trew Chriſtianis vniuerſalie al tyme and place refauit: without al dout ſa doing, yai had win ye cauſe, and al our pley hald an end, and we and al wtheris profeſſing our commoun crede, war

## TO YE MAIST GRATIOUS SOUERANE,

compellit to confeſs thame tobe ye trew catholikis, and our felfis to hef errit. Bot fen yai can neuir do that, and zit wald be haldin fones of the haly catholik kirk : it followis neceffarlie, yat yai fuld leue yare awin phantafie and condefcend with thame, quha can preue yare doctrine to ye wthir contrarious tobe catholik, be ye famin lyne. And fua as yis reul dounthrawis ye errour, fa incontinent it fettis wp ye treuth on ye wthir fyde : yat nocht without caufe we nameit it bayth a waippin and a werklume to ftrek doun a faa, yat is, an errour quhatfumeuir, and in the mein tyme, to big wp thir haly wallis of vnitie and confent, in ye trew catholik fayth.

And zit nocht oulie may yis my inftrument proffet to a godly concord aganis al errouris: bot alfo in al wther effairis, may ftrenthe mekle ye famin vnitie. Quhilk fpecialie is conqueft and keipit, gif euery perfoun in ilk ftate fal leue worthelie, as occafioun feruife, according to his vocatioun : as gif yat ye paftouris fuld vnabaifitlie gainftand ye woulfis, quhenfoeuir be yat meanis yai ar perfuadit, yat yai may faue ye flok : yat ye Princes be thare auctoritie manteame al Godlines and richt, and fuppres al impietie and wickitnes : yat ye nobilitie fuld ftoutlie affift yairto reddy euir to defend ye fayth, law and peace of thare lauchful and catholik Souerane, yat fua yare airis may lauchfullie to thame fuccede : yat ye burgeffis and craftifmen fuld remember on ye auld prouerb (faifing dew honour to zour Maief. I name it) *Ne futor vltra crepidam :* and take na mair reuling on thame aboue wtheris, yan yai haif commiffioun frome yare Souerane yairto : and breuelie yat al fuperiour poueris fuld Godly reul, and inferiouris humelie obey, euery ane contening himfelf in yat reul,

Sap. 6. 20.
13.
Ephes. 4.
1. Cor. 7.
12.

quhareto he is callit. For only fa may ye wallis of our Ierufalem be biggit wp, and aganis ye force of al Enimeis be defendit. For yat yis ordour conforme to my reul in Godis houfe fuld be keipit, *Oueralquhare, at al tymes, and be al trew Chriftianis is beleuit.*

And albeit zour G. excellence, befydis zour eruditioun in the Latin toung, is fik a mirrour of al Godlines, conftance, and continence, integritie, wifdum, and of al hæroical vertewis, and a nurifear be al poffible meanis of yis vnitie and peace, yat ye trompet of zour fame (to ye almychty be al gloir) is blawin loud amangis al Chriftiane nationis, to the grete confort of zour G. trew fubiectis: yat I neidit nocht to hef tane thir my labouris heirin for zour Maief. caufe: zit be reffoun yis my auctour makis fa mekle to that Godly concord, quhareof zour G. is fa defyrous: I richt humblie and hertlie dedicatis my fmal labouris heirin to zour Hienes: be quhais name and auctoritie yis anciant father may haif place in difputatioun, according to his dignitie, to help to difcufs the treuth veray neceffar at this tyme tobe outfet and manteamit, of the quæftioun exagitat præfentlie in zour G. Realme. Quhilk is, *quhow the awin proper fenfe, and mynd of ye haly Gaift in ye fcriptuir, may be difcernit fra ye erroneous fenfe, confauit yairof be ye wickit,* Of this mater I heir of a buke fet furth certane zeris paffit be an honorable confeffour of ye trew catholik fayth M. Quintine Kennedie, a werk commendit be findry cunning men als weil of Ingland as of Scotland. And alfo laitlie I hef fein certane clatteris and I wate nocht quhat, nameit contumeliouflie in hie contempt of ye kirk of God, *A confutatioun of ye faid M. Quintinis Papiftical counfelis.* Put out be ane of our windfallin brethir, laitlie fnapperit in the cummerance of Caluin M. Iohne Dauidfone. Quha for his parte of the new padzeane of his defperat brethir, wald be haldin a Dauidfone fa douchty, yat with a puft of his mouth he micht be iudgeit to cleik fra ye counfelis, als weil general as wtheris, al auctoritie: in yat he dar be fa temerarious as to cal yame papiftical: yat is, as he intendis contumeliouflie be yat terme, diffaitful, wickit, leing and erroneous. And fua impudentlie dar he affirme few Godly counfelis to hef bene othir, fen Sylueftris days or afore: and agane nameis yame fa few, and fa few, yat nocht only he makis him to mifknaw ony ane of yat fort: bot ye firft and principal general counfel efter ye Apoftolis haldin at Nice, as he can nocht cal it a general counfel, fa he apperis to infinuat yat ye haly fatheris aggreit nocht yare amangis yame felfis: be reffoun yat certane wickit confentit nocht to thame, bot to ye blafphemie of Arrius yare condemnit. As he wald fay nixt (for certane is it yat fik men decays euir to worfe) ye Apoftolis war nocht of ane confent and mynd in Chrifte, becaufe Iudas left yame. And finalie concluidis he, yat nocht only general counfelis may erre, bot tobe a dreme to think yat euir yai hef bene a counfel vniuerfal præfenting ye kirk of God, fen ye Apoftelis days: and zit he thinkis nocht al yat venum aneuch: bot affirmis als that yai hef bene few guid paftouris in ye kirk fen ye faid Syluefter. *O ingentem confidentiam!* My toung treulie, Madame, failzeis me to expres ye zele yat a faythful Chriftiane fuld haif, for ye houfe of God, aganis yir fchameles learis, aganis ye folie, zea ye phrenefie of yir proud peftilent proteftantis, euery day defcending a ftep feryer to yare maifter in hel. Layng may yai heir proteft, or ony man quha hes cuir of his faul, be moueit for fik a proteftatioun. For quhat war yat ellis, bot to admit place to ye difcipulis of Arrius, Macedonius, Euticbes, Neftorius and wtheris iuftlie condemnit be general counfelis? and to cal abak agane yare hærefeis fa mony C. zeris erdit in hel? Bot yis manis folie is fufficientlie declarit be ye maift cunning wrytearis of Caluinis and of Luthdris fect: quha almaift appreuis ye firft four general counfelis, and teftifeis yat al ye Bifchopes of Rome qubil Bonifacius, quha fuccedit to Gregore ye grete about .iijC. zeris efter Syluefter, war cunning and Godly paftouris. And quhatkin wtheris paftouris yai war fen fyne, the lichtis and lampis of ye kirk of God, Athanafius, Gregore, Nazianzene, S. Hierome, Ambrofe, and Auguftine, Bafil, Chryfoftome and Cyril with mony wtheris in thare dayis, fen ye tyme of Syluefter teftifeis be thare writtingis. Bot this my auctour, as he had forefein the vanitie or rather impietie of this man, makis al thir materis almaift, fa cleir aganis him: that M. Quintine neidis na wthir Apologie nor nane wthir man to waift paper and ink for yis porpofe. For the quhilk caufe, I mak mentioun of thame bayth to zour G. yat ye treuth of thare pley be fupport of yis father mot be tryit, and filence put to ye erroneous. And yis fpecialie I do, to confirme ye wyfe and graue fayng, quhilk I hard zour Maief. fumtyme fpeik on yis manere: *Sen of wryteing of buikis* (as witneffis Salomon) *yair is na end, and fen ye veritie in al thingis is bot ane, and vnuariable: yai ar buikis anew alrady put furth, gif thai war weil vnderftand.* Quhais fayng (fen the hertis of princis ar in ye handis of God) I wnderftuid, as proceding of ye haly Gaift, and conforme to zour G. mynd hes fpecialie, according to my fmal talent, labourit fen fyne, as I gat oportunitie, befydis fum wthir mater yat I had than begun, yat fum tractatis writtin be anciant fatheris mony zeris ago, micht be, for a Godly vnitie in zour G. Realme vnderftand be thame,

Eccle. 12.

Prouerb. 21.

be quhome yai micht nocht afore. Of ye quhilkis as I cheifit yis auctour firſt ſa ye mater of ye wechty quæſtioun foreſaid, cunninglie tretit be him, is neceſſarlie firſt, efter my iudgement, for an vnitie in ye trew religioun tobe vnderſtand. To ye quhilk vnitie, Madame, beſydis ye help and aid that we hef afore expreſſit, it wald help mekle, gif twa thingis war to addit : Firſt yat worthy puniſment war tane of ſchameles oppin learis and treuth brekaris, and of yame, quha ar knawin on ſet porpoſe wriſtearis of ye veritie, and nuriſearis of diſcord. The ſecund yat the grete Gentrice of zour Maieſ. wald perſuade to certane deſperat perſonis, yat ze ar an hertlie and a compatient mother to thame (as na faythful Subiect doutis, bot ſa is in deid) and yat zour G. nothir ſeikis ye lynes nor landis of certane of ye vnleirnit nobilitie, and wtheris ſeduceit be yir diffaitful foxis, and rauenous woulfis thare fals techearis. For ſuythlie ſa it becumis, and equitie yat requiris : ſen be ye negligence and inordinat affectioun of zour Hienes forebearis (quhat is zour awin parte thairin præſentlie, I am incertane) in the promoueing of vnqualifeit Prælatis in ye kirk : al this perturbatioun, trible, and hie interpryſeis, in Scotland, as the lyke for ye lyke cauſeis alſo in vtheris partes, ar wpſproung. Inſameke yat the peple houngerit throw inlake of the heuinlie and neceſſare fuid of Godis word, and haifand a vehement houngir and thriſt thairof, entering vnhappelie tobe refreſchit in ye cumpanie of yir neu techearis, as it war in an apothecaris buyth ful of al kynd of droigis, bayth of delicat ſpycerie and of rady poyſoun : quare yai without ony conſyderatioun or reſpect of ye guid or the ewil, hes tane ſa gredy a fil, bot ſum mair and ſum les of ye poyſoun, yat certane ar fallin as it war in an apopleſie nothir heiring, ſeing, nor feling thare infirmitie: wtheris as in a phreneſie, rinnand and ruſcheand without knaulege quhat yai othir do or ſay : wtheris alſo as it war in a licht flummir eaſelie tobe walkinnit. Of quhome mony ar, as I am be euident reſſonis perſuadit, fra al perel ſa recouerit : yat with litle craft and diligence of a guid medicinar, yai may be cuirit fra al infirmitie, and without al ſcrupuloſitie accumpaniit with the kirk of God, bot that zit mair ſpedelie thai wald do, gif thai war deliuerit from feir of yare former plays. Thir meanis, gratious Souerane, being prouideit, and ye trew ſenſe of myn actour deulie embraceit, thare is na dout, bot thir wallis of vnitie, Madame, be zour gratious affiftence falbe vpbigit and defendit, with fik expeditioun and fortitude, as wes the wallis of Ierufalem be Nehemias. The quhilk mot grant ws ye only auctour of vnitie and peace our Lord IESVS CHRISTE: quha mot hald zour Celfitude in his continual protectioun. Amen.

Of Antuerp the .2. of Decemb. 1568.

¶ In ye catalog of Gennadius, quhilk is conionit with ye catalog of S. Hierome of ye Ecclesiastik wrytearis, yis testimonie is of Vincentius Lir.

*Vincentius natione Gallus, apud Monasterium in Lirinensi insula presbyter: vir in scripturis sanctis doctus, et notitia ecclesiasticorum dogmatum sufficienter instructus, composuit ad euertenda hæreticorum collegia, nitido et aperto sermone validissimam disputationem, quam absconso nomine suo, attitulauit Peregrini aduersum hæreticos: cuius operis quia secundi libri maximam in schedulis partem à quibusdam furatam perdidit, recapitulato eius paucis sermonib. sensu, primò compegit, et in librum vnum œdidit. Moritur Theod. et Valentiniano regnantib.*

¶ Tritemius in his buke of ye Ecclesiastik men, wrytis yis:

*Vincentius Monachus et Presbyter Monasterij Lirinensis insulæ, natione Gallus, vir in diuinis scripturis eruditissimus, et sæcularium literarum non ignarus, vita et moribus clarus. Exstat eius insigne opus, quod sub Peregrini nomine composuit, à veteribus doctoribus percelebre laudatum, De erroribus et collegiis hæreticorum fugiendis, lib. ij. Alia quoque nonnulla scripsisse legitur, quæ ad notitiam meam non venerunt. Claruit sub Theodosio et Valent. regnantib. An. D.* 480.

## TO THE REIDAR.

<small>* Of ye qubilkis we reid sum of yame to hef maidagrete parte of ye ground of thare werk.</small>

To eschew al occasioun of wane stryse with aduersaris, for * Iimpis of Grammar or sik triflis: I hef behauit me in ye translatioun of yis tractate sa, yat I hef bene scrupulous to vse ye ful libertie of a translatour: bot hes geuin labour als weil to expres almaist ye samin self wordis of myn auctour, as his ful sense and mynd. And zit I hoip yat yow sal think me to speik propir langage conforme to our auld brade Scottis. As to my fidelitie, I referre it to ye godly cunning. I hef vseit twyse only ye iugement of Cos-

<small>* In yir wordis, Cuius scientiæ cum Græcia cederet, and, Qui artem totius scientiæ conscendisset.</small>

terius concerning * ye text: quhare he planelie apperis to deliuer ye wordis of Vincentius. Gif in wthiris places ¯ vseit his iugement or myn awin, I inserit it within sik twa ( ) circulis, a.. alterit na thing of ye text: as sumtyme I did ye lyke, eiking sum thing to explane an obscuir word: and anis notit my apperence in ye margin. And yat al mot be mair facil, les tedious, and mair attentlie consideril: I hef distinctit ye first and principal parte in cheptouris, proponing sum breue argumentis yairto. Quhilk thing I suspect na leirnit man to repreue. Bot sen my labouris heir ar for ye vnleirnit only: I exhort ye zoung scoleris to reid yis auctour in his awin toung, yat yai may bettir knaw his godly eruditioun: quhilk makis mekle at yis tyme for ye first step fra errour, to a haly concord in our lord Iesus. Quhais spirit mot induce and conserue the, and thame in al treuth. Amen.

# VINCENTIVS LIRINENSIS,

OF YE NATIOUN OF GALLIS,

FOR YE ANTIQUITIE AND VNIUERSALITIE OF YE CATHOLIK FAYTH, AGANIS YE PROPHANE NOUATIONIS OF AL HÆRESEIS.

*The cauſeis yat moueit ye Auctor to wryte yis tractat. Cap. I.*

THE ſcripture ſayand and commandand, Demand thy fatheris and yai ſall tell the : yi eldaris, and yai ſall ſchaw ye : And agane, To ye wordis of ye wyſe apply yi ere : and ſiklyke, My ſone forzet nocht thir ſayngis, bot yi hert mot keip my wordis : it apperis to me ye Pilgrum ye leift of Godis ſeruandis, yat it be Godis help, ſall nocht be a mater of litle proffet, gif yai thingis quhilkis I hef refauit fra haly fatheris, I put in writt, weray neceſſare at ye leift to my awin waiknes : as quhen it mot be in reddines, quhareby ye imbecillitie of my memorie, be continuall reiding may be ſupportit. To ye quhilk biſſines nocht onlie ye fruit of ye werck, bot alſo ye confideratioun of tyme, and commoditie of place prouoikis me : The tyme, be reſſoun all manlie thingis ar reuiſſit be it, we alſo euery ane to wthir ſum thing fuld reuiſs fra it, that mot proffet to ye lyfe eternall : ſpecialie ſen bayth a terrible expectatioun of ye diuine iugement requiris gretumlie ye ſtudie of religioun tobe eikit, and ye fraudfull diſſait of new hæretikis hes mekle neid of thocht and attendence. Bot ye place, inſamekle yat we fleand ye frequent cumpanie of townis and wtheris vnquietnes, remanis in ye ſecret duelling place of a quiet village, and monaſterie in it : quhare without grete diſtractioun yat may cum to paſs, quhilk is foung in ye Pſalme, *Waik and ſe, yat I am God.* Bot ye cauſe alſo of our porpoſe makis to yis end, yat I quha ſumtymes wes inuoluit with ſindry and ſorrouful cummeris of yis warldlie weirfair, at ye laſt be ye help of Chriſte, I hid me ſelf in ye heuinning place of religioun, to all man at all tymes maiſt ſuir : yat yair ye blaſtis of vanitie and pryde being put doun, be ye ſacri-

Deut. 32.

Prouer. 22.

Prouerb. 8.

Be ye name of a Pilgrum he firſt intitulit this buke.

The vtilitie. The tyme.

Note.

The place.

Pſal. 45. Vincentius wes in his zowtheid a man of weir, and efter dreu him to monaſtik life :

fice of Chriſtiane humilitie, I ſatisfiing my God, nocht onlie mycht eſchew ye ſchipbreking of yis præſent lyfe, bot alſo ye fyrie flambis of ye warld tocum. Bot now in ye name of ye Lord will I begin yat thing, quhilk is in reddines : to witt, yat I may wryte thai thingis be our forbearis til ws deliuerit, and amangis ws laid vp in keiping and ſtoir, and yat rather be ye fayth of a trew reherſar, yan be ye præſumptioun of an auctour, yis law of writting nochtyeles obſeruit, yat nocht all, bot onlie all materis neceſſare I mot collect : and yat nocht in an ornate and exquiſit, bot in a facill and commoun ſtyle, yat mony thingis may rather appere ſigniſiit, yan explanit. Lat yame wryte delicatlie and exquiſitlie : quha to yat porpoſe ar moueit, othir be bauldnes of ingyne, or be reſſoun of yair office : bot it ſal ſuffice me for ye ſupport of my memorie, or rather forzetfulnes, to hef præparit to me ſelf yis memorial : quhilk pece and pece reduceing to memorie, I intend daylie, God willing, ya thingis quhilkis I hef lerit to correct and complete. Bot yis fer heir hef I afore aduertiſit, yat gif peraduenture ony thing ouerſlippit be me, cum in ye handis of haly men (or of iudges) ya na thing ſuld repreue without cauſe : forſamekle as ya ſee, yat zit be a promiſt emendatiouni, yis is tobe maid mair trim.

*Aganis errouris and hæreſeis al trew Chriſtiane ſuld ſtrenth him ſelf with double armour : yat is, with ye haly ſcriptuir, and with auctoritie of ye haly catholik Kirk, tueching ye trew wnderſtanding yairof. Cap. II.*

I HEIRFOR oftymes with grete diligence and maiſt attendence, feirceand at veray mony men of excellent halines and doctrine, be quhat manere I be ſum ſuir, and as be ſum general and reulful way, micht diſcerne ye treuth of ye catholik fayth, fra ye falſet of hæretical wickitnes : ane anſſuer on yis manere gat I almaiſt euir of al men : that gif othir I, or ony wthir wald perſaue the diſſaitis, eſchew the ſnairis of the wpſprouting hæretikis, and in ye hail fayth wald found and hail perſeuere, on double manere ſuld he, be help of ye hieaſt, ſtrenthe his fayth. Firſt to wit, be ye auctoritie of haly ſcriptuir : ſyne yaireſter be ye traditioun of ye catholik Kirk. Heir peraduentuir ſum man may ſpeir : ſen ye canoun of ye ſcriptuiris is

## YE NOUATIONIS OF AL HÆRESEIS.

perfyte, and to ye felf, till all thingis anewche and largelie fufficient: quhat neid is, yat till it be ionit the auctoritie of ye Kirk? Becaufe to wit, that all man refauis nocht ye haly fcriptuiris for ye heich hid fenfe yairof, in ane and in ye famin fence: bot the fayingis of ye famin wtherways yis man, and yat man interpretis: yat almaift quhow mony men yai ar, that fa mony fentences apperis may be drawin thairof. For wthirways exponis it Nouatianus, wthirways Photinus, wthirways Sabellius, wthirways Donatus, wthirways Arrius, Eunomius, Macedonius, wthirways Apollinaris, Prifcillianus, wthirways Iouinianus, Pelagius, Celeftius, wthirways finalie Neftorius. Bot heirfor for werray neceffare it is, for fa grete dangerous flonkis of findry errouris, yat ye lyne of Propheticall and Apoftolik interpretatioun be directit, according to ye rewll of ye Ecclefiaftik and catholik vnderftanding. Siklyke in ye catholik Kirk felf, cuir is gretumlie to be hald, yat we retene yat thing, quhilk ouer alquhare, quhilk at all tymes, quhilk be all men is beleuit. For yat is treulie and properlie catholik (quhilk thing ye felf ftrenthe and propirtie of ye name declairis) quhilk verelie and vniuerfalie comprehendis all. Bot yis thing onlie fua cumis to pafs, gif we follow vniuerfalitie, antiquitie, and confent. We fall follow vniuerfalitie trewlie on this maneir, gif we confes yis ane fayth tobe trew, quhilk ye haill Kirk ouer all ye compas of ye erd confeffis: antiquitie fuythlie fua, giue we diffiuir nawais fra yis vnderftanding, quhilk our haly forebearis and forefatheris is knawin to hef appreuit and renounit: confent alfo fiklyke, gif in ye antiquitie felf, we fall follow ye diffinitioun and fentence of all, or at ye leift of almaift all ye Preiftis togiddir and ye techearis.

*The famin spirit of diuerfitie is nou betuix ye Lutheranis and ye Caluiniftis, betuix yame twa and ye Anabaptiftis, betuix yame thre and ye Suinkfeldianis, betuix yame four and ye Serueticania. of quhilkis euery fect callis thame the trew kirk, and ait ya al ar out of ye way. Catholik a Greik terme signifiis ouer al. The catholik fayth is knawin of vniuerfalitie, antiquitie, and confent of bayth.*

*Sindry quæstionis tueching yis mater worthy tobe obferuit. Cap. III.*

QVHAT fall heirfor a Chriftiane catholik do, gif ony portioun of ye Kirk, fall cut ye felf fra ye commonioun of ye catholik fayth? Quhat treulie bot yat he præfer ye helthe of ye haill body, to ane poyfonnit or corruptit membre? Quhat gif fum cankir makis to defyle nocht onlie a portioun, bot the haill kirk at anis? Than fiklyke fall he prouide, yat he inhere to ye antiquitie, quhilk aluterlie may nocht now be ony fraud of noueltie be

1  *Four gol-din reulis.*

2

3 diffauit. Quhat gif in ye antiquitie felf, ye errour of twa or thre men, or of a citie, or alfo of fum prouince be perfauit? Than fall he aluterlie do diligence, yat he to ye fuilhardines or ignorance of a few numbre, præfer
4 ye decreis of ye vniuerfal kirk, gif ony vniuerfalie be of ye auld. Quhat gif ony fiklyke thing brek out, quhare na decre of yat kynde may be found?

*The vniforme confent of ye doctouris.* Than fall he do diligence to inquire and ferce ye fentences of our forefatheris conferrit amang yame felfis, and yat of yame only quha albeit in diueris tymes and places, nochtyeles perfeuerand in ye communioun and

*Obserue.* fayth of ane catholik kirk, wes prouable or laudable techearis : and quhatfumeuir nocht ane or twa onlie of yame, bot all togidder with ane and ye famin confent, he fall knaw planelie, frequentlie, perfeuerantlie to hef haldin, writtin and techeit : lat him vnderftand that thing alfo without all dout, fuld be beleuit be him.

*Exemples of ye præmiffis, and firft of ye Donatiftis. Cap. IIII.*

Bot yat yir thingis, quhilkis we fpeik, may be maid mair plane, be exemplis feueralie yai ar tobe illuftrate, and a litle mair largelie tobe dilatit : lefte be ye ftudie of immoderat fchortnes, ye wecht of ye mater be fwiftnes of fpeche fuld nocht be perfauit.

In ye tyme of Donatus, of quhome are ye Donatiftis callit, quhen a grete part of Aphrik had wappit doun ye felf in ye furious rage of his er-

*Donat⁹ allegeit yat yair wes na kirk of Chrifte in his days, bot yame in Aphrik of his sect.* rour, and quhen it vnmyndfull of ye awin name, religioun, and profeffioun, præferrit ye curfit fuilhardines of ane man, to ye kirk of Chrifte : than quhaeuir wes in Aphrik detefting ye prophane fchifme and diuifioun, war accumpaniit to ye haill vniuerfal kirkis of ye warld, yai onlie of al within ye fanctuarie of ye catholik fayth, micht be faifit : leuand but dout an excellent forme and exemple to yair eftercummeris. to wit, quhow yairefter be a guid cuftum ye helth of al mot be præferrit to ye wodnes of ane, or always of few.

*Of ye Arrianis. Cap. V.*

*Arrius a Preist in Alexandria* Siklyke quhen ye venom of ye Arrianis had nocht yan infectit a certane portioun, bot almaift ye haill warld : infafer yat a certane mift wes zet

vpon ye myndis of al ye Bifchopes of ye Latin toung almaift, partlie dif- *puft vp in his awin*
fauit throw ignorance, and partlie throw fraud, quhat thing in fa grete *confait be opinioun of*
confufioun of materis wes fpecialie tobe followit: yan quha euir become *his science, inuentit ye*
ye trew luuear and worfchipar of Chrifte, præferring ye auld fayth to ye *damnable errour, yat*
new wnfaythfulnes, be na peftilence of yat contagious cankir wes defylit. *ye sone of God wes*
Be experience trewlie and dainger of ye quhilk tyme it is sufficientlie and *nocht of equal sub-*
mair furthfchawin, quhoumekle calamitie is inbrocht be ye inductioun of a *stance with ye father.*
new doctrine: fen yan nocht onlie fmal thingis, bot ye maift heich wes *Of ye grete calamiteis*
doung almaift to nocht. For nocht onlie affinitie, confanguinitie, freind- *in ye kirk throu ye*
fchip, houffis: bot alfo townis, peple, prouinces, nationis, and breuelie ye *Arrianis.*
haill Romane Empyre fra ye ground wes fchaikin, and moueit out of ye
place. For quhen ye prophane nouatioun of ye Arrianis as ye goddace
of battel, or as a furie, ye † Emperour of all firft being maid captiue, had *† Constantius or Va-*
fubdewit yairefter al ye hie turretis of ye palice be new lawis, naways efter *lens, quha bayth de-*
yat ceiffit to mingle throw wthir and confound all, bayth priuat and pub- *fendit the Arriane*
lict, bayth hallowit and prophane, na regard nor difference to haif of ye *impietie, and cruelie*
guid and ye trewth, bot quhomefoeuir it pleifit, as it war furth of a fupe- *persuitit ye trew catho-*
riour place to bete doun to ye ground. Than wes mariit women defilit, *likis, bot specialie ye*
wedowis fpulzeit, virginis prophanit, monafteriis deftroyit, clerkis wappit *religious men in ye*
findry, ye minifteris of ye kirkis ftrikin, ye Preiftis dryuin away and *desertis.*
baniffit, ye prefonis, pittis, and mettal places fillit ful of ye fanctis of God. *The Caluinianis at*
Of ye quhilkis a grete parte, ye townis being forbiddin yame: wes hurlit *this present intendis in*
out and baniffit, and amang ye defertis, coiuis, wild beiftis, and rolkes, be *yis part to follow the*
naikitnes, hungir and thrift wes worne away and confumit. Bot come all *Arrianis vnfenzet-*
yir thingis for ony wthir caufe, bot treulie quhen for ye heuinlie doctrine *lie.*
manlie fuperftitioun is introducit, quhen ye weill foundit antiquitie for a
curfit noueltie is ouerquhemlit, quhen ye ftatutis of ye fuperiouris ar violatit, quhen ye decreis of ye fatheris ar cuttit away, quhen ye determinationis of ye eldaris ar rugit vp, as it war be ye ruitis, quhen within ye
maift chaft boundis of ye haly and vndefylit antiquitie, ye luft of prophane
and new curiofitie contenis nocht ye felf.

*He citis for yis porpofe ye authoritie of S. Ambrofe: and techis yat ye conftancie and fayth of ya catholikis tribulit be ye Arrianis, be ws is tobe followit. Cap. VI.*

Bot peraduentuir throw ye haitrent of noueltie and luue of antiquitie we imaginat yir thingis. Quha euir iugeis yat, lat him haif traift at ye leift to bliffit Ambrofe, quha in ye fecund buik to ye Emperour Gratiane, deplorand ye bittirnes of ye tyme, fays: Bot now fufficientlie, fays he, O omnipotent God, be our extreme calamitie, and be our bluid we hef wefchin away ye flawchtir of ye confeffouris, ye baniffing of ye Preiftis, and the horrible cryme of fa grete impietie. It is maid manifeft anewch, yat yai quha violatit yair fayth, micht nocht be fuir. Siklyke in ye thrid buik of ye famin werk: Lat ws keip heirfor, fays he, ye præceptis of our eldaris, and lat ws nocht violat ye hæritable felis be temeritie of a brutal fuilhardines. For that felit Prophetical buik, nocht ye eldaris, nocht ye poteftatis, nocht ye Angelis, nocht ye Archangelis durft oppin: to Chrifte allane wes referuit yat prærogatiue to explane it. Quhilk of ws dar oppin ye preiftlie * buik felit be ye confeffouris, and confecrat now be ye martyrdome of mony? Quhilk buik quha wes compellit to oppin, efter yat nochtyeles ye diffait being condemnit, feilit it: quha præfumit nocht to violat it, become confeffouris and martyris. Quhow fall we deny ye fayth of yame quhais victorie we preche? We preche, I fay, O wirfchipfull Ambrofe, we preche planelie and in louing yame we ar eftonift. For quha is fa woud, quha albeit he may nocht attene to yame, will nocht defyre to follow yame, quhome fra ye defence of ye fayth of yair eldaris, na violence repellit nor put abak? Nocht manaffing nor plefand flattrie, nocht the lyfe, nocht the dethe, nocht ye court, nocht ye garrifoun, nocht the Emperour, nocht ye Empire, nocht men, nocht ye deuillis. Quhome I fay, for ye fuir gripping to ye religious and godlie antiquitie, ye Lord iugeit worthy fa grete reward, that be yame he wald raifs vp his Kirkis afoir wappit doun, wald quikin his fpiritual peple afoir flane, wald place vp agane the multitude of Preiftis afoir caffin fra yair dignitie, wald delete yai curfit nocht writtingis bot wriftingis of ye new vngodlines, be ye fontane of faythfull teris pourit in ye Bifchopes frome ye heuin : and finalie wald cal agane almaift ye hail warld, yan fcatterit be a cruel ftorme of a fuddane hærefie, to ye auld faith fra ye new vnfaithfulnes, to ye auld helth of mynd fra ye neu woudnes, fra ye blindnes of noueltie to ye auld licht.

*Aganis ye abominable impietie of Arrius determinate ye haly fatheris according to ye mutual confent of vniuerfalitie and antiquitie. Cap. VII.*

Bot in yis diuine ftrenthe of confeffioun, yat thing till ws alfo is maift fpecialie tobe confiderit, yat yan in ye famin antiquitie of the Kirk, nocht the defence of ony ane part yairof, bot of ye vniuerfal kirk wes tane on yame. For it wes nocht lefum yat fa grete and fiklyke men fuld affirm with fa grete force and feruour, ye wauerand fufpicionis of ony ane or twa men, and yai contrarious to yame felfis : or zit yat yai fuld ftriue for the fulege confpiracie of ony ane prouince : bot yai following ye decreis and determinationis of al Preiftis of ye haly Kirk, and of ye Apoftolik and catholik veritie, had leuir hef lofeit yame felfis, yan ye fayth of ye vniuerfal antiquitie. Quharthrow yai hef deferuit to attane to fa grete gloir, yat yai nocht onlie confeffouris, bot the principalis of confeffouris be al reffoun fuld be haldin. Grete heirfor and manifeftlie diuine is yis exemple of the famin maift bliffit fatheris, and be al trew catholikis in continual meditatioun tobe rememberit : quha in maner of ye feuinfauld chandelar fchinand be ye feuinfald licht of ye haly gaift fcheu afoir a maift cleir forme to ye eftercumeris, on quhat maner yairefter amang euery vane clattir of errouris, be ye auctoritie of haly antiquitie ye malepeirtnes of prophane nouveltie, mot be trampit vnder fute. This is fuythlie na new thing, fen yis confuetude fluriffit euir in ye Kirk, yat quhoumekle euery man wes mair godlie in religioun, infafer ye mair reddelie he gainftuid new inuentionis. *Obserue yis, O ze luuearis and slaueis of sour awin phantasie. He alluidis to the goldin chandelar in ye 25. of Exo.*

## VINCENT. LIRIN. AGANIS

*According to ye confent of vniuerfalitie and antiquitie determinat Pape Stephanus with wtheris Bifchopes aganis yame of Aphrik, quha techeit to baptize agane yame quha wes baptizit be hæretikis. Cap. VIII.*

OF fik exemplis al hiftoriis ar ful. Bot yat my mater be nocht prolixt: a certane exemple, and yat fra ye Apoftolik fait fpecialie wil we tak, yat all men mair cleirlie yan ye licht may fe, be quhat feruour in al tymes, be quhat diligence, be quhat erniftnes, ye bliffit fucceffioun of ye bliffit Apoftolis hes euir defendit ye integritie of ye religioun anis refauit. Sumtyme heirfor Agrippinus of worfchipful memorie Bifchope of Carthage, the firft of all men contrare ye diuine canoun, contrare ye reul of ye vniuerfal Kirk, contrare ye vnderftanding of al wtheris Preiftis, contrare ye confuetude and ftatutis of his eldaris iugeit to baptize agane. Quhilk præfumptioun fa grete damnage inbrocht, yat nocht onlie it gaue an exemple of facrilege to al hæretikis, bot alfo occafioun of errour to certane catholikis. Quhen heirfor on al fydis yai cryit out al on the noueltie of ye mater, and al Preiftis oueralquhare euery man for his awin diligence gainftuid: yan Pape Steuin of happy memorie, Prælat of the Apoftolik fait with wtheris his collegis, bot zit he mair than the reft maid obftacle: eftemand it worthy (as I think) gif he nicht ourcum fafer al ye reft be deuotioun of fayth, fafer as he furmontit ye reft be auctoritie of his place. And breuelie in an epiftil quhilk yan wes fend to Aphrik, he decretit in yir wordis, yat na thing fuld be alterit: bot yat † keipit quhilk wes be tradiţioun commandit. For the haly and prudent man vnderftuid that godlines admittis na wthir thing, bot yat al thingis in yat famin fayth fuld be confignit and deliuerit to ye fones, in quhilk fayth, yai war refauit fra yair fatheris. And yat it becumis ws nocht to leid ye religioun quhat way we wald, bot yat we rather fuld follow it, quhat way it wald leid ws: and yat tobe ye propirtie of a Chriftiane modeftie and conftancie, nocht to deliuer yair awin thingis to ye eftercumeris, bot to keip yai thingis refauit fra the forbearis. Quhat end heirfor wes of ye haill biffines? Quhat treulie bot ye vfeit and accuftomit end? That is to wit, ye antiquitie is referuit, and ye noueltie is fchot to ye duir.

<small>Agrippin⁹ bischope of Carthage wes ye first yat causit to baptize ugane.</small>

<small>Pape Steuin in the tyme of Cypriane.</small>

<small>Quhilk epistil is ye seuint in numbre of the secund buik of Cypria. epistolis.
† In Lat. *exem. riusmodi vox desyderari videtur.*
A trim and a godly saying.</small>

*Of ye excellent leirning, eloquence, &c. in yir hæretikis: quhilkis wes eſtemit nochtis aganis ye conſent of ye vniuerſal antiquitie. And quhou ye inuentaris of yis hæreſie ar ye ſones of God, and ye defendaris yairof efter, ye ſones of perditioun. Item quha now ar ye ſones of Cham. Cap. IX.*

Bot perchanſe at yat tyme ye new inuentioun wantit aid and ſupple. Bot erar yai war yan ſa grete quiknes of ingyne, ſa grete fluidis of eloquence, ſa grete multitude of defendaris, ſa grete apperence of ye trewth, ſa mony auctoriteis of ye law of God, bot planelie of a new and of an euill maner vnderſtandit, yat it apperis to me, yat al yat conſpiracie naways micht be deſtroyt, except yat profeſſioun ſelf of ye noueltie anis reſauit, anis defendit, anis appreuit had left ye cauſe of ſa grete an interpriſe. At laſt quhat wes ye ſtrenthe of yat counſel or decre of Aphrik? Be Godis gift it was nane, bot al as dremis, as fabellis, and vaniteis aboliſſit, annullit, and trampit vnder ſute. And O meruolous turning of materis! ye inuentouris of ye famin opinioun ar haldin catholikis, and ye followaris ar haldin hæretikis. The maiſteris ar abſoluit, and ye diſcipulis ar condemnit. The wrytaris of yir buikis ſalbe ye ſones of ye kingdome of heuin, bot ye hellis fyre ſal reſaue ye defendaris yairof. For quha is he ſa woud, quha may dout, bot that ſchyning licht of al the ſanctis bayth of Biſchopes and Martyris, maiſt bliſſit Cypriane I mein, with ye reſt of his collegis ſal ring æternalie with Chriſte? Or contrarie quha is ſa wickit, that he may deny the Donatiſtis and the reſt of yat peſtilent band, quha craikis and wanetis yame be ye auctoritie of yat counſel to baptize agane, with the deuil euir tobe brint. Quhilk iugement to me ſuythlie apperis to hef bene pronunceit and declarit frome aboue, for yair falſet ſpecialie, quha quhen vnder an wthir manis name, imaginis to dek vp hæreſie, takis oftymes ye writtingis of ſum auld aunciant man weil dirklie † ſetfurth, quhilkis for ye obſcuritie yairof as yai ſuld aggre to yair doctrine, yat yat thing quhatſumeuir, I wate nocht quhat, quhilk yai put out, yat yai nothir firſt, nor zit allane ſuld appere to vnderſtand it ſua. Quhais wickitnes I think worthy double hatrent: bayth becauſe yai feir nocht to propyne ye venum of hæreſie til wyeris, and becauſe alſo yat yai ſchaik vp in ye wound with yare

*Of obſtinate pertinacitie in arrour.*

*Cypriane conſentit to ye firſt prouincial counſel of Cartha. quhar it wes ſtatut yat quha wes baptiſit be heretikis, ſuld be baptiſit agane: and ſit he wes na hæretik ſen nathing wes determinat in yat queſtioun contrare him afoir his days be ye kirk.*

*† As all heretikis dois at yis preſent.*

<small>Note. Quha ur yis day ye sones of Cham. Genes. 9.</small>
curfit handis ye memory of euery haly man, as it war ye muildis of yame now laid on fleip : followand aluterlie ye fuitftepis of yair fathir Cham, quha nocht onlie neclectit to couer ye baernes of venerable Noë, bot alfo maid ye famin patent to wtheris tobe fcornit. Quharethrow he deferuit fa grete difplefour for ye violatioun of natural honour, yat his eftercum-
<small>+ The peple of Chanaan deftroyit be ye Israelitis.</small>
aris † alfo wes thrallit to the curfe of his fin : ye wthir brethir being bliffit and fer vnlyke, quha wald noyir defile with yare ene, nor zit haif patent to the fyth of wtheris, the baernes of yair worfchipful father : bot turning yair faces abak couerit him, as it is writtin. yat is, yat yai nothir appreuit ye falt of the haly man, nor maid it oppin till wtheris, and yairfor wes rewardit with an happy blifling to yair eftercumeris.

*The terrouris pronunceit be the Apoftole aganis al fickil of fayth, apoftatis, fchifmatikis, and hæretikis. Cap. X.*

Bot lat ws return to ye purpofe. wyth grete dreidour heirfor is the horrible cryme of a changeit fayth, and violatit religioun be ws tobe ferit : fra ye quhilk nocht onlie ye difcipline of ecclefiaftik ordinance geuis ws terrour, bot alfo ye iugement of ye Apoftolik auctoritie. For it is knawin to al men, quhow greueouflie, quhow feueirlie, quhow vehementlie inweys ye bliffit Apoftil Paul contrare certane men, quha be meruolous inconftancie, ouer fuddanlie wes turnit fra him, quha callit yame vnto the fa-
<small>Galat. 1.</small> uour of Chrifte, vnto an wthir Euangell, quhilk is nocht an wthir : quha
<small>2. Tim. 4.</small> had heipit vp to yame felfis, maifteris till thair awin defyris, turning away
<small>1. Tim. 5.</small> fuythlie yair hering fra ye trewth, wes turnit to fabellis : haifand yair damnatioun, for yat yai violatit yair former fayth. Quhome yir men had
<small>Rom. 16.</small> begylit, of ye quhilkis ye famin Apoftil to the Romane brethir wrytis. Bot I praye zow brethir, that ze mark yame, quha makis diffenfioun and impediment, by ye doctrine quhilk ze hef lerit : and decline fra yame.
<small>2. Tim. 3.</small> For thir kynd of men feruis nocht the Lorde Chrifte, bot yair awin belly :
<small>* For wyirways this day God wald nocht permit sa mony to fall.</small> and be fuet fpeche and bliffingis diffauis ye hertis of ye innocent. Quha enteris in houffis and leidis in bondage women ladin * with fin, quhilkis women ar led with findry luftis, euir lerand, and to ye knaulege of ye
<small>Tit. 1.</small> trewth neuir cumand. Wanetalkand men and diffauearis, quha peruertis

hail houffis, techeand yat becumis nocht, for filthy lucres caufe: men of
corruptit mynd, and reprobat as concerning ye fayth, proud and but all
knawlege, bot tribuland yair wit about quæſtions and ſtryfe of wordis, 2. Tim. 3.
quha ar denudit of verite, eftemand lucre tobe godlines: and with yat alſo 1. Tim. 6.
ydil, leris to ga fra houſs to houſs: and nocht allanerlie ydill, bot alſo
clatterand and curious, ſpeikand that becumis nocht: Quha repelland fra 1. Tim. 5.
yame guid conſcience, as concerning fayth yai ar ſchipbrokin: Quhais 1. Tim. 1.
prophane vane clattir makis mekle to vngodlines: and ye ſpeche of yame 2. Tim. 2.
creipis as a cankir. Bot weill is it, that it is writtin of yir on yis maner. 2. Tim. 3.
Bot langer ſall yai nocht increſs: for ye fulechenes of yame ſalbe manifeſt
to al men, as it wes of the wthyr. Quhen heirfor fiklyke men paſſand
about cuntreis and citeis, and cariing about thair errouris tobe ſauld come Errouris to
alſo to ye Galathianis: And yir men being hard, ye Galathianis almaiſt An allu-
irkit of ye veritie, layand aſyde ye heuinlie fuid of ye apoſtolik and catho- sion of licht
lik doctrine, with ye filthynes of hæretical noueltie wes defylit, ye auctoritie of ye Apoſtolik pouer put out ye heid ſua, yat with maiſt hie ſeueri-
tie it decretit. Bot albeit othyr we, ſays he, or an angell frome, heuin Galat. 1.
preche to zow, by it quhilk we hef prechit, lat him be as accurſit. Quhat
is it yat he ſays, bot albeit we? Quhy nocht erar bot albeit I? That is,
zea, gif Petir, zea gif Andro, zea gif Iohne, zea finalie gif all ye haill cum- A quik de-
panie of ye apoſtolis, wald preche to zaw by it quhilk we hef prechit, lat of ye apos-
yame be as accurſit. A feirful charge for to defence ye perſeuerance of dis.
ye firſt faith, yat he noyir ſparit him ſelf, nor the reſt of the apoſtolis. This
is bot ſmal. Zea, gif an angel, ſays he, from heuin wald preche to zow
by it quhilk we hef prechit, lat him be as accurſit. It had nocht bene ſufficient to ye conſeruatioun of ye faith anis techit, to hef nameit ye natuir
of manlie ſtate, except he had comprehendit alſo ye excellencie of angelis:
Albeit we, ſays he, or an angell frome heuin. Nocht yat ye Angelis or
Sanctis of heuin may now fin: bot this is it, yat he ſays. Zea, gif it war
done, quhilk may nocht be done. Quhaſoeuir wald attempt to change ye
fayth anis techit, lat him be as accurſit. Bot paraduentuir he hes ſpokin
yir thingis raſchelie, and hes breſtit out erar of a manlie paſſioun, yan decretit be heuinlie reſſoun. God forbid: For it followis, and the famin
thing he oft repetis, with a vehement feruour of ferther declaratioun. As

we hef faid afoir, fays he, and now I fay agane: Gif ony man fal preche
to zow, by it quhilk ze hef refauit, lat him be as accurfit. He faid noth
gif ony man wald fchaw to zow, by it quhilk ze hef refauit, be he bliffit,
be he louit, be he admittit: Bot be he as accurfit, fays he, that is diuidit,
fegregat and fchot out: left the contagious fcab of ane fcheip be peftiferous accumpaniing, mot fmit ye hail innocent flok of Chrifte.

*Quhat wes commandit to ye Galathianis, wes commandit to all
Chriftianis. Cap. XI.*

BOT peraduentuir yir thingis ar onlie commandit to ye Galathianis. Heirfor alfo yir thingis to ye Galathianis only ar commandit, quhilkis in ye

Galat. 5. places follouing of the famin epiftil ar red: of quhilk kynd ar thir: Giue
we leue of the fpirit, lat ws walk in the fpirit. Be we nocht maid defi-
rus of vane gloir ane prouokand ane wthir, ane inwying ane wthir: And
ye reft. Quhilk thing gif it be an abfurditie, and to al men yai thingis
ar commandit alyke: it reftis yat lyke as yir præceptis of maneris, fua alfo
the wtheris, quhilkis ar decretit of fayth, fuld comprehend al men on lyke

Note. maner. And as it is nocht lefum to ony man to prouoke an wyir, or to
inwy an wyir: fua it mot nocht be lefum to ony man, to refaue ony doctrine by yat, quhilk ye catholik Kirk in al partis hes precheit. Or peraduentuir it wes at yat tyme commandit, gif ony man had precheit, by it
quhilk wes precheit, tobe accurfit: bot now it is nocht fua commandit.

Heirfor alfo yat thing quhilk he on lyke maner fays yair: Bot I fay
walk ze in ye fpirit, and ye luftis of ye flefche ze fal naways wirk, yan only
wes commandit, bot now efter is nocht fua commandit. Gif it be bayth
vngodlie and pernicious with yat alfo, to beleue: it followis neceffarlie,
yat as al yir, ar in al aiges tobe obferuit: fua alfua yai thingis quhilkis ar
ordanit, for nocht changeing of ye fayth, in al aiges ar commandit. To

An illa- preche heirfor ony thing to Chriftiane catholikis, by it quhilk yai hef re-
tioun or
conse- fauit, wes neuir lefum, neuir is lefum, nor neuir falbe lefum. And to
quence. accurfe yame, quha precheit ony thing by it quhilk wes anis refauit, wes
neuir vnlefum, neuer is vnlefum and neuir falbe vnlefum. quhilkis thingis
fen fua ar, is yair ony man of fa grete fuilhardines, quha fuld preche by it,

quhilk is precheit in ye Kirk? or of sa grete lychtnes, quha suld resaue by
it, quhilk he hes resauit fra ye Kirk? Lat him cry, and cry agane, and
yat to al men, and at al tymes, and oueralquhare, and be his writtingis lat
him cry, he quha is ye choisin weschell, he quha is maister of ye gentilis,
he quha is ye trompet of ye Apostolis, he quha is herald of al cuntreis, he
quha knawis ye secretis of heuin, yat gif ony man sal preche ony new doctrine, lat him be accursit. And on ye wthir syde contrare cryis certane
padokis, filthy verming, and fleis præparit to the dethe, of ye quhilk sort
are ye Pelagianis, and yat to ye catholikis? Be our auctoritie, say yai,
be our dominioun, be our expositioun, condemne yat thing quhilk ze held,
hald yat thing quhilk ze condemnit, cast away zour auld fayth, ye determinationis of zour fatheris, ye pledgeis of zour eldaris, and resaue: quhat
materis I pray zow? I wg to tell. For yai ar sa prydeful, yat nocht onlie
yai appere, yat yai may nocht be affirmit, bot nocht tobe confutit without
sum horrible cryme.

*S. Paul.*

*An illu-sioun of the plagis in Ægipt.*

*Ar nocht ye Caluin-ianis yis day as proud in Scotland?*

*Quhy ar sum cunning men sufferit be God sumtymes to preche errouris.
Item yat hæresèis ar callit also strange Godis.    Cap. XII.*

Bot sum man will say: Quhy oftymes heirfor ar yai sufferit be God sum
excellent persones placeit in ye Kirk, to preche new thingis to the catholikis? This is an apt quæstioun, and worthy tobe tretit mair diligentlie
and mair largelie: to ye quhilk nochtyeles it becumis to satifie nocht of
my awin ingyne, bot be auctoritie of ye diuine law, and be ye doctrine of
an ecclesiastik maister. Lat ws yairfor heir ye haly man Moyses, and lat
him teche ws, quhy cunning men, and quha for ye gift of science, be ye
Apostil ar callit also Prophetis, ar permittit sumtyme to setfurth new doctrine, quhilk the auld testament be an allegorik speche vseis to cal strange
Godis, for yat cause to wit, yat sua be hæretikis yair opinionis ar haldin in
reuerence, as be ye gentilis wes yair Godis. Thairfor blissit Moyses wrytis
in Deuteronomie: Gif a Prophet, says he, sal ryse in ye middis of the, or
quha sal say, yat he hes sein a dreme. That is a techear * placeit in ye
Kirk, quhome his discipulis or auditouris beleuis to teche, be sum reuela-
tioun. Quhat yairefter? And gif he sal forespeik, says he, a signe or

*S. Paul callis ye exposi-touris of ye scriptuir prophetis. Strange godis ar callit erro-neous doc-trine. Deut. 13. An allego-rik speche is, quhen an wyir thing is meanit, yan ye wordis planelie signifiis. * Zea bot ye new techearis takis ye place at* foretaking, and it fal chanfe, as he hes fpokin. I wate nocht treulie quhattin a grete maifter is fignifiit, and of fa grete fcience, yat he mot appere to his awin fcoleris to knaw nocht only manly thingis, bot alfo yat he may knaw afoir yai thingis, quhilkis ar aboue man. Of quhilk kynd yair difcipulis, almaift bragis to hef bene Valentinus, Donatus, Photinus, and Apollinaris, and ye reft of yat fort. And quhat yairefter? And he fal tel to ye, fays he, Lat ws go and follow ftrange Godis, quhome yow mifknawis: and lat ws ferue yame. Quhat ar ftrange Godis, bot ftrange errouris, quhilkis yow mifknew, and is new and nocht hard? And lat ws ferue yame: yat is, lat ws beleue yame, and follow yame. Quhat yan finalie? *Thou fall nocht heir*, fays he, *the wordis of yat Prophet, or dremar.* And quhy I pray the, is yat thing forbiddin be God nocht tobe techeit, quhilk be God is forbiddin to be hard? Becaufe, fays he, ye Lord zour God temptis zow, yat it mot be plane, quhidder ze luue him or nocht in all zour hert, and in all zour faul. Mair cleirlie yan the lycht the caufe is oppinnit, quhy fumtymes the prouidence of God fufferis fum reularis of ye kirkis to preche fum new doctrine: that the Lord zour God, fays he, mot preue zow. And fuythlie it is a grete temptatioun, quhen that man, quhome thow beleuis tobe a Prophet, a Difciple of the Prophetis, a Doctour and affirmar of the veritie, and quhome thow hes embraceit in grete veneratioun and luwe, the famin man fra hand fuld inbring in hidlingis peftilent errouris, quhilkis haiftelie yow may noth parfaue, quhilis you is led be ye præiudice of ye auld doctrine: and iugeis noth lefum efalie to condemne it, fa lang as yow is empefcheit be ye affectioun of yi auld maifter.

*Exemples of temptatioun in ye lauchful miniſteris of ye Kirk: and firſt of ye hæretik Neſtorius, quha wes a Biſchope lauchfullie ordinat. Cap. XIII.*

Heir perchanfe fum man wald afk, that yir thingis quhilkis ar allegeit be haly Moyfes, be fum ecclefiaftical exemples war maid plane. It is a iuft requeift and nocht lang tobe delayt. For yat I may begin at the nerraft and maift manifeft: quhattin a temptatioun think we it to hef bene, quhen that mifcheuous Neftorius haiftelie of a fcheip turnit in ane wowlf, began to ryue ye flok of Chrifte? quhen yir famin men quha wes revin and gnawin be him, beleuit yat he hald bene ane of Chriftis fcheip, and thairfor war thai mair patent to his byting. For quha wald efalie beleue yat man to erre, quhome he faw electit be fa grete iugement of ye Empyre, and haldin in fa grete fauour of ye Preiftis? quha with fa grete luue of ye fanctis, with fa grete fauour of ye peple, daylie wes renounit, quha oppinlie tretit ye word of God, and confutit alfo the peftiferous errouris of ye Iowis and Gentilis. Be fik a maner as yis, I pray zow quhome wald he nocht caufe trow, yat he techit ye trewth, precheit ye trewth, and vnderftuid ye trewth? Quha yat he mycht oppin ye way to his awin ane hærefie perfuitit ye blafphemeis of al hærefeis. Bot yat wes it, yat Moyfes fays: The Lord zour God temptis zow, gif ze luue him, or nocht.

*A greatear temptatioun, nor quhen a rennigat and a voluptuous preift, or munk makis his affalt aganis the trewth.*

*A delitio⁹ venum.*

## *Of ye hæretik Photinus.  Cap. XIIII.*

AND yat we fett Neftorius afyde, in quhome wes euir mair admiratioun, yat proffet: mair fame and name, yan experience: quhome be ye opinioun of ye peple a certane tyme throw manlie fauour mair yan godlie, wes haldin in æftimatioun: lat ws mak mentioun of yame rather quha being excellent in grete actis, and grete diligence, become nocht a litle tentatioun to ye catholik men: as in Pannonia in ye memorie of our eldaris, Photinus is rememberit to hef temptit ye kirk of Sirmitane, quhare quhen with grete fauour of al men, he wes promotit to ye dignitie of Preiftheid, and certane tyme maid miniftratioun yair as a catholik, fra hand as yat euil Prophet or dremar, quhome Moyfes fignifiis, began to perfuade ye peple of God committit to him, yat yai fuld follow ftrange Godis, yat is ftrange errouris, quhilkis afoir yai mifknew. Bot yis is a commoun thing, bot yis wthir a pernicious: infafer as to fa grete a wickitnes, he vfeis nocht a mein and a vulgar fupport. For he wes bayth potent in quiknes of ingyne, excellent in ye riches of leirning, and weray piffant in eloquence: as he quha had copiouflie and grauelie bayth reffonit and writtin in bayth ye toungis, quhilk thing is maid manifeft be his bukes zit refting, quhilkis he partlie maid in Greik, and partlie in Latin. Bot it chanfeit weil, yat

*Pannonia wes yai landis quhilk nou ar callit Vngarie and Auftrik. Photinus a cunning hæretik.*

*Ye ingyne, leirning, and eloquence of Photinus.*

ye fcheip of Chrifte committit to him, gretumlie and warlie walkryfe, for
ye catholik fayth, haiftelie had refpect to ye faynges of Moyfes afoir wair-
ning: And albeit yai meruelit at ye eloquence of yair Prophet and Paftour, zit yai mifknew nocht ye temptatioun. For quhome yai afoir as ye
belwodder of ye flok followit, ye famin yairefter as a woulf, yai began
to flie.

*Deut. 13.*

### *Of ye hæretik Apollinaris. Cap. XV.*

AND nocht onlie be exemple of Photinus, bot alfo of Apollinaris leir we
ye perel of yis temptatioun in ye Kirk, and togidder ar aduertifit mair diligentlie to obferue ye faifgaird of ye fayth. For he engenerit to his fcoleris richt vehement cummeris, and grete perplexitie: as quhen ye auctoritie of ye Kirk drew yame fra yis fyde, and ye familiaritie of yair techear
drew yame abak agane fra ye wthir fyde: fua yai fweand and fwounand
betuix thame twa, determinatis nocht quhat wes fpecialie eraft tobe chofin
be yame. Bot peraduentuir yat man wes of fik fort, yat he wes worthy
lychtlie tobe contemnit. Zea, trewlie he wes fa excellent, and fik a man,
to quhome yai micht ouer haiftelie hef geuin credit in mony thingis. For
quha wes mair excellent yan he in quiknes of ingyne, in exercife, and
leirning? Quhow mony hærefeis in mony volumis oppreffit he, quhow
mony errouris inimeis to ye fayth confutit he, ane figne yairof may be yat
noble an large werk, of na les yan of thretty buikis, in ye quhilk be grete
heip of probationis he confoundit ye woud fals allegeance of Porphirius.
It war a lang tyme to reherfs al his werkis, be ye quhilkis trewlie he
micht hef bene æquall to ye grete bigaris of ye kirk, war nocht be yat prophane luft of hæretik curiofitie, I wate nocht quhat noueltie he had found,
be quhilk, as be ye admixtioun of certane lepre, he defylit al his labouris:
yat his doctrine mycht be callit nocht fa mekle ædificatioun, as temptatioun of ye kirk.

*The excel-
lencie of A-
pollinaris.
Of his large
writtingis
aganis Por-
phirius.*

### *Of ye principal hærefeis of ye forenameit: and firft of Photinus*
### *errour. Cap. XVI.*

HEIR perchanfe it may be afkit at me, yat I declare ye hærefeis of fum of

## YE NOUATIONIS OF AL HÆRESEIS.   149

yame afoir nameit, to wit of Neftorius, Apollinaris, and Photinus. Bot ye is thing treulie to ye mater of ye quhilk we now talk, pertenis nocht. For we hef tane porpofe nocht to difcufs ye errouris of euery man, bot to produce ye exemplis of few, be quhilkis euidentlie and cleirlie it mot be fchawin, yat quhilk Moyfes fpeikis: that is to wit, gif ony techear in the Kirk, he being a Prophet alfo in the interpreting ye myfteriis of ye Prophetis, attemptis to inbring ony nouatioun in ye Kirk of God. yat ye prouidence of God, fufferis yat thing tobe for our probatioun. It falbe profetable heirfor in the bypaffing, quhat the foirnamit hæretikis thinkis, fchortlie to expone, that is Photinus, Apollinaris, and Neftorius. This heirfor is the fect of Photinus. He affirmis that God is fingle † and folitare, and tobe confeffit of ye Iowis manere: he denyis ye fullines of ye trinitie, and nothir thinkis he tobe ony perfoun of ye Sone of God, or ony perfoun of ye haly fpirit: bot affirmis Chrifte tobe only a man allane, to quhome he afcriuis ye beginning tobe of Marie, and fua on al manere techeis he, yat we fuld worfchip onlie ye perfoun of God ye father, and worfchip Chrifte only as a man.

*Thir auld hæretikis barkit fpecialleaganis Chrifte our heid: bot ye new aganis the kirk his mystical body, and sumtymes aganis bayth.*

*† That is without distinctioun of persones.*

### *Of the hærefie of Apollinaris.  Cap. XVII.*

THIR thingis heirfor techis Photinus. Bot Apollinaris in a manere crakis and waintis that he confentis in Deid to the vnitie of the trinitie, and yat trewlie be full hailnes of fayth, bot be oppin profeffioun he blafphemis ye incarnatioun of ye Lord. For he fays that in the body of our Saluiour, yat othir aluterlie yair wes nocht a manis faul, or at the leift, that yair wes fik a faul, quhilk wantit mynd and reffoun. Atouer he faid yat ye flefche of ye Lord, wes nocht refauit of ye flefche of ye haly virgine Marie, bot defcendit frome heuin in ye virgine. And he all tymes flowand and doutfum fumtyme precheit it tobe coæternal, and euir alyke leftand with ye fone of God, and fumtyme it to hef bene maid of the diuinitie. For he wald nocht twa fubftances tobe in Chrifte, ane diuine and an wthir humane, ane of ye father, an wthir of the mother: bot he beleuit that ye felf natuir of the fone of God wes cuttit findrie: as that ane part perfeuerit in God, and ane wthir part wes turnit in ye body: as quhen ye veritie fays of twa fubftances, tobe ane Chrifte, he contrarious to ye veritie, of ane diuinitie of Chrifte, wald affirm twa fubftances to hef bene maid. hiddirtillis fua dremis Apollinaris.

*Of Neftorius errour. Cap. XVIII.*

Bot Neftorius be a contrarious feiknes to Apollinaris, quhen he imaginatis him felf to diuide twa fubftances in Chrifte, he bringis in fra hand twa perfones, and be an vnhard wickitnes, he will that yair be twa fones of God, twa Chriftis: ye ane tobe God, and ye wthir man: ye ane of ye father, ye wthir quhilk is generat of the mother. And yairfor affirmis he, haly Marie nocht tobe callit θεότοκον (yat is ye mother of God) bot χριστότοκον (yat is ye mother of Chrifte:) for that caufe to wit, yat nocht yat Chrifte, quhilk is God, wes borne of hir, bot that, quhilk wes man. Gif ony man thinkis him in his writtingis to name ane Chrifte, and to preche ane perfoun of Chrifte: Lat him nocht beleue him fulechelie. For othir hes he inuentit that be craft of diffauing, yat be guid, he mycht mair efalie perfuade ye euill, as ye Apoftill fays: Be guid he hes wrocht to me dethe: or yairfor as we hef faid, for diffait, in fum places of his writtingis he bragis yat he beleueis tobe ane Chrifte, and ane perfoun of Chrifte. Or at ye leift efter ye birthe now of ye virgine he fays, yat twa perfones conuenis fua in ane Chrifte: yat nochtyeles in the tyme of the conceptioun and birthe of ye virgine, and a litle yairefter, he contendis to hef bene twa Chriftis: and quhen to wit Chrifte wes firft borne a commoun man and man allone, and nocht zit marrowit be the vnitie of ye perfoun of ye fone of God, yat yairefter the perfoun of the fone of God, refauing him to ye felf defcendit: and albeit now he refauit remanis for atyme in ye glore of God, zit that na difference fuld be hald betuix him and wthir men. Thir thingis fua Neftorius, Apollinaris, and Photinus as woud doigis, barkis contrare ye catholik fayth. Photinus nocht confeffing ye trinitie, Apollinaris fayng ye natuir of the fone of God tobe conuertible, and nocht confeffing twa fubftances tobe in Chrifte, and othir denying ye hail faul of Chrifte, or at the leift denying mynd and refoun tobe in ye faull, and affirming ye word of God to hef bene for the knaulege of the mynd: Neſtorius allegeing twa Chriſtis oyir euir tobe, or ſumtyme to hef bene.

*Quhat is ye trew catholik fayth aganis yir hæretikis. Cap. XIX.*

Bot ye catholik Kirk vnderſtanding bayth richt of God and of our Saluiour, nothir blaſphemis contrare ye myſterie of the trinitie, nor contrare ye incarnatioun of Chriſte. For it worſchipis ane diuine ſubſtance in fulnes of ye trinitie, and æqualitie of the trinitie in ane and in the ſamin maieſtie: and ane Ieſus Chriſte, and nocht twa Chriſtis, and ye ſamin tobe bayth God and man. It beleuis ſuythlie tobe in him ane perſoun, bot twa ſubſtances: twa ſubſtances ſuythlie, bot the twa ſubſtances tobe ane perſoun: becauſe the word (or ſone of God) is nocht changeable, that he may be changeit in a body. It beleuis ane perſoun, left profeſſing twa ſones it mot be iugeit to worſchip a quaternitie, and nocht ye trinitie. Bot it is weray proffetable that we explane ye ſamin thing agane and agane, mair diſtinctlie and expreſlie. In God is ane ſubſtance, bot thre perſones: in Chriſte twa ſubſtances, bot ane perſoun. In ye trinitie is ane wthir and ane wthir, bot nocht ane wthir ſubſtance and ane wthir ſubſtance. In our Saluiour is ane wthir ſubſtance and ane wthir ſubſtance: bot nocht ane wthir and ane wthir. Quhow is yare in the trinitie ane wthir and ane wthir, and nocht ane wthir ſubſtance? Becauſe to wit, ane wthir is ye perſoun of ye father, ane wthir of ye ſone, and ane wthir of ye haly gaiſt: bot zit yair is nocht ane wthir and ane wthir, bot ane and ye ſamin natuir of ye father, and of ye ſone, and of ye haly gaiſt. As in our Saluiour yair is ane wthir ſubſtance and ane wthir ſubſtance, bot nocht ane wthir and wthir. Becauſe to wit, ye ſubſtance of ye diuinitie is ane, and of ye humanitie ane wthir: bot zit ye diuinitie and humanitie is nocht ane wthir Chriſte, bot ane and ye ſamin Chriſte, ane and ye ſamin ſone of God, and of ane and ye ſamin Chriſte and ſone of God, is ane and the ſamin perſoun. As in a man the body is ane thing, and ye ſaul an wthir thing: bot ye ſaul and body is ane and the ſamin man. In Petir and Paul ane thing is ye ſaul, an wthir thing is ye body: and zit ye ſaul and ye body ar nocht twa Petiris: or ye ſaul is ane Paul, and ye body ane wthir Paul: bot Petir is ane and ye

*Note the godly erudition of ye wrytear, in ye hie myſterie of ye haly trinitie, and of our Saluiour.*

*Ane wyir and ane wyir: yat is, in perſonis. In ye diuinitie is ane ſubſtance and thre perſones: bot in Chriſte ane perſoun and twa ſubſtances, diuine and humane.*

*A ſimilitude.*

famin, and Paul is ane and the famin, being of twa and diueris naturis of faul and body. Sua heirfor in ane and ye famin Chrifte, ar twa fubftances : bot ane is diuine, and ane wyir is humane : ane of God the father, ane wyir of ye virgine ye mother : ane coæternal and æqual with ye father, ye wthir in tyme les yan ye father : ane of ye famin fubftance with ye father, ane wthir of ye famin fubftance with ye mother : zit bot ane and ye famin Chrifte is in bayth ye fubftances. Heirfor Chrifte God is nocht ane, and Chrifte man an wthir : nocht ye ane nocht creat, and ye wthir creat : nocht the ane impaffible, and the wthir paffible : nocht ye ane æqual with ye father, and ye wthir les yan ye father : nocht ye ane of ye father, and ye wthir of ye mother : bot ye ane and ye famin Chrifte is God and man : ye famin nocht creat and creat : ye famin vnchangeable and impaffible : ye famin changeit and fufferit : ye famin æqual to ye father, and les : ye famin of ye father afoir al warldis begottin : the famin in the warld generat of the mother : perfyte God, and perfyte man : in him as God ful diuinitie, in him as man ful humanitie. Humanitie, I fay, ful as it quhilk hes bayth faul and body, bot a weray body, zea our body, and body of ye mother : a faul trewlie endewit with vnderftanding, ftrenthit with mynd and reffoun.

*In Chrifte Iefus is na commixtioun nor changeing of diuinitie in humanitie, or contrare : bot bayth ye twa naturis vniit in ane perfoun, without al præfenting of ony wther perfoun. Cap. XX.*

THAI ar heirfor in Chrifte ye word, ye faul, and body : bot al yis thing is ane Chrift, ane Sone of God, ane Saluiour, and our Redemar. Bot ane nocht be, I wate nocht quhat, corruptible confufioun of the diuinitie and humanitie, bot be ane hail and certane fingular vnitie of perfoun. For yat coniunctioun changeit nor conuertit nocht ye ane in ye wthir, quhilk errour is propre of ye Arrianis : bot fua ionit yame bayth in ane, yat ye fingularitie of ye ane and ye famin perfoun, euir remaneing in Chrifte, for euir alfo mot perfeuere ye proprietie of euery ane of baith ye natuiris : to wit yat God neuir beginnis tobe ye body : quhilk thing alfo is maid plane be exemple of ye ftate of man. For nocht onlie in yis præfent lyfe, bot in ye lyfe tocum alſo euery man ſal confiſt of body and ſaul: zit neuir ſal ye body be turnit in ye ſaul, nor ye ſaul in ye body. Bot euery man being to leue without end, in euery man without end neceſſarlie ſal perſeuere ye difference of bayth ye ſubſtances. Sua in Chriſte alſo ye proprietie of bayth ye ſubſtances, is tobe retenit to euery ane yairof, ſaifing zit ye vnitie of perſoun. Bot quhen we name oftymes ye perſoun, and ſays yat ye perſoun God wes maid man, gretumlie is tobe ferit, yat we appere nocht to ſay yis, yat God the ſone be only imitatioun of doing, hes tane vpon him our natuir: and quhateuir yat thing be of manlie leuing, quhilk he did, yat he did it as ouerſchaddowit, and nocht as a weray man: as it vſeis tobe done in ye playng places, quhare a man ſchortlie plays ye partis of ſindry perſones, of quhilkis nane is he in deid. For quhouoft euir yat ony imitatioun of wyir menis doingis is tane vpon ony, ſua ye offices or werkis of wtheris ar done, yat yir zit quha dois yame, ar nocht ye ſamin perſones, quhome yai præſent. For lat ws nocht vſe, as for demonſtratioun, ye exemplis of ſecularis, and of ye Manicheis: quhen ye playar of a tragedie præſentis ye perſoun of a Preiſt, or of a King, he is nocht a Preiſt, or a King. For efter yat he hes endit ye part of his play, yai thingis alſo ceiſſis, quhilkis he tuke on him be yat perſoun. God ſtay fra ws yat wickit and curſit mokrie. Lat that be the madnes of the Manicheis, quha precheand phantaſeis ſays, yat the ſone of God become nocht the perſoun of a man in ſubſtance, bot be a certane apperand gyſing and conuerſatioun, finzeit ye ſamin. Bot ye catholik fayth ſua ſays ye ſone of God tobe maid man, yat he tuke nocht our natuir on him finzetlie and vnder a ſchaddow, bot verelie and manifeſtlie: and yat he præſentit nocht yai thingis, quhilkis pertenit to man, as of an wthir, bot exerceit yame as his awin, and aluterlie wes yat thing, quhilk he præſentit. As we our ſelfis alſo in yat we ſpeik, vnderſtand, leuis, and in ſubſtance ar, we præſent nocht wthir men, bot ar men in deid. For Petir and Iohne, that I may name yame ſpecialie, wes nocht men be præſenting wtheris, bot men in weray ſubſtance. Siklyke Paul nocht feinzetlie præſentit an Apoſtil, or feinzit him tobe Paul, bot wes an Apoſtil, and in weray ſubſtance wes Paul. Siklyke alſo ye ſone of God takand on him and haifand ane body in ſpeiking, doing, and ſuffering be ye fleſche, zit without al corruptioun of his natuir, he deinzeit him aluterlie to do yis in deid, nocht yat he be imitatioun fchew or finzeit him tobe man, bot trewlie gaue him felf a perfyte man, nocht yat he fuld appere or be iugeit, bot yat he fuld be and that in weray fubftance a perfyte man. Heirfor as the faul adunit to the body, bot nocht zit turnit in ye body præfentis nocht an wthir man, bot is a man, and a man nocht be feinzeing, bot be fubftance : fua alfo ye fone of God without al changeing of ye felf, be vniing him felf to man, nocht be commixtioun of natuiris, nor be præfenting an wthir, bot in ye felf fubftance wes maid man. Heirfor lat al ye vnderftanding of fik a perfoun aluterlie be wappit away, quhilk be finzeing and præfenting an wthir, is tane on hand : quhare ane thing euir is in trewth, and ane wyir thing is finzeit, quhare yat man quha præfentis ye perfoun, neuir is he, quhome he præfentis. God forbid, yat be yis diffaitful maner, ye fone of God mot be beleuit, to hef tane on him ye perfoun of man : bot rather fua, yat his fubftance remanyng vnchangeable, and takand ye natuir on him of a perfyte man, he mot be ye body felf, ye man felf, and ye felf perfoun of ye man, nocht a fenzeit, bot a trew perfoun : nocht in præfenting, bot in fubftance : nocht fchortlie yat mot ceifs with ye præfenting, bot quhilk aluterlie remanis in fubftance.

*That ye vnitie of perfoun in our Saluiour wes complete in ye virginis bofum. And yat ye propirteis of ye humane natuir in our Saluiour, ar catholiklie attribute to his godheid : and ye propirteis fiklyke of his godheid, to his manheid : be reffoun yat ye fone of God and man, is ane Chrifte only in perfoun. And yat ye bliffit virgin deulie is callit ye mother of God. Cap. XXI.*

HEIRFOR this vnitie of perfoun in Chrift, naways eftir the birthe of the virgine, bot in ye felf wombe of the virgine wes coniunit and perfytit. For we man gretumlie be war, that we confes Chrifte nocht onlie ane : bot alfo euir tobe ane : becaufe it is an intolerable blafpheme, yat gif yow affirme yat he is now ane, zit fumtyme yow wil contend yat he hes nocht bene ane, bot twa : yat is ane eftir ye tyme of baptime, bot twa about ye tyme of his natiuitie. Quhilk botumles facrilege na wyirways trewlie may we efchew, except we confes man vnit to God, in vnitie of perfoun, nocht in his afcenfioun, or refurrectioun, or in baptim, bot yan in ye motheris wombe, yan quhen ye virgine confauit. For ye quhilk vnitie of perfoun, indifferentlie to him and alyke bayth thai thingis, yat ar propir to God, ar attribute to man, and quhilkis ar propir to ye body, ar appropriat to God. For frome yis ground is it, yat is reuelit in writ be God : bayth ye fone of man to hef defcendit frome heuin, and ye Lord of gloir to hef bene crucifiit in erth. Fra that ground is it alfo, yat ye body of ye Lord being maid, ye body of ye Lord being creat, yat ye fone of God him felf mot be callit maid, ye complete wifdome of God mot be callit ye creat knawlege, as in ye foreknaulege his handis and feit ar fchawin to be peirfit. Be yis vnitie, I fay of perfoun, yat thing alfo is perfytit be reffoun of ficlyk a myfterie, yat ye body of ye fone of God being borne of an immaculat mother, God him felf in ye fecund perfoun, mot be beleuit maift catholiklie to be borne of ye virgine, and maift wickitlie denyit to hef bene borne. Quhilk thingis fen yai ar, God forbid yat ony man preifs to defraude ye haly virgine of ye priuilegis of ye grace of God, as of hir fpecial gloir. For fche be a fpecial gift of oure Lorde and God, bot of hir fone, maift treulie and bliffitlie is tobe confeffit tobe θεότοκος (yat is, ye mother of God). Bot nocht on yat manere ye mother of God, as fum vickit hærefie fufpectis : quhilk affirmis hir to be callit be name onlie ye mother of God, as fche quha buir a man quha efterwart was God : as we cal ye mother of a Preift, or ye mother of a Bifchope, nocht now in ye bering of a Preift or a Bifchop, bot in ye bering a man, quha eftirwart wes maid a Preift or Bifchope. Nocht fua I fay, haly Marie is ye mother of God, bot yairfor rather, becaufe, as it is ellis faid, yat in hir confecrat bofum, yat maift haly myfterie wes wrocht, quhilk for a fingular and onlie vnitie of perfoun, as ye fone of God in manly nature is man, fua man in God, is God.

*A repetitioun of ye errouris præceding : with a congratulatioun to ye trew catholik Kirk, for hir fynceritie of fayth. Cap. XXII.*

Bot now to yai thingis, quhilkis of ye forefaidis hærefiis ar of ye catholik fayth fchortlie fpokin afoir, for ftrenthin of oure memorie, lat ws fchortliar and mair narroulie reherfe : to wit, yat ye thingis reherfit agane may be bayth mair fullelie vnderftand, and preffit in memorie mair firmlie may be kepit. Lat it be heirfor an accurfe to Photinus, quha nocht refauis ye fullines of ye Trinitie, and quha prechis yat Chrift is man onlie. Lat it be an accurfe to Apollinaris, quha affirmis, yat yair is corruptioun of ye Trinitie changeit in Chrift, and quha takis away the proprietie of ye perfyt manheid in him. Lat it be an accurfe to Neftorius, quha denyis God tobe borne of ye virgine, and affirmis tobe twa Chriftis, and ye fayth of ye Trinitie being fchote away, introducis til ws a Quaternitie. Bot bliffit is ye catholik Kirk, quha wirfchipis ane God in fullines of Trinitie, and fiklyk æqualitie of ye Trinitie in ane diuine fubftance : yat noyir ye fingularitie of ye fubftance, mot confund ye proprietie of perfones, nor zit fiklyk ye diftinctioun of ye Trinitie, mot diuide ye vnitie of ye godheid. Blift, fay I, is ye Kirk, quha in Chrift beleuis tobe twa weray and perfyte fubftances, bot ye perfoun of Chrift to be ane : yat nothir ye diftinctioun of naturis mot diuide ye vnitie of perfoun, nor zit alykways ye vnitie of perfoun mot confound ye difference of fubftances. Blift, I fay, is ye Kirk, quhilk yat it mycht grant bayth euir to be, and to bef bene ane Chrifte, confeffis the manheid vnitit to the Godheid, nocht eftir ye birthe, bot ewin in ye felf wombe of ye virgine. Blift, I fay, is ye Kirk, quha vnderftandis God maid man, nocht be changeing of natuir, bot be reffoun of ye ane perfoun, of ye perfoun trewlie nocht finzeit, appering, and vaniffing away : bot of ye fubfifting perfoun, and euir permanent. Blift, I fay, is ye Kirk, quhilk prechis yis vnitie of perfoun to haif fa greit power, yat yairthrow be a meruolous and intellable myfterie, it attributis ye godlie propirteis to man, and ye manlie to God. For yairthrow yat man defcendit from heuin as concerning God, it denyis nocht : and beleuis yat God as concerning man, wes in ye erd maid, fufferit, and crucifiit. Thairthrow breuelie it confeffis bayth man to be ye fone of God, and God ye fone of ye virgine. Blift heirfor and worfchipful, fanctifiit, and maift haly is yat confeffioun, aluterlie to be comparit to yat fupernal louing of ye Angelis, quhilk be ane threfald bliffing glorifiis ane Lord God, for fpecialie yairfor it furthfchawis ye vnitie of Chrift : yat ye myfterie of ye trinitie exceid nocht in

## YE NOUATIONIS OF AL HÆRESEIS. 157

numbir. Thir thingis ar fpokin, as it war be ye way, ane wyer tyme mair fullelie to be tretit and explanit.

*He returnis to ye temptatioun of ye faythful be erroneous doctrine, techeing al guid Chriftiane, yat he fuld refaue ye doctouris aggreing with ye Kirk, and nocht leue ye fayth of the Kirk with ony ane doctour quhatfumeuir. And firft of Origine. Cap. XXIII.*

Now lat ws return to our porpofe. We faid thairfor in the former partis yat in ye Kirk of God, tentatioun of ye peple wes ye erroure of ye techear: and infamekle the tentatioun gretar, quhowmekle he war cunningar, quha had errit. Quhilk thing firft be authoritie of fcripture, yairefter be exemplis of the kirk we declarit: to wit be the reherfing of yame, quha quhen fumtyme war eftemit of hail fayth, and at lenthe zit othir fel in an wther manis fect, or yame felf inuentit yair awin hærefie. A gret mater trewlie and proffetable to be lerit, and neceffare to be brocht in memorie: quhilk thing diligentlie be abundance of exemplis we fuld mak cleir, and ding in ye eris of men: yat al catholikis almaift hes knawin, yat yai fuld refaue ye doctouris with ye kirk, and nocht with ye doctouris leue ye fayth of the kirk. Bot I think yis, yat fen we may produce mony in yis kynd of tentatioun, yat almaift nane is that may be comparit to the tentatioun of Origine: In quhome yai war mony thingis fa fer excellent, fa fingular, fa meruolous yat in ye begynning ony man efalie mycht iuge credit to be geuin to al yat he affirmit. For gif lyfe makis authoritie, he wes a man of grete labouris, of grete chaftitie, of grete patience and fuffering: Gif gentrice or leirnyng, quha was mair noble yan he? Firft quha was borne in yat houfs, quhilk wes maid noble be martyrdome? and yairefter for Chriftis faik nocht onlie wes denudit of his father, bot of al his geiris alfo, fa mekle proffetit in the ftryte way of haly pouertie, yat he for confeffing the Lord oftymes (as yai fay) wes afflictit. Bot zit thir thingis allane war nocht in him: quhilkis all efterwart mycht be temptatioun, bot fa grete alfo quiknes of fa profound, fa fcharpe, fa gentil ingyme, yat almaift he gretumlie and fer ourcome al wtheris: and of fa gret excellencie of leirnyng and of al eruditioun, yat yai war litle of diuine philofophie, and

Note.

Of Origine.

Of the singular proprieteis in Origine.

Sa mony excellent proprieteis wes nocht knawin, amangis al our renningatis: quharefor mair mischeantlie wes ye feble of fayth vincust.

almaift peraduentuir nane of humane philofophie, quhilk he had nocht throwchlie knawin. To quhois knawlege quhen the Greikis gaue place, the Hebrew literis alfo war exornat be him. Bot quhairto fal I tel of his eloquence? quhais fpeche wes fa plefand, fa iocund, fa fueit, yat to me apperit out of his mouthe, nocht wordis fa mekle, as certane hwnie to hef flowit. Quhat thingis difficil to perfuade, be ftrenthe of difputatioun maid he nocht plane? Quhat thingis difficil to be done dreffit he nocht, yat yai mot appere maift facil. Bot perchanfe, be knottis onlie of argumentatioun he dreffit his allegeance. Ze planelie neuir wes ony of the doctouris, that vfeit may exemplis of Godis law. Bot I trow yat he wrate bot litill: na mortal man wrate mair: yat it apperis to me yat al his writtingis may nocht onlie nocht be perfytlie red, bot na wayis may be found. To quhome yat na thing fuld inlake to ye occafioun of fcience, ye fowthe of age aboundit alfo. Bot peraduenture he wes litle happy be his fcoleris: quha ewir was mair happy? furth of his bofum treulie become innumerable Doctouris, innumerable Preiftis, confeffouris, and Martyris. Bot quhou gret wes yan ye admiratioun of him amangis al men, quhow grete the gloir, quhou grete ye fauour, quha can declair? quha weil ftudious of religioun come nocht fleand to him, fra ye vtmaift partis of ye warld? quhat Chriftiane worfchipit nocht him, as a Prophet? quhat Philofophour worfchipit him nocht, as a maifter? Quhow worfchipful wes he, nocht onlie to ye priuat eftate of men, bot to ye Empyre felf alfo, ye hiftoriis declaris: quhilkis fchawis that the mother of Alexander ye Empriour callit him in hir cumpanie and that for the merit trewlie of heuinlie wifdome, with gift and luue of ye quhilk he was inflammit. Bot his epiftolis alfo beris witnefs, quhilk he be authoritie of his pouer in Chrifte, wrate to Philip ye Empriour, quha wes ye firft Chriftiane of ye Romane Princis. Of quhais incredible knawlege gif ony refauis nocht a teftimonie be report of ws Chriftianis, lat him at ye leift refaue ye confeffioun of ye Ethnikis, according to ye witneffing of Philofophouris. For wickit Porphyrius felf mouit be ye name of him, almaift in his barneage paffit to Alexandria, and yair faw him yan ane aigeit man bot planelie fik a ane, and fa excellent yat he had afcendit ye heich toure of al fcience. Tyme fal fonear failze me, nor I may collect anis, for ye leift part, yai excellent thingis, quhilkis fprang of yat man: quhilkis al nocht onlie zit pertenit to ye gloir of religioun, bot alſo to ye a grete cauſe of tentatioun. For quha is he quha wald hef ſchaikin fra him a man of ſa grete ingine, of ſa greit leirnyng, of ſa gret beutifulnes, and nocht rather vſe yis ſentence: yat he had leuir erre with Origene, yan with wtheris to vndirſtand ye trewth? And quhat neidis mair? the mater declinit heirto, that nocht a manly, bot as the mater ſchew, a weray perelous tentatioun of ſa grete a perſoun, of ſa grete a doctoure, of ſa grete a Prophete, dounled mony fra the integritie of fayth. Quhairfor the famin Origene ſa excellent and ſik a man, quhylis he inſolentlie abuſeis the grace of God, quhylis he lippinnis ouermekle to his awin ingyne, and creditis til him ſelf largely, quhylis he eſtemis lytle ye auld ſimplicitie of ye Chriſtiane religioun, quhylis he præſumis to haif vnderſtanding by all wyeris, quhylis he contemnand the eccleſiaſtik traditionis, doctrine, and auctoritie of ye forefatheris, interpretis of a new manere certane heidis of ſcripturis, he deſeruit yat of him alſo, to ye Kirk of God it mot be ſaid: Gif a Prophet ſal ryiſs in ye middis of the: and a litle eftir: Thow ſal nocht heir (ſays he) ye wordis of yat Prophete: and ſiklyke, Becauſe ye Lorde zoure God (ſays he) temptis zow, quhiddir gif ze luue him, or nocht. Trewlie nocht onlie a tentatioun wes it, bot alſo a grete tentatioun, quietlie and ſtep and ſtep to draw away be admiratioun of his ingyne, eloquence, conuerſatioun and fauoure, ye kirk of God til him ſubmittit, and on him dependand, and na thing ſuſpectand of him, na thing fering him, haiſtelie fra the auld religioun til a new prophanatioun. Bot ſum man wil ſay, yat ye bukis of Origene ar corruptit. yis I ganeſtand nocht, bot erar wald ye famin, for yat is techit be ſum and alſo writtin, nocht be catholikis onlie, bot alſo be hæretikis. Bot that is the thing quhilk we ſuld now conſider that albeit him ſelf wes nocht, zit the buikis ſet furth in his name, is a grete tentatioun: quhilkis braiſtis owt in mony woundis of blaſphemeis, nocht as wther menis, bot as his ar red and luueit: yat albeit it wes nocht ye mynd of Origene in ye confaiting of ye erroure: zit to perſuade the erroure, ye authoritie of Origine mot appere to mak mekle.

*Of Origenis fal, and of ye cauſe yairof.*

*Origenis buikis be wtheris corruptit.*

## Of the fall of the grete leirnit man Tertulliane. Cap. XXIIII.

*His erudi-tioun.* Bot the famyn is ye cafe of Tertulliane: for as ye wther amangis ye Greikis, fua he amangis ye Latinis, is to be iugeit neir ye principal of al oure men. For quha wes bettir leirnit yan wes yis man, quha in ye diuine and humane materis wes mair exerceit? He trewlie al ye Philofophie, and al ye fectis of Philofophouris, ye authoris and appreuearis of the fectis, and al thair doctrine, al ye veritie of hiftoriis and of excercifeis, be a meruolous capacitie of mynd, perfytlie vnderftude. Bot excellit he nocht of folide and hie ingyne: that na thing almaift he fet him to, quhilk he othir peirfit nocht be fcharpenes of wit, or be wechty reffonis diftroyit nocht. Ferther quha may dewlie exprefs ye louing of his eloquence? *Quhais errouris he confutit.* quhilk is dreft be fa grete, and be, I wate nocht quhat, force of reffonis, yat it may fchuit men forduart to ye confent yairof, quhome it may nocht † *Sua na-meit for oftenta-tioun of yare sci-ence, quben yai war maist vane, quha in yat parte now hes mony discipulis. In 5. Math.* aluterlie tyift: Of quhome yai ar almaift fa mony fentences as wordis, quhow mony fentences fa mony victoriis. This thing knawis the Marcionis, Apelles, Praxeæ, Harmogenes, Iowis, Gentilis and yai callit † Gnoftici, and ye reft, quhais blafphemeis he be mony and grete wolumis, as be certane fyireflachtis brak doun to nocht. And zit yis man alfo eftir al thir thingis, yis man, Tertullian I mein, litil grippand and ftikand to the catholik doctrine of the vniuerfal auld aunciant fayth, and mair eloquent yan happy, his iugement yaireftir changeit, did at lenthe, yat of him the bliffit confeffor Hilarius in a certane place wrytis. Be his errour follow-*Tertulliane apprenit ye dremis of Montanus.* ing, fays he, fra his louable and approuable wrytingis he plukit away ye auctoritie: and he alfo in ye kirk wes a grete tentatioun. Bot of him I wil fpeik na mair. This thing onlie wil I reherfe, that contrare ye command of Moyfes in yat he affirming the new furious madnes of ane Montanus fproutand vp in ye Kirk, and yai woud dremis of new doctrine of certane voud women to be trew Propheciis, he deferuit, yat of him and of his wrytingis it fuld be faid: *Gif a Prophete ryfe in ye middis of the,* And eftir: *Thou fal nocht heir the wordis of yat Prophete.* Quhy? *Becaufe,* fays he, *ye Lord zour God temptis zou, quhidder ze luue him, or nocht.*

## YE NOUATIONIS OF AL HÆRESEÍS.

*Quha is to be callit a Catholik. Of ye miserable state of ye wauering in fayth: and quhou in ye haly catholik Kirk only is suir rest of conscience. Cap. XXV.*

BE thir heirfor sa mony, and sa grete, and wtheris siklyk mony wechty ecclesiastical exemplis, we suld euidentlie persaue, and according to ye law writtin in Deuteronomie mair cleirlie yan ye lycht vnderstand: yat gif ony tyme ony techear in ye kirk, sal wauer and aberre fra ye fayth, yat ye prouidence of God sufferis yis to be to ye temptatioun of ws, quhidder we luue oure God or nocht, in al oure hart, and in al oure saul. Quhilkis thingis sen yai ar sa, he is a trew and a weray Catholik, quha luuis ye trewth of God, ye Kirk of God, and ye bodie of Christ. Quha præferris na thing to ye religioun of God, nor to ye catholik fayth: nocht præferring ye auctoritie of ony ane man, nocht ye luue, nocht ye ingyne, nocht ye eloquence, nocht ye philosophie: bot dispyseand al thir thingis, and perseuerand firme and constant in fayth, quhateuir thing he sal knaw ye catholik Kirk vniuersalie, to hef haldin of auld, yat thing onlie decretis he to be haldin, and to be beleuit be him. Bot quhatsumeuir thing yaireftir be ony ane man, by al, and contrare al haly men to be brocht in of new, and nocht hard asoir: yat thing lat him vndirstand to pertene nocht to religioun, bot rather to tentatioun, and yat specialie that he is instructit be ye mynd and sayngis of Sanct Paul, for yis is it, quhilk he wrytis in ye first to ye Corynthianis: It behuifis (says he) hæresiis tobe, yat quha ar prouin mot be manifest amang zow. As he wald say, for yis cause, ye auctouris of hæresie ar nocht haistelie be God ruitit out, yat ye prouin mot be maid manifest: yat is yat euery man mot appere quhow grippand, faythful, and constant luuear he be of ye catholik fayth. And in deid quhen euery noueltie springis out, fra hand is persauit ye wecht of ye corne, and lychtnes of ye caf: than without gret difficultie is it blawin out of ye barn fluir, quhilk without wecht wes haldin within ye samyn. For sum ar quhilkis fra hand aluterlie blawis away: bot wyeris aluterlie schakin out bayth seriss to pereis, and thinkis schame to returne, woundit, half deid, and half leuing: as yai quha hes drunkin sik quantitie of wyne, quhilk noyir hes micht to flay, nor zit may be digestit: nothir causis to de,

*margin notes:* Quhy permittis God errouris and hæreseis to spring vp. — Lat ye erroneous yis day, lay to thair doctrine to this lyne, and reul. — The corne, ye caf. — The half slane anis: nothir hait nor cauld. — A similitude.

nor fufferis to leue. O miferable ftate! O with quhou grete violence and feruour of cairis, and with quhou grete troublous blaftis ar yai cacheit and careit! For now quhat way ye wind blawis, be fuddane erroure ar yai reueift: now returnit to yame felfis, as certane contrarious wallis ar doung abak: now be fuleche præfumptioun yai thingis alfo quhilkis apperis incertane, yai appreue: now be an vnreffonable dredoure alfo yai thingis quhilkis ar fuir, yai feir: incertane quhat way yai fuld pas, or quhat way fuld return: quhat they fuld couet, or quhat fuld efchew: quhat yai fuld hald, or quhat yai fuld lat flip. Quhilk afflictioun trewlie, of thair doutfum and euil hung hart is a medicine of Godis rewth towart yame, gif yai war wyife. For heirfor without ye maift fuir heuinning place of ye catholik fayth, be findry tempeftuous ftormis of thochtis and cuiris ar yai fchaiking, ftruking, and almaift flane, yat yai mot lat doun ye failis of thair proud confait, fchaikin out to heicht, quhilkis vickitlie thai had dilatit to ye windis of noueltie: and mot reduce and hald yame felfis within ye maift fuir raid, and harbery of yare haly mother ye Kirk, and womet out agane fra ye ground yai bittir and tribulous feis of errouris, yat eftir yai micht drink ye fluidis of ye quick fpringand wattir. Lat yame forzet weil, yat yai haif lerit nocht weil: and of al ye doctrine of ye kirk, quhilk be vndirftanding may be tane, lat yame tak: quhilk may nocht, lat yame beleue.

*Aganis ye inconftant and curious new forgearis of fectis and errouris.*
*Cap. XXVI.*

QVHILKIS thingis fen fa ar, I gretumlie reuoluand and panceand ye famin thingis with me felf, may nocht merwel aneuch of fa gret wodnes of fum men, at fa gret impietie of yair blindit mynd, and fchortlie at fa gret luft to erre and wauer, yat yai nocht content of ye rewl of beleif anis of ye auld techit and refauit, bot feikis noueltie fra day to day, and euir ar defyrous to eik fum thing to religioun, to change, or to pluk fra it. As it war nocht ye heuinlie doctrine, yat fufficeis anis tobe reuelit, bot manlie doctrine, quhilk may nocht bot be daylie mending, zea rather be repreuing be perfitit. Sen Godis word cryis, Pafs nocht ouer yai boundis (proptis, or marcheis) quhilkis thy fatheris hes putt. and: Aboue ye Iuge, iuge

yow nocht. and: The ferpent fal byte him quha cuttis ye haige. And **Eccle. 9.**
yat alfo of ye Apoftil, be ye quhilk al ye vickit noueltéis of al hærefiis, as **Eccle. 10.**
be a fpiritual fuord, hes oftymes bene ftowit away, and oftymes ar tobe
ftowit. O Timothe, faue that thing, quhilk is geuin ye to keip: efchew- **1. Tim. 6.**
and ye prophane noueltéis of woceis, and ye contradictioun of fcience
falflie fa callit: quhilk fcience quhen fum men promifis, thai hef errit, as
concernyng fayth. And eftir yir thingis ar yai ony found fa indurat, fa **A grete**
inueterat, and of fa fchamelis a forret, of fik obftinat vnfchamefulnes, of fa **ye trewth**
ftanerie ftubburnes, quha fuld nocht fubmit yame felfis to fa gret plentu- **tour.**
oufnes of thir heuinlie wordis? To fa gret force and wecht fuld nocht
bow? be fa ftrang mellis and hemmeris quha fuld nocht be betit doun?
with fa gret fyreflachtis breuelie fuld nocht be dung to ye ground? Efchew fays he, the prophane noueltéis of woceis. He fayd nocht ye anti-
quiteis, he fayd nocht the thingis haldin of bald: zea, rather planelie quhat
contrarie mot follow, he furthfchew. For gif noweltie is to be efchewit,
antiquitie is to be haldin: and gif noweltie is prophane and vngodlie, antiquitie is haly and fanctifiit. And oppofitionis, fays he, (or obiectionis) **Of ye fals**
of fcience falflie fa nameit. Treulie the name is falfs in the doctrine of **of science**
hæretikis, that ignorance be ye name of fcience, mift be ye name of brycht **hæretikis.**
and fair wedder, mirknes be ye name of lycht mot be colorit and clokit.
Quhilk fum men (fays he) quhen yai promifeit, yai errit, as concernyng
faythe. Quhat thing promifeit yai quhen yai errit? bot ane new and, I
wait nocht quhat, vnknawin leirnyng. For yow may heir fum of yame
felfis fay: Cum ze, O ignorantis and miferable, quhilkis ar commonlie **The proud**
callit catholikis, and leir ye trew faythe, quhilk except ws, nane vnder- **hæretikis**
ftandis, quhilk mony lyftymes of men afoir hes lyin hid: bot it is laitlie **thing.**
reuelit and furthfchawin: Bot leir it thiftuoulie and fecreitlie, for it fal
delyte zow. And fiklyke quhen ze hef lerit it, teche it in hidlingis, lefte **Sa began**
ye warld heir, left ye kirk knaw. For it is geuin to few men to vnder- **gatis.**
ftand ye fecrete of fa grete a myfterie. Ar nocht yir ye wordis of yat
huir, quhilk in ye prouerbis of Salomon callis til hir men by ye way, quhen
yai had ye gait. Quha is (fays fche) ye maift fulefche amangis zow, lat **Prouerb. 9.**
him cum by ye way to me. Bot fcho callis ye puir of witt, fayng: Tak
to zow glaidlie ye hid breidis, and drink in hidlingis ye fueit watter.

Quhat followis? Bot he wate nocht, fays he, quhow erthlie creaturis
paffis in hir cumpanie. Quha ar ye erthlie creaturis? Lat ye Apoftil declare it. Quha hes errit, fays he, as concernyng fayth.

*The wechty command of ye Apoftil:* Depofitum cuftodi. *yat is: Saue
ye thing geuin ye to keip, is difcuffit. Cap. XXVII.*

Bot it makis mekle to ye porpofe, to treit mair diligentlie, ye hail fentence felf of the Apoftil. O Timothe, fays he, faue yat, quhilk is geuin
O. ye to keip: efchewand ye prophane nouelteis of woices. O, yis exclamatioun is bayth of knawlege of thingis to cum, alyke and of cheritie. For
he faw afoir ye errouris to cum, for ye quhilkis he alfo afoir wes forie.
Timothe Quha is Timothe this day? Bot other generalie ye vniuerfal Kirk, or
fpecialie ye hail cumpanie of Prælatis: quha awcht at ye leift to haif ye˙
hail knawlege of Godis religioun yame felfis, or to teche it to wtheris?
Saue, &c. Quhat is, Saue yat thing quhilk is geuin ye to keip? Saue, fays he, for
theuis, for inimeis, yat quhen men flepis, yai faw nocht fetcheis vpon that
Matth. 13. guid feid of the quheit, quhilk the fone of man hes fawin in his croft.
Saue yat thing quhilk is geuin ye to keip. Quhat is ye thing, yat is geuin
ye to keip? That is, quhilk is committit to ye, nocht yat quhilk is inuentit be ye: quhilk yow hes refauit, nocht that quhilk thow hes imaginat: a mater nocht of ingyne, bot of techement: nocht of priuat vfurpyng,
bot of publict traditioun: a mater brocht to the, nocht pronunceit be
the: in quhilk thow fuld nocht be an actour (inuentour or forgear) bot a
keipar: nocht a lawmakar, bot a lawkeipar, nocht a gyde, bot a followar,
Saue, fays he, yat quhilk is geuin to ye, faif ye talent of ye catholik fayth
vnbrokin and incorrupt. Quhat wes committit to ye, lat yat remane in
thy poifs, lat yat be randerit agane be ye. Thow hes refauit gold, rander
agane gold: I wil nocht yat yow in ye place of ane thing, flip in ane
other: I wil nocht yat yow othir for gold fchameleflie put doun leid, or
diffaitfullie brafe: I wil nocht haif ye apperance, bot ye natuir planelie of
Note. gold. O Timothe, O yow Preift, O yow Techear, gif ye grace of God
hes maid ye apt and ganeand be ingyne, exercife, and leirnyng: be yow a
Befeleel
wes enduit Befeleel of the fpiritual tabernacle, graif owt ye precious ftanis of godlie

doctrine, faythfullie set yame, wyslie trim yame, eik to yame licht, brycht- *be ye spirit of wisdum and science, to dres al thingis to ye ornament of ye tabernacle. Exod. 36.*
nes, beutifulnes and plesance. Lat it be vnderstand be thy expositioun,
mair cleirlie, quhilk afoir was beleuit obscuirlie : lat ye eftircumeris reiose
yat yai vnderstand be ye, quhilk the antiquitie afoir had in reuerence,
quhen yai vnderstude it nocht. Zit teche sa the samyn thing, quhilk thow
hes lerit, that quhen thow speikis newlie, yat yow speik na new thingis. *Neulie, bot na neu thingis, to be techit.*

*That it is proffetable to incress in religioun and knawlege yairof, bot aluterlie vnlesum to alter or change ony thing yairin. Cap. XXVIII.*

Bot perchanse sum man wil inqueir : Suld yair be heirfor in ye kirk of *O quhou godly and cunninglie.*
Christ na incress of religioun ? zis lat incress be hald, and yat weray grete.
For quha is he sa inwyous to man, sa odious to God, quha wald preifs to
stay yat thing ? Bot zit sa, yat ye incress trewlie may be of fayth, and *The incres of religioun.*
na change yairof : sen to incress pertenis onlie, yat euerie thing bydand
in ye self mot be amplifiit : bot it is proper to changeing, yat ane thing *Changeing.*
mot be transferrit and turnit in ane wther. It is expedient heirfor yat
knawlege, science, and wisdome gretumlie and mekle mot grow and incress, als weil of euerie man, as of al : als weil of ane man, as of ye hail
kirk : and yat in al greis of aigis and tymes : bot zit onlie in the awin
kynd, to wit, in ye awin doctrine, in ye awin vnderstanding, and in ye
awin sense. Lat ye religioun of saulis follow ye natuir and maner of ye *A similitude of ye incres of bodyis and of religioun.*
bodyis, quhilkis albeit be proces of zeris turnis ouer, reknis, and fwrth-
schawis yair number and compt, zit thai remane stil ye samin thing, yat
thai war. Thair is a gret difference betuix ye floure of barneage and ye
maturitie and rypnes of ye eild. Bot zit ye samyn ar auld men, quha afoir
wes childer : yat albeit ye state and forme of ye ane and ye samyn man
be changeit : zit nochtyeless ane and ye samyn natuir, ane and ye samyn
persoun remanis. Litle ar ye membris of infantis, grete of ye zoung men :
zit ya ar ye samyn self membris. Quhou mony iuncturis and membris ar
yai of barneis, sa mony ar yai of men : and quhat euery thingis yai ar,
quhilkis be proces of ye rypear aige ar generit, yai war yan sawin in ye
strenthe of ye seid : yat na thing yairefter wes produceit in ye auld men,
quhilk yan lay nocht hid afoir in ye barneis. Quhair by thair is na dout

bot yis is ye lauchful and rycht reul of increſs, bot yis is ye fuir and maiſt gay ordoure of grouing, gif the partes of the aige weiwe out yai membris, fchape, and forme in ye mair of aige, quhilkis ye wifdum of the makar of al, had formit afore in ye zoung anis. For gif manis fchape, be eftir turnit in ony forme nocht of his awin kynd, or always ony thing be eikit to ye numbir of ye membris, or ocht tane fra ye famin : force it is yat oyer ye hail body decay and perife, or be monftruous, or at ye leiſt be waikit. Sa it is alfo decent, yat ye doctrine of ye Chriftiane religioun mot follou yir lawis of increfs and grouing, to wit, yat be zeris it mot be ftrenthit, be tyme dilatit, and be aige vpheit : nochtyeles yat it perfeueir incorrupt and vndefylit, and in ye hail mefoure of ye partis yairof, and in al ye membris and al fenfis mot be ful and perfyte, quhilk by yat mot admit na interchange, na damnage of ye proprietie, nor refauing na vthir definitioun yan afoire. As for exemple, oure eldaris of auld hes fawin in yis feid tyme of ye Kirk, the feid of fayth, as of clene quheit, is weray iniuſt and vngan- and, yat we yair eftircumaris for ye felf veritie of ye quheit mot cheis ye errour of fitches, and put in ye place of ye wther. Quhy rather is nocht yis rycht and followis bettir, yat ye first and laſt procedingis difaggre nocht amang yame felfis, yat of ye increfs of ye firſt inſtitutioun, as it war of fawing of guid quheit, we mot alfo fcheir the fruit of ye doctrine of quheit : yat quhen ony thing of ye natiue begynning of yai feidis, be proces of tyme be alterit in forme, and fumtyme be plefing, rank, and grow to maturitie : zit nochtyeles na thing be changeit of ye propirtie of ye firſt feid. albeit ye fchap, zea, forme and difference be eikit : zit ye famyn natuir of euery kynd fuld perfeueir. For God forbid, yat ye rofe plantis of ye catholik fenfe, be turnit in thirfillis and thornis. God forbid, I fay, yat in yis fpiritual paradife, of ye graiwis of cannal and balme, fra hand fpring wp guild and humlokis. Quhat ewir heirfor in this Kirk, be ye hufbandrie of God, and be ye fayth of the fatheris is plantit : it becumis, yat yis famin thing be ye diligence of ye fones be laborit, nuriſt and kepit : lat yis famin thing flureis and wax rype : lat this famin thing proceid, and be perfytit. For it is lefum yat ye auld doctrine of ye heuinlie philofophie be proces of tyme be labourit, trimmit, and polifit : bot aluterlie vn- lefum yat it be changeit, aluterlie vnlefum that it be mankit, or maid mu-

## YE NOUATIONIS OF AL HÆRESEIS. 167

tilat. Lat it refaue plainnes, lycht, and diftinctioun: bot, yat it retene fullines, integritie, and ye propir fenfe, it is aluterlie neceffare. For gif anis falbe admittit yis licence of diabolical diffait, I wg to talk it, quhou gret perel fal follou, to cut away and abolifhe ye hail religioun. For ony part of ye catholik doctrine being refufit, and fchot away: wtheris thingis alfo, and wtheris agane ficlyk, and thaireftir wtheris and wtheris, yan as of a confuetude, and as of a lefum maner falbe fchote away. Bot ferther ye partis being feueralie refufit, quhat wther thing fal follou at lenthe, bot yat ye hail mater to gidder be refufit? Bot alfo contrarie, gif we fal begin to mixt noueltie with antiquitie, vncouth and ftrange thingis with domeftical materis, and prophaniteis with thay thingis, quhilkis ar haly: force it is, yat yis maner fprig vp vniuerfalie, yat na thing eftir this in ye kirk may be left vntwecheit, na thing vndefylit, na thing hail, na thing vnfpotit, bot yat heireftir be thare a bordal of abominable and filthy errouris, quhair afoir wes an haly temple of ye chaft and vndefylit veritie. Bot ye pietie of God mot turn away yis horrible cryme fra ye myndis of his peple, and grant yat yis be rather ye madnes of ye wickit and of ye reprobat. Bot ye kirk of Chrifte a diligent and a war keipar of yat doctrine to it deliuerit, in it neuir changeis ony thing, na thing diminufis, na thing eikis: it cuttis nocht away ye thingis neceffare, eikis to na fuperfluitie, it tynis nocht ye awin, nor vfurpis na wther manis: bot with al diligence labouris yis ane thing, yat faythfullie and wyiflie treting ye auld, gif ony thingis be techit of auld and begun, yat it mot fet out and polife ye famin: gif ony thing be expres and outfett, yat it mot ftrenth and confirme ye famin: gif ony thing be confirmit and determinat, yat it mot kepe ye famin. And fchortlie quhat wthir thing euir intendit ye kirk be ye decreis of counfelis, bot yat thing quhilk afoir wes fimple and planelie beleuit, to be eftir beleuit mair diligentlie: yat afore wes precheit flawlie, ye famin thing eftir to be precheit mair feruentlie: yat afore wes baldin in litil reuerence, ye felf thing eftir to be baldin in mair reuerence. This thing, I fay, ye catholik kirk fterit be ye nouatioun of inuentionis of hæretikis, perfytit euir be ye decreis of counfelis, and na thing ellis: bot yat quhilk fche had refauit fra hir forefatheris be traditioun only, eftir ye famin thing to hir pofteritie alfo, fche mot confirme and mak fuir be hir hand-

*A notable sentence.*

*Zit stay, O ze deformearis of ye catholik kirk.*

*A bordal of filthy errouris.*

*Ye diligence and deuitie of Godis kirk.*

*Quhat decretit euir ye counfelis.*

writ: comprehending a gret fumme of materis in fchort writtingis, and fumtymes for ye lycht of vnderftanding, be ye proprietie of a new name makand na new fenfe of fayth.

1. Tim. 6.

*He returnis to ye wordis of ye Apoftil afore difcuffit: exhorting to perfeuere in yat doctrine of religioun anis be al Chriftianis refauit. Cap. XXIX.*

Bot lat ws return to ye Apoftil. O Timothe, fays he, faue yat thing geuin ye in keiping, efchewand ye prophane nouelteis of woices. Efchew, fays he, as fra a viper, as fra a fcorpioun, as fra a cokintrace, lefte yai flay ye nocht onlie be tueching, bot alfo be yair ficht and venemo$^9$ aind. quhat is to efchew? with fiklyk men nocht to refaue mete. Quhat is it, efchew thow? Gif ony man cumis to zow, fays he, and bringis nocht this doctrine. Quhat doctrine, bot ye catholik, ye vniuerfal doctrine, ye ane and ye famin doctrine, quhilk be incorrupt traditioun of ye trewth, perfeueris be al fucceffioun of aiges, and quhilk fal but end perfeuer in al aiges to cum? Quhat mair? refaue him nocht in zoure hous, nor bid him nocht guid day: for quha biddis him guid day, communicatis with his wickit werkis. Efchew, fays he, ye prophane nouelteis of woices. quhat is prophane? quhilk hes na halines, na godlines, ftrange and plane outlay fra ye inwart chalmer of ye kirk, quhilk is ye temple of God. Prophane nouelteis of woices (fays he) of woices, yat is of nouelteis of doctrine, of materis, of fentences, quhilkis to anciantie, quhilkis to antiquitie ar contrarious. Quhilkis gif yai be refauit, force it is, yat ye fayth of ye bliffit fatheris, other in ye hail, or in a grete parte be corruptit: force it is, yat al ye faythful of al aiges, al ye fanctis, al ye chaft, ye continent, ye Virginis, al Clerkis, Diacones, and Preiftis, fa mony thowfand Confeffouris, fa grete oiftis of Martyres, fa grete anciant multitude of Tounis and Peple, fa mony Ilis, Prouincis, Kingis, Clannis, Realmis, Nationis, and finalie almaift ye hail cumpafe of ye erth be ye catholik fayth now incorporat to Chrift thair heid, mot be pronunceit be fa grete proces of aiges to hef bene ignorant, to hef errit, to hef bene blafphemous, to hef mifknawin, quhat yai fuld hef beleuit.

Efchew.
1. Cor. 5.

2. Ioan. 1.

Prophane nouelteis,

Of woices.

A doctrine tobe faft lockit this day in the breift of a Christiane.

Recant, recant, O ze blafphemous and maist curfit Caluiniftis. For be zour doctrine, this is force to be said.

*That neuir wes hæresie inuentit bot only be him, quha separatit him self,
fra ye vniuersal consent of Godis kirk: and certane exemples yairof. Cap. XXX.*

Eschew, says he, ye prophane noueltie of woices: quhilkis to resaue and
follow, wes neuir ye custome of catholikis, bot of hæretikis. And trewlie
quhat hæresie euir hes bullerit out, bot onder a certane name, a certane
place, or a certane tyme? Quha euir set out hæreseis, bot he, quha first
separat and disiunit him self, fra ye consent of ye vniuersalitie and antiquitie of ye catholik kirk? Quhilk thing sa to be, exemplis makis mair
cleir yan ye lycht. For quha euir asoir yat wickit man Pelagius præsumit <small>Pelagius.</small>
sa grete pouer of ye fre vil of man, yat to help it in al guid materis, in <small>Ye Caluinianis fleis to ye contrar errour of ye Ma-</small>
euery doing, thocht nocht ye grace of God necessare? Quha euir asoir his
monstruous disciple Cæleftius denyit al mankynd to be bund with ye sin of <small>nicheis, denying ye frewil of man.</small>
ye transgressioun of Adam? Quha durst asoir blasphemous Arrius diuide
ye vnitie of ye trinitie? or asoir cursit Sabellius confound ye trinitie of ye <small>Cælestius. Arrius. Sabellius. Nouatian⁹</small>
vnitie in Godheid. Quha asoir ye maist cruel Nouatianus affirmit God to
be cruel, insamekle yat he had leuir ye dethe of ye deand sinnar, yan yat
he suld returne, and leue. Quha asoir Simon ye weche, quha wes strukin <small>O Scotland mair than xiij. C. lx. zeris a chast virgine to Christe, suld you be nou a strompet to this blasphemous harlot Simon? or to ony sik a knaue?</small>
be ye Apostolis cursing, of quhome yat auld swellie of filthines be conti-
nual and secret successioun, sprang euin to ye last of yat sect Priscilliane,
durst cal God ye creator of al, to be ye auctour and wirkar of euillis: yat
is, of our sinnis, vngodlines and crymes? As quhome he allegis to hef
maid with his handis ye natuir of men of sik sort, quha be yair awin propir
motioun, and be impulsioun of a certane wil led be necessitie may do na
wther thing, may wil na wthir thing, bot sin: be ressoun yat yis wil cariit
about, and inflammit with a certane furious raige of al wices, in al ye botumles potis of filthines, be an insatiable concupiscence violentlie is drewin.
Thai ar intellable wtheris thingis, quhilkis for schortnes cause, we pas
ouer: be quhilkis al, it is euidentlie and cleirlie schawin, this thing almaist <small>Heretikis ar euir desyrous of noueltels, and fascheit of antiquitie: and the catholikis contrarie.</small>
amang al hæreseis, tobe as a maist praisit and a lauchful thing, yat euir yai
reiose in prophane noueltels, irkeis of ye determinationis of antiquitie, and
be ye oppositioun of a fals name of science, passis as schipbrokin fra ye
sayth. Bot contrarie yis is ye propirtie of ye catholikis, to saue yai thingis

z

## YE NOUATIONIS OF AL HÆRESEIS.

Quhat is the germountis of ye fcheip, bot ye fayngis of ye Prophetis and Apoftolis, quhilkis yai as in fyncere integritie of ye fcheip hes wowein, and maid as certane fleifis of wow, to yat immaculat lambis behalf, quha takis away ye finnis of warld. Quha ar ye rauenous woulfis, bot ye wyild and fauage vnderftanding of hæretikis: quha euir inuadis and trublis ye faldis of Godis kirk, and ryues in fchundir the flok of Chrifte in al yat yai may. Bot yat yai mot fteil mair fraudfullie vpon ye vnwar fcheip, quhylis thai keip the crueltie of the voulfis, yai lay of ye voulfis fchape: and faldis yame about, as it war with certane fleifis of ye woul: yat quhen ony man firft felis ye foftnes of ye wowl, naway fuld feir ye venemous fcharpenes of yair tethe. Bot quhat fays oure Saluioure? Of thair fruitis fall ze knaw yame: yat is, quhen yai begin nocht onelie to crak and brag of ya wordis, bot alfo to interprete yame: yan yat fournes, yan yat bittirnes, yan yat furie is vnderftandit, yan the new wenum ftewis out, yan ye prophane nouelteis ar oppinit: yan firft yow may fe ye haige cuttit, yan ye boundrodis of oure elderis tranflatit and changeit, yan ye catholick fayth to be cuttit and diuydit, yan ye doctrine of the kirk to be reuin. Of yis fort war ya men, quhome ye Apoftil Paul in ye fecund to ye Corinthianis twechis, fayand: For thir kynd of fals prophetis, fays he, ar diffaitful werkaris, transfiguring yame felfis in the Apoftolis of Chrifte. The Apoftolis produceit exemplis of Godis law, and ye wtheris produceit yame alfo: The Apoftolis produceit ye authoritie of ye Pfalmes, and ye wtheris produceit yat ilk: ye Apoftolis produceit ye fentenceis of ye Prophetis, and ye wtheris nochtyeles produceit yame. Bot quhen yai begane nocht to interprete alyke manere, quhilk yai alyke manere produceit: yan ye fimple fra ye diffaitful, yan ye feinzet fra ye vnfeinzet, yan ye richteous fra ye peruerft, yan finalie ye trew Apoftolis fra ye fals Apoftolis war difcernit. And na meruel, fays he: for Sathan him felf transfiguris him in ye Angel of licht: it is nocht heirfor a grete mater gif his minifteris ar transfigurate, as ye minifteris of rychtuoufnes. Heirfor eftir ye doctrine of ye Apoftil S. Paul, quhowoft foeuir fals Apoftolis, or fals Prophetis, or fals Techearis produceis the fentenceis of Godis law, be ye euil vnderftanding of ye quhilkis yai preifs to confirme yair errouris, it is na dout bot yai follow ye fubtel inuentionis of yair maifter: quhilk thingis he neuir but dout

*margin notes:* Ye scheipis garmont. — The rauenous woulfis. — Sawaris of difcorde. — Thare craft. — The fruitis of the hæretikis. — 2. Cor. 11. — Note. — To transfigure yame in the Apoftolis of Chrifte, quhat it is.

Ye radiast way to dissaue.

wald hef inuentit, except yat he had knawin aluterlie na radiar way til diffait, yan quhair ye fraude of a curfeit erroure is quietlie brocht in, yat yair ye auctoritie of Godis word mot be allegeit.

*Quhow Sathan temptit our Saluiour : and of ya wordis of Sathan to him :* Wap thy felf doun: *and quhow yat fentence is oft inculcate in our eris be ye minifteris of Sathan, yat is, hæretikis : and of that fentence :* Thow fal nocht offend thy fute at a ftane. *Cap. XXXII.*

Bot fum men wil fay : Quhairby is it prouin yat ye deuil accuftomis to vfe ye exemplis of Godis law ? Lat yat man reid ye Euangel quhairin it is writtin : Than ye deuil tuke him, yat is, ye Lorde oure Saluioure, and fet him aboue ye prik of ye temple, and faid to him : Gif yow be ye fone of God, wap yi felf doun : for it is writtin, yat God hes geuin his angelis charge ouer the, that thai mot keip ye in al thy ways. Thai fal lift ye wp in thair handis, yat perchance yow offend nocht thy fute at a ftane. Quhat fal he do to fillie miferable men, quha affaltit be teftimonie of fcriptuir ye Lord felf of maieftie? Gif yow be, fays he, ye fone of God, wap thi felf

Quhat is it to wap thi self doun. Obserue.

doun. Quhy ? For it is writtin, fays he. The doctrine of yis place is gretumlie to be markit and haldin in memorie : yat be fa grete exemple of ye Euangelical authoritie, quhen we fal fe ony men produce ye wordis of ye Apoftolis or Prophetis, contrare ye catholik fayth, yat we fuld naways dout bot ye deuil fpeikis be yame. For as ye heid fpak yan to ye heid, fua now alfo ye membris fpeikis to ye membris : the membris to wit of the deuil fpeikis to the membris of Chrifte, apoftatis and remigatis to ye faythful, ye wickit to ye godlie, ye hæretikis breuelie to ye catholikis. Bot quhat, I pray zow, fays he? Gif yow be, fays he, ye fone of God, wap thi felf doun. That is, gif yow wil be yè fone of God, and refaue ye hæretage of ye heuinlie kingdome, wap yi felf doun : yat is, put doun thi felf fra ye doctrine and traditioun of yis heich kirk, quhilk is eftemit to be alfo ye temple of God. And gif ony wald demand ony of ye hæretikis, quha perfuadit him fik thingis : Quhairby preuis yow, quhairby techis yow, yat I fould leue ye vniuerfal and anciant fayth of ye catholik kirk ? Fra hand fal he anfueir : For it is writtin. and but delay dreffis he a thow-

## YE NOUATIONIS OF AL HÆRESEIS. 173

fand teftimoniis, a thowfand exemplis, a thowfand authoriteis out of ye Pfalmes, out of ye Apoftolis, out of ye Prophetis, be ye quhilkis interpretit of a new and wickit manere, ye miferable faul fra ye toure of ye catholik religioun, mot be wappit heidlingis in ye pot of hærefeis. Bot yan with yai promiffis quhilkis followis, ye hæretikis accuftomis to diffaue ye vnwar and incircumfpect men, on a meruolous manere. For yai dar promife, and teche, yat a grete, fpecial, and planelie a fingular grace of God is in ye conuenticle of thair congregatioun and communioun: infafer yat without ony laboure, without ony diligence, ze albeit yai feik it nocht, afk it nocht, nor zit knok yairfor, quha euir pertenis to yair flok, zit fua yai ar ordanit frome aboue as cariit vp be ye handis of Angelis, yat is, faifit be Angelical protectioun, yat yai neuir may offend yair fute at a ftane, yat is, neuir may be fclanderit. *Fra ye catholik caftel to be wappit in ye botumles pit of hæreseis. Note. To offend thy fute at a stane.*

*Gif ye deuil or his membris ye hæretikis allegeis ye fcriptuir in a wrang fenfe, to tempt a Catholik to erroure, quhat fuld be done. Cap. XXXIII.*

Bot fum man wil fay, gif ye deuil and his difcipulis fa vfeis ye fpeche, ye fentenceis, and promifis of God, of ye quhilkis fum ar fals Apoftolis, fals Prophetis, fals Doctouris, and al fullelie hæretikis: quhat fal ye catholik men and fones of ye Kirk of God do? Be quhat maneir fal yai difcerne in ye haly fcriptuiris the veritie fra falfet? This thing planelie fal yai maift diligentlie laboure to do, yat in ye begynning of yis Memorial we hef writtin haly and cunnyng men to hef techit, yat yai interprete ye diuine canoun of ye fcriptuir, according to ye traditioun and techement of the vniuerfal Kirk, and according to the reulis of ye catholik doctrine: in ye quhilk fiklyk neid is yat yai follow ye vniuerfalitie, antiquitie, and confent of ye catholik and Apoftolik Kirk. And gif ony tyme ane part fal rebel contrare ye vniuerfalitie, and noueltie contrare antiquitie, or ye diffenfioun of ane or few erroneous contrair ye confent of al, or at ye leift of fer may catholikis: lat yame præfer ye integritie of ye vniuerfalitie to ye corruptioun of a part: and in ye famin vniuerfalitie lat yame præfer ye religioun of ye antiquitie to ye prophanatioun of noueltie: and fiklyke in *In thir .ij. heidis following besyds ye rest, is a godly and cunning declaratioun of the first of our lxxxiij. quæstionis proponit to ye Caluinianis. A trim oppositioun.*

ye antiquitie felf, lat yame fet firft afoir ye general decreis of ye vniuerfal counfel gif ony beis, to ye temeritie and fuilhardynes of ane, or of a few numbir. Than eftir gif yat be to litil, lat yame follow yat is narreft ye myndis and iudgement in ane confent of ye monyaft and greteaft Doctouris, quhilk thingis be ye help of God, faythfullie, fobirlie, and cairfullie being obferuit, we fal but grete difficultie, confider al the venemous errouris of wpftarting hæretikis.

*Quhou be vniforme confent and mynd of ye Doctouris and anciant Fatheris in ye Kirk new hærefeis may be knawin, and condemnit. Cap. XXXIIII.*

HEIR now I fe it conuenient confequentlie to mak plane, be quhat manere ye prophane nouelteis of hæretikis, be ye fentenceis and myndis togidder aggreing, of ye auld Doctouris produceit and conferrit, may be knawin and condemnit. Quhilk auld confent zit of ye haly fatheris, nocht in al quæftionis of ye law of God, bot onelie, or at ye leift principalie, in ye reul of faith with grete diligence be ws is bayth for to be ferceit, and followit. Bot noyer in al tymes, nor zit al hærefeis ar on yis manere to be impugnit, bot ye new and ye lait onelie: yat is quhowfone yai fprout vp, afoir yai begin to falfifie ye reulis of the anciant fayth, fuddanlie in that mein tyme lat yame be ftayit, and afore with yair vennum mair largelie brefting out, yai mak yame to corrupt ye buikis of our eldaris. Bot ye hærefeis fpraid alrady abreid, inueterate and auld, naway on yis maneir ar to be affaltit: becaufe be lang proces of tyme, lang occafioun to yame to fteil ye veretie hes bein patent. And yairfor it becumis on naways to conuict and fuppres ony of yai wyld awld prophanationis, othir of fchifme or hærefeis: except othir be onlie auctoritie of ye fcriptuiris, gif it beis expedient, or at ye leift to efchew yame as of auld be general counfelis of catholik Preiftis alrady conuict and condemnit.. And heirfor quhowfonefoeuir ye rottin ftink of a wickit erroure quhatfumeuir fal begin to breft out, and to fteil ye wordis of Godis law to ye defence of it, and falflie and diffaitfullie to expone yame: fra hand ye fentenceis of oure eldaris ar to be gadderit to interpret yat canoun or reul, be ye quhilkis fentenceis yat

*[marginal notes:]* That ye confent of the anciant doctouris is fufficient to conuict al new hæreseis. Of auld hæreseis. Note.

quhatſumeuir noueltie, and thairthrow prophane ſal wpryiſs without al hæſitatioun or dout bayth lat it be maid patent, and without ony retractatioun be condemnit. Bot ye iudgement of yai fatheris ar onelie to be conferrit and collectit: quha in fayth and in ye communioun of catholikis halelie, vyſelie, conſtantlie, leuand, techeand, and perſeuerand oyer meritit to dee in Chriſte faythfullie, or for Chriſt to be ſlane happely. To quhome nochtwithſtanding it is tobe beleuit on yis conditioun, yat quhatſumeuir thing yai al, or moniaſt be ane and ye ſamin ſelf ſenſe and mynd, maniſeſtlie, frequentlie, and perſeuerantlie, as be a certane counſel of maiſteris and techearis aggreing amang yame ſelfis, hes be refauing, halding, and teching confirmit: lat yat thing be haldin for vndoutit, ſuir, and firme veritie. Bot quhat ſumeuir ony ane, albeit haly and cunnyng, albeit byſchope, albeit confeſſoure and martyr, ſal wnderſtand by al, or alſo contrare al: lat yat be ſett aſyde fra ye authoritie of ye commoun publict and general vnderſtanding, amang his awin hid and priuat opinionis: and lat ws nocht follow with extreme perel of æternall ſaluatioun, eftir ye curſit cuſtome of ſchiſmatikis and hæretikis ye erroure of ane man, ye veritie of ye catholik doctrine caſſin at oure helis. Of ye qubilkis bliſſit fatheris halie and catholik conſent, leſt ony man iuge perchanſe, yat he ſuld fulefchlie contemne, ye Apoſtil in ye firſt to ye Corynthianis ſays: Certane men ſuythlie God hes placeit in ye Kirk, firſt ye Apoſtoles, of quhome he wes ane: nixt ye Prophetis, of quhat ſorte we reid in ye Actis of ye Apoſtolis to hef bene Agabus: thridlie ye Doctouris, quha now ar callit expoſitouris, quhome yis ſamin Apoſtil alſo ſumtymes callis Prophetis, for yat cauſe, yat be yame ye myſteriis of ye Prophetis ar oppinnit to ye peple. Heirfor quha euir ſal contemne yir men ordanit frome aboue, be tymes and places in ye Kirk of God, vnderſtanding ony ane thing in ye ſenſe of ye catholik doctrine, contemnis nocht man, bot God: frome quhais trew vnitie yat na man ſuld diſſent nor diſſeuir, the ſamin Apoſtil maiſt erneſtlie requeiſtis, ſayand: Bot I beſeik zow brether yat ze al ſay ye ſamin ſelf thing, and yat yai be na ſchiſme amangis zou: bot yat ze be perfyte in ane mynde and in ane meanyng. Gif ony man diſſentis fra ye communioun and participatioun of thair mynde, he ſal heir yis of ye ſamin Apoſtil: He is nocht God of diſſentioun, bot of peace: yat is, nocht God

<small>Ye ſentence of quhat fatheris ſal we follow.

Obſerue yis goldin reul, of na man, except of a weray apoſtate tobe denyit.

Of yis priuat opinioun ſays Tertulliane: Ex perſonis probamus fidem an ex fide perſonas? and nocht of ye vniuerſal consent.

Note.

1. Cor. 12.

1. Cor. 1.

Ibidem. 14.</small>

of him, quha diffeueris fra ye vnitie of confent: bot of yame, quha ſal perſeuir in peace of confent. As I teche in al ye kirkis, fays he, of ye fanctis : yat is, of ye catholikis : quhilkis kirkis heirfor ar fanctifyit (or halie) becauſe yai perſeueir in communioun of faith. And lefte, ony man perchance lychtly and wtheris arrogantlie afcriue to him felf, yat he onlie ſuld be hard, and he onlie ſuld be beleuit: he fays a litle efter: Quhidder gif ye word of God procedit of zow onlie? or amangis zow onlie is it cum? And left yis fayngis ſuld be refauit as lychtlie fpokin, he eikit: Gif ony, fays he, is iugeit to be a Propheit, or a fpiritual man, yat is a Techear of fpiritual thingis, lat him be with al diligence a worfchepar of æqualitie and vnitie : to wit, yat he nother præfer his opinioun to wtheris, nor diffent fra ye vnderftanding of ye vniuerſal Kirk. The command of ye quhilk mater (fays he) quha myfknawis : yat is, quha other leris it nocht quhen he myfknawis, or contemnis it, quhen he knawis, he ſalbe myfknawin : yat is, he ſalbe iugeit vnworthy, yat he mycht be fene frome aboue amangis yame quha ar vnyit be fayth, and maid æqual be humilitie : yan ye quhilk euil, I wate nocht gif ony wthir may be eftemit mair pernicious. Quhilk thing according to ye manaffing of ye Apoftil, we fee to hef hapnit to Iuliane ye Pelagiane, quha other neglectit to incorporat him felf to ye vnderftanding of his collegis, or præfumit to feparat him thairfra. Bot now tyme is, yat we fet furth the exemple be ws promyfit: quhair and quhou ye myndis of ye halye fatheris war aggreit, that accordyng to thame be decrete and auctoritie of ye counfel, ye reul of faith in ye Kirk mot be maid ſtable. Quhilk thing that it may be mair commodiouflie done, latt heir be an end of this Memorial : that ye reft quhilkis followis, we maye tak of an other ground.

*Iuliane ye Pelagiane.*

*Heir endis ye firſt parte.*

## YE NOUATIONIS OF AL HÆRESEIS. 177

¶ *The fecund Memorial is loift, and na thing yairof mair vnperifit, bot a litle of ye laft parte, that is, a recapitulatioun onlie : quhilk heir alfo followis.*

QVHILKIS thingis fen fa ar, now tyme is yat we reduce yai materis quhilkis we hef fpokin in thir twa Memorialis in ye end of this fecund, to a breif fumme. We hef faid aboue that yis hes bene, and is alfo this day ye confuetude of ye catholikis, yat be yir twa wayis yai fuld appreue the trew fayth. Firft be auctoritie of ye diuine canoun of ye fcriptuir : fecundlie be ye traditioun of ye catholik kirk : nocht that ye canoun allane may nocht be fufficient to ye hail wair, bot becaufe mony interpretand ye wordis of God, euery man efter his confait, confauis findry opinionis and errouris : and yairfor it bebuifis yat ye vnderftanding of ye heuinlie fcripture mot be directit to only ane ecclefiaftical reul and meaning of ye Kirk, in yir quæftionis maift fpecialie, on ye quhilkis dependis ye fundament of ye catholik doctrine. Atouer we hef faid, yat agane in ye Kirk felf, it is neceffare yat ye confent of vniuerfalitie and of antiquitie, alyke be confiderit, lefte other fra ye integritie of vnioun, we be brokin in fum part of diuifioun, or out of ye religioun of antiquitie we be wappit heidlingis in ye noueltie of hærefeis. Sua we hef faid, yat in the antiquitie felf of ye Kirk twa certane thingis ar gretumlie and diligentlie to be obferuit, to ye quhilkis aluterlie yai fuld inhere, quha wald nocht be hæretikis. Firft gif ony thing of auld, be al the Preiftis of ye catholik Kirk, be ye auctoritie of a general Counfel be decretit : thairefter gif ony new quæftioun vpftartis, quhare yat may nocht be found, we mone hef recourfe to ye iugementis of ye haly fatheris : of yame onlie, of quhome euery ane in yair tymes and places, perfeuerand in ye vnitie of communioun and fayth, become tryit and louable maifteris. And quhateuir yai in ane fenfe and confent, mot be found to hef haldin, lat that be iugeit but al fcrupulofitie to be ye treuth and catholik iugement of ye kirk. Quhilk thing left we appere mair be our præfumptioun, yan be the auctoritie of ye Kirk to furthfet, we hef applyit an exemple of the haly Counfel, quhilk afoir yis almaift thre zeiris wes celebratit at Ephefus in Afia,

*The trew catholik fayth is twa wayis approuin.*

*Ane principal sense of ye scriptuir in materis concerning fayth.*

*Recourse to the general counsellis. Consent of the doctouris. Note for ye first of our .lxxxiij. questionis.*

*Quhen wes yis tractat writtin.*

2 A

<sup>*</sup> Be yis name war twa of the principal magistratis zerlie choi- sin in Rome callit.
<sup>*</sup> Sua callis he the bi- scopes.

quhen ye renounit men Baffus and Antiochus war <sup>*</sup> Confulis. Quhare quhen it was difputit of the reulis of fayth to be conftitutit, lefte perchanfe ony prophane noueltie mot crepe in yair, eftir ye maner of ye vnfaythful- nes of Ariminia, to al ye <sup>*</sup> Preiftis quha conuenit yair to ye number of twa hundreth almaift, yis thing apperit maift catholik, maift happy, and beft tobe done, yat ye iugementis and fentences of ye haly fatheris mot be produceit oppinlie, of ye quhilkis fuld be knawin fum Martyris, fum Confeffouris, bot al Catholik Preiftis to hef bene, and perfeuerit: yat is, yat ye religioun fetfurth of auld be ye confent and decrete of yame mot be deulie and folemlie confirmit, and the blafphemie of prophane noueltie con- demnit. Quhilk thing quhen fua wes done, be al fkil and reffoun ye wickit Neftorius wes iugeit tobe contrarious to the catholik antiquitie, bot bliffit Cyrillus to be aggreing to ye famin maift halie. And yat na thing fuld inlake to confirme ye treuth of ye mater, we fchew alfo ye names and ye number (albeit we flippit the ordour yairof) of yais fatheris, according to quhois ordour aggreing yare amangis yame felfis, and concording iugement and myndis, bayth ye wordis of Godis haly law wes exponit, and ye reul of godlie doctrine eftabiliffit. Quhilkis fatheris to reherfe heir alfo for ye ftrenthing of our memorie is naways fuperfluous. Thir heirfor ar yai men qubais writtingis as of iugeis, or as of witneffis in yat counfel wes red. Sanct Petir Bifchope of Alexandria an excellent doctour and maift bliffit Martyr: Sanct Athanafius Prælat of the famyn toun, a maift faythful Techear

Ye consent of quhat fa- theris wes produceit at Ephesus.

and maift renounit Confeffour: Sanct Theophilus Bifchope fiklyke of ye famyn toun, a man of fayth, lyfe, and knawlege honorable aneuch: to quhome fuccedit wirfchipful Cyrillus, quha at this præfent decoris ye Kirk of Alexandria. And lefte peraduentuir yat it mot hef bene iugeit, to hef bene ye doctrine of ane toun, or prouince: yair was adiunit alfo ye lichtis and lampis of Cappadocia S. Gregore Bifchope and Confeffour of Nazan- fum. Sanct Bafil Bifchope of Cæfarea in Cappadocia, and a Confeffour: and fiklyke ye wthir Sanct Gregore Bifchope of Nyce, be merit of fayth, conuerfatioun, integritie and wifdum, maift worthy of his brother Bafil ye Grete. Bot lefte Grece allone, or ye Orient onlie, and nocht the Weft and Latin parte alfo mot hef bene prouin euir fua to hef vnderftand: yair wes red yair lykeways fum epiftolis to certane men, of Sanct Fœlix ye

Martyr, and of Sanct Iulius Bifchopes of ye toun of Rome. And yat nocht onlie ye heid of ye world, bot alfo ye fydis mot beir witneffing to this iugement, maift blifit Cypriane ye Bifchope of Carthage, and Martyr wes adiunit fra ye fowth: fra the Northe, Sanct Ambrofe Bifchope of Millane. Thir ar heirfor al in ye haly number of that table of ten fum at Ephefus produceit as Maifteris Counfeleris, Witneffis and Iugeis. Quhois doctrine yat haly Conuentioun halding, quhois counfel following, quhais teftimonie beleuing, to quhois iugement obeyng without irking (or hatrent) præfumptioun, or fauour, pronunceit of ye reules of fayth. Albeit a fer gretear number of ye aunciant mycht hef bene to yame accumpaniit, bot yare wes na neid, for it wes nocht conuenient, that the tyme fuld hef bene occupiit with multitude of witneffis of ye mater: and na man doutit, bot yai ten hald na wther mynd nor iugement, yan the wtheris yair colleggis. Efter ye quhilkis al, we eikit alfo the bliffit fentence of Cyril, quhilk is contenit in ye procedingis felf of ye kirk. For quhen ye epiftil of Sanct Capreolus Bifchope of Carthage wes red, quha intendit and prayt na wyer thing, bot yat ye noueltie being ftrampit doun, antiquitie fuld be defendit, fua the Bifchope Cyril forefpak and definit: quhais fayngis to put in heir alfo amangis the reft, apperis nocht tobe impertinent. For he fays yis in ye end of yare procefs: And yis Epiftil quhilk is red, fays he, of ye venerable and weray Godlie Bifchope of Carthage Capreolus, mot be inferit for the treuth of thir thingis, quhais fentence is plane: for he defyris the doctryne of the anciant faith to be confirmit, bot the nouelteis, and al thingis inuentit fuperftitiouflie, and vngodlie fet furth, to be repellit, and condemnit. Al ye Bifchopes with loude woce affentit: Thir ar the wordis of ws al, we al fays the famyn, yis is ye feruent defyre of al. Quhat, I pray zow, wes the woceis and woteis of al, bot that ye thing quhilk wes techeit of auld fuld be haldin? and that quhilk wes neulie inuentit, fuld be explodit, and hyit away? Efter ye quhilkis we meruelit, and fchew quhow grete wes ye humilitie and halines of yat Counfel, and quhow mony Preiftis in number, almaift for ye maift parte \* Metropolitanes, of fa greit eruditioun, and of fa grete doctrine, yat neir al micht hef difputit of materis determinate in religioun. To quhome quhen ye conuentioun in ane mynd wes iugeit to geue a bauldnes, to take on yame,

*Seu ye Calunianis ap- preuis yis counsel of Ephesus: suld thai nocht admitt ws ye consent of yir samin fatheris in ye materis now in controuersie? quhilk gif ya syncerlie did, our pley war almaist endit.*

\* That is principal Bischopes of ye first principal Christiane tounis, cal-

*lit yan motheris of ye rest: as with ws nou ar Archebischopes.*

and to ftatute fum thing of yair deuyfe: zit na thing wald yai mak new, na thing wald yai præfume, na thing wald yai aluterlie afcriue in arrogance to yame felfis, bot always wald be war and efchew, that yai fuld deliuer na thing to yair pofteritie, quhilk yai had nocht refauit fra thair foirfatheris: and nocht onlie wald thai difpone the mater weil for the præfent tyme: bot alfo wald geue exemple to the eftercummeris, yat yai alfo fuld hald in reuerence ye doctrine of ye haly antiquitie, and condemne ye inuentiones of prophane noueltie. We hef inueyit alfo contrare ye wickit

*The proud hert of Nestorius.*

præfumptioun of Neftorius, infafer yat he awantit him afore al wtheris, and allane to vnderftand ye haly fcripture, and al yame to hef bene ignorantis, quha afore hald ye office of preching, and tretit ye word of God:

*See ye proud and blafphemous heretikes at yis tyme pyntit be exemple of Nestorius.*

yat is, vniuerfalie al Preiftis, Confeffouris, and Martyris: of quhome fum had techeit the law of God, and wtheris' had confentit or beleuit to ye techearis: and finalie for yat he affirmit ye hail kirk now to erre, and euir to hef errit, quhilk as he thocht, had follow it and followis ignorant and erroneous Doctouris. Quhilkis al, albeit yai be largelie and abundantlie fufficient to tramp doun, and flokin out al prophane noueltis: zit yat na thing fuld appere to inlake to fa greit plentuoufnes of defencis, laft of al we hef eikit ye double auctoritie of the Apoftolik fait: to wit ane of Sanct Xiftus the Pape, quha now rycht wirfchepful lychtnis the Roman kirk, the other of Pape Celeftinus of haly memorie, his prædeceffor. On

*Xistus.*

this maner fays Pape Xiftus in an epiftil, quhilk he fend tweching the caufe of Neftorius to ye Bifchope of Antiochia: Heirfor, fays he, be-

*Ephes. 4.*

caufe, as ye Apoftil fays, ye faith is ane, quhilk euidentlie hes obtenit (and haldin) quhilkis ar to be faid: lat ws beleue, and beleue we ya thingis, quhilkis ar to be haldin, at ye laft he procedis to ya heidis, quhilkis ar to be haldin and to be trowit, and fays, Lat na ferther be lefum to noueltie, becaufe it becumis to eik na thing to antiquitie. Lat ye cleir fayth and credulitie of our elders be na mixing of glar or mude be tribulit (and maid drumlye) and this aluterlie as become an Apoftolik man fpeikis he, yat he be the lycht (and name) of clerenes mot ornate (and fetfurth) ye

*Celestinus.*

faith of our elderis: bot ye new prophanationis he mot difcriue be ye mixing (and name) of glar (and mwde) Bot alfo the Pape Celeftinus on lyke manere and in ye famin fentence procedeis. For he fays in an epiftil, quhilk he fendis to ye preiftis of ye Gallis repreuand, yat thai wynkit and bure with fum, leueand be yair filence ye auld fayth without defence, fuffered prophane nouelteis to fprout vp. Iuftlie, fays he, ye caufe is laid to our charge, gif be filence we fofter an errour. Heirfor lat yir kynd of men be reprewit, lat na fredome be, to talk at thair plefuir. Heir peraduenture fum men may dout, quha ar thir quhom he wald forbid to fpeik frelie at yair plefuir: quhidder ye precheouris of antiquitie, or ye inuentouris of nouèltie: lat him felf fpeik and folue ye quæftioun of ye reidaris. For it followis: Lat it ceis, fays he, gif ye mater be fua: yat is, gif it be fua as fum men heir, blaymes zour townes and prouincis: yat ze caufe thame be a weray hurtful diffimulatioun to confent to certane nouelteis. And fa, fays he, lat nouèltie hald ye peace, and reproche nocht antiquitie. This heirfor wes ye bliffit fentence of bliffit Celeftinus: nocht yat antiquitie fuld ceifs to downtrampe nouèltie, bot rather yat nouèltie fuld ceifs to accufe antiquitie. To ye quhilkis Apoftolik and Catholik decreis quha ewer ganeftandis, force it is, firft of al that he owtrageouflie reproche ye memorie of fainct Celeftinus quha ftatutit, yat nouèltie fuld defift to accufe antiquitie: and fyne yat he mok ye determinatioun of fanct Xiftus, quha iugeit that na thing ony ferther fuld be lefum to nouèltie: becaufe it becumis nocht to eik ocht to antiquitie: and alfo difpyfe ye ftatutis of blift Cyrillus quha be grete louing commendit ye zeil of the venerable man Capreolus: becaufe he defyrit ye auld doctrine of fayth to be confirmit, and ye new inuentionis to be condemnit. And alfo he mot trampe vnder fute the Counfel of Ephefus, that is the iugement and determinatioun of ye haly Bifchopis of almaift ye hail Orient, quhome it plefit be diuine inftinctioun to decrete na other thing tobe beleuit be ye efter cummeris, except yat, quhilk ye fanctifiit antiquitie of ye halye fatheris confenting amangis them felfis in Chrifte, had beleuit: and quha alfo crying, and with loud woce affirming witneffit with ane mouth yir to be ye woces of al, al man to defyre yis, al man to iuge yis: yat as ye vniuerfal hæretikis almaift afoir Neftorius contemning ye antiquitie and affirming nouèltie, wes condemnit: fua Neftorius alfo him felf ye auctor of nouèltie and impugnar of antiquitie fuld be condemnit. † Quhais maift halie confent infpirit be ye gift of heuinlie grace, to quhome is difplefand: quhat other thing fol-

<small>That na man fuld be fa bauld, to inpugne ye confent of ye haly fatheris, or of a general counfel. S. Xiftus ye Pape.

† Yis argument iuftlie may be proponit to al erroneous this day, tuechiug al hærefeis condemnit: gif yai refaue ye counfel bot in yat parte only quharein ony hærefie wes con-</small>

lowis, bot that he affirme ye curfit wychkitnes of Neftorius nocht to hef bene iuftelie condemnit? And finale alfo he mot lichtlie as wyle and contemptibil ye vniuerfal kirk of Chrifte, and ye Doctouris of it, ye Apoftolis and Prophetis, and zit fpecialie the Apoftil Paul: the Kirk, becaufe it newir departit fra the religioun of the honoring and furthfetting of that fayth, anis be it reffauit: and Paul, quha hes writtin, O Timothe faue yat thing quhil is geuin ye in keping, efchewand ye prophane noueltie of woices. And ficlyke, Gif ony man fal fchaw to zow by yat, quhilk ze haue refawit, lat it be as accurfit. Gif nother ye ordinance of ye Apoftolis, nor the decreis and ftatutis of ye kirk ar to be violatit, be ye quhilkis efter ye maift halye confent of the uniuerfalitie and antiquitie, al hæreticis euir, and at ye laft Pelagius, Cæleftius and Neftorius be al reffoun iuftlie war condemnit: force is futhlie to al catholikis yairefter, quha intendis to preue yame felfis lauchful fonnes of the mother ye kirk, yat thai adheir, be glewit, and dee with the halye faith of the haly fatheris: and deteft treulie, abhorre, and perfew ye prophane nouelteis of prophane men. Thir almaift ar the thingis, quhilkis in thir twa Memorialis mair largelie ar difcuffit, bot now fum thing mair fchortlie efter ye maner of recapitulatioun ar drawn to gidder, that my memorie, for fupport of ye quhilk we hef thir thingis brocht to pafs, be daylie aduertifment mot be helpit, and be fafcheous prolixitie nocht ouirlaidin.

*denunit: us yai do expreslie in al counsels that euir hes bene maist auncunt amangis the catholikis.*
*1. Tim. 6.*

*Galat. 1.*
*Note.*

F I N I S.

*Pacis amator habes, pacem vt Vincentius vnus*
*Tutatur fufis hoftibus innumeris:*
*Eripit arma truci, rabida obftruit ora draconi,*
*Detegit et fraudes: pax quibus exul erat.*
*Morte fua Chriftus pacem, fera fchifmata Dæmon*
*Fraude parit: pacem, pacis alumne, foue.*

*In defence of yis auctour aganis certane mockaris the sones of Cham and mekle wors.*

VINCENTIVS be a proper applicatioun, conuenientlie callis thame ye sones of Cham: quha knawing ony licht falt or negligence in yare forefatheris, reuelis it fra hand til wtheris: as thai wald fchaik wp (yat I may vfe his wordis) ye muildis of yame deceifit wnto ye wind. Bot quhais fones fal we propirlie cal thame, quha dar accufe yair fatheris til wtheris of a falt, quhen thair is nane? We knaw ye principal of this fort tobe ye angel of dirknes: quha as he is callit the father of leis, fa is he callit for the wther falt, fathan: that is, a calumniator, a fals accufear. Gif his follouaris in this parte, ar tobe callit his fones: quhais fone fal that vnkynd fpark and vnnatural monftre of man be, quha labouris al his wittis, and ryueis his heid ftudiing to thraw be his mokrie and bairding the mekle vertew and honor of his father tobe a vyce? his godlines tobe haldin impietie? This I wryte, forfamekle as fum blafphemous bairdis, conuict in confcience be the inuincible treuth in this litle buke, wald draw ye cunning auctour thairof, in a contempt and lichtlie be thare iefting, tanting and rayling: thinkand yat yai hef anffuerit fufficientlie to ony thing obiectit to thame of him, gif thai cal him anis a munk, and imagin thame to rug of his clathis, as thai war playng with him pluk at the craw. For fuythlie quhiddir he wes a Preift (as fum wryteis) amangis ye haly munkis of his tyme, as wes * S. Hierome a litle afore him: or an Abbate (as wtheris wil) he is naway tobe reprocheit, bot gretumlie tobe commendit thairfor. For it is manifeft that the munkis fra the Apoftolis daye, quhil his tyme and mony zeris efter, war munkis in dede, throw wilful and glaid pouertie, conftance of fayth and continence of body, befydis continual ftudie prayer, or wthir Godly exercyfe that al the warldlie and flefchelie myndit, or Apoftate munkis knichtis of Venus court in our days, and wtheris fiklyke clerkis of roy-

* In the monasterie of Bethleem he witnesis in Epitaph. Paul. The large writtingis of S. Hierome, Aug. Chrys. and Basilius in commendatioun of ye monastik lyfe, and ye ryche fundationis maid to ye

<small>efter cum-meris of yir munkis throu opinioun of thare godlines, preuis this to be trew.</small> tous and licentious lyfe, quha wald be haldin mair haly than yai war, and thareby makis thame reformearis of wtheris, fuld be efchameit of thare parte. This I eik, Chriftiane Reidar, that thow be nocht temerouflie fclanderit, nothir in this porpofe nor in wtheris be euery wane manis trittil trattilis.

www.ingramcontent.com/pod-product-compliance
Ingram Content Group UK Ltd.
Pitfield, Milton Keynes, MK11 3LW, UK
UKHW031417221224
3821UKWH00042B/653